ASPECTS OF SHEFFIELD
1

ASPECTS *of* SHEFFIELD

Discovering Local History – 1

Edited by
Melvyn Jones

Wharncliffe Publishing Limited

First Published in 1997 by
Wharncliffe Publishing Limited
an imprint of
Pen and Sword Books Limited,
47 Church Street, Barnsley,
South Yorkshire. S70 2AS

Copyright © Wharncliffe Publishing Limited 1997

For up-to-date information on other titles produced under the
Wharncliffe imprint, please telephone or write to:

> **Wharncliffe Publishing Limited**
> **FREEPOST**
> **47 Church Street**
> **Barnsley**
> **South Yorkshire S70 2BR**
> **Telephone (24 hours): 01226 - 734555**

ISBN: 1-871647-40-1

A CIP catalogue record of this book is available from the
British Library

Cover illustration: 'Sheffield from Psalter Lane, Brincliffe Edge'
by J. McIntyre, by courtesy of Sheffield Arts & Museums Department.

Printed in Great Britain by
Redwood Books, Trowbridge, Wiltshire

Contents

INTRODUCTION

by Melvyn Jones

THE PUBLICATION OF THIS VOLUME marks the latest stage in the development of the *Aspects* series. The series began in 1993 with the publication of *Aspects of Barnsley* edited by Brian Elliott, the overall series editor. Its outstanding success led to the publication of *Aspects of Barnsley 2, 3* and *4* in 1994, 1995 and 1996 respectively. The second stage began in 1995 with the appearance of *Aspects of Rotherham* edited by Melvyn Jones. The runaway success of the latter led to *Aspects of Rotherham 2* which appeared in 1996. This year – the third phase of the development of the series – sees the extension of the series to Sheffield, Doncaster and Leeds. Further volumes on Barnsley and Rotherham are planned for 1998 and a second Sheffield volume will appear in 1999.

The concept of the *Aspects* series is simple. Interest in and enthusiasm for family and local history continue to grow. Not only is there an unprecedented level of research activity – by professionals and amateurs alike – but there is a potentially large readership for the fruits of that research. With this in mind volumes in the *Aspects* series contain original articles on aspects of economic, social, cultural, community and landscape history and historical biography by both new and experienced writers.

Not surprisingly, articles on industrial themes loom large in this volume. Geoffrey Tweedale's meticulous analysis of the claims and counterclaims over the origins of the electro-plate industry not only shows the intense rivalry between Sheffield and Birmingham but also the important roles played in the unfolding tale by two leading Sheffielders of their day: the larger than life Sir John Bingham, senior partner in the firm of Walker & Hall and leading figure in the Sheffield cutlery trade, and Robert E. Leader, Sheffield's foremost local historian at the time. The story reads like a rattling good Edwardian whodunnit.

Two further articles on industrial themes deal with industries that many local residents will not associate with the city. Dennis Smith's carefully researched study of buttonmaking reveals the one time importance of this forgotten industry to the local economy; likewise Chris Morley's survey of the stove grate and light castings industry shows that for a century and a half, Sheffield's foundries produced stove grates and kitchen ranges that graced the dining rooms, drawing rooms, bedrooms and kitchens of the highest to the lowest in the land, with examples holding pride of place at the Great Exhibitions of 1851 and the International Exhibition of 1862.

Finally on an industrial theme, Trevor Lodge – a regular *Aspects* contributor – using the oral testimony of Sheffield's last puddler, records the production process in the wrought iron industry, a manufacturing process older than Sheffield itself. Also making full use of oral testimony as an historical source, Valerie Answer has interwoven family and social history to recount the story of a Sheffield family with a military, farming and light steel trades background.

A spirit of independence, a non-conforming attitude and dissent have all been marked features of local society at various junctures in its history and these themes are taken up in different ways in three of the articles in this volume. Stephen Cooper, another regular *Aspects* contributor with a particular interest in Tudor history and litigation, outlines the legal battle over tithes between the sixth Earl of Shrewsbury and the tenants of Meadowhall, all couched in evocative Shakespearean language. Malcolm Mercer's study of religious non-conformity in Tudor and Stuart Sheffield records a critical period in the social and cultural development of the town, while David Hey's article on Mahlon Stacy reveals aspects of the development of Quakerism in the local area and the part played by members of this movement in the European settlement of one small part of the then American colonies.

Transport problems have always been close to the hearts of Sheffielders, and in the past particularly to Sheffield manufacturers. Howard Smith's study of the development of turnpike roads records the first important attempts to put Sheffield on the transport map.

Social history has not been neglected either. Tim Caulton's and Julie Goddard's studies of Sheffield Workhouse and Endcliffe Hall respectively, reveal the two ends of the social spectrum in nineteenth century Sheffield.

Finally, three articles are concerned with landscape history. Sue Turton's article recounts the changing face of Darnall in the nineteenth century, Melvyn Jones reveals the all-pervading significance of woodlands and their products to eighteenth century Sheffield, and Joan Sewell records the rise and decline of a number of local landscape jewels: the city's parks and gardens.

What all fourteen contributions have in common are: enthusiasm for the subject, rigorous research in primary sources, and a clear and direct writing style. Although aimed at the general reader, the volumes already published contain studies of considerable local and regional historical importance. The present volume is no exception.

The book could not have been produced without the help and support of a number of key individuals. I would like to thank Charles Hewitt of Wharncliffe Publishing for his continued support for the project. Brian Elliott, as the originator of the series, has been a great source of encouragement. The sterling efforts of Barbara Bramall and Roni Wilkinson at the production end are also gratefully acknowledged. I also acknowledge the help of Hazel Undy and Jane Scothorne in word processing and Neil Donovan for technical help with disks. Bob Warburton has produced a number of key maps. The assistance given to contributors by staff in Sheffield Archives and Sheffield Local Studies Library, particularly Doug Hindmarch, is also gratefully acknowledged. I also wish to thank Sheffield Arts & Museums Department for permission to reproduce J. McIntyre's 'Sheffield from Psalter Lane, Brincliffe Edge' as the cover illustration. Finally, I would like to thank the contributors for meeting deadlines and for producing articles of infinite variety and interest.

Anyone interested in making a contribution to Aspects of Sheffield 2 *should, in the first instance, contact Melvyn Jones, Editor, Aspects of Sheffield, c/o Wharncliffe Publishing Ltd, 47 Church Street Barnsley S70 2AS, enclosing a brief description of the proposed work.*

1.   THE EARL OF SHREWSBURY AND THE TITHES OF MEADOWHALL[1]

by Stephen Cooper

MEADOWHALL, leviathan of South Yorkshire in the reign of Elizabeth II, features little in the annals of history, except as the Meadow Hall homestead from which the Roman Rig earthwork could best be seen in 1875;[2] but during the reign of the first Elizabeth there was a lawsuit concerning its tithes. The 6th Earl of Shrewsbury sued two local men and the case came before the Consistory Court in York in 1584, when it was claimed that the tithe of hay was worth two shillings. The author wonders what the tithes of the modern shopping mall would be worth.

The 6th Earl of Shrewsbury

GEORGE TALBOT, 6th EARL OF SHREWSBURY between 1560 and 1590 (Figure 1), dominated Hallamshire and South Yorkshire. His ancestors had inherited the manors of Sheffield and Ecclesfield as early as 1406 and his immediate predecessors in the Earldom had built the family's fortune by loyal service to the Tudor dynasty. The 4th Earl was Steward of the Royal Household from 1502, and helped King Henry VIII to put down the Pilgrimage of Grace in 1536. He had a castle and a park in Sheffield and built a fine lodge there – 'Sheffield Manor Lodge' – whose ruins can still be visited.[3] After the dissolution of the monasteries, the King granted him all the possessions of Rufford Abbey, partly to compensate for the loss of his estates in Ireland, following a decision to impose direct rule there; and this grant included the manor of Rotherham. The 5th Earl further consolidated the family estates by acquiring more Church land in the area after the dissolution of the chantries in 1549, and acquired the lordship, manor, park and fair of

Figure 1. The sixth Earl of Shrewsbury.

Kimberworth in 1552.[4]

The 6th Earl was the wealthiest peer in England, with an income of £10,000 a year in 1586, £3000 deriving from Yorkshire alone. Professor Collinson tells us that he was the nearest thing the Elizabethan age had to a tycoon:

> *He was the largest demesne farmer of whom we have any record. He had shipping interests. He was the largest single lead smelter in the country. He made most of the steel which supplied the Sheffield cutlery trade. He owned coal-mines and glassworks.*

The Earl was powerful as well as wealthy, maintaining a large household and holding high office. He was a Knight of the Garter and a member of the Privy Council, Earl Marshal, and Lord Lieutenant of Staffordshire and Derbyshire:

> *A mighty man he was, in wealth he did abound*
> *Of all his howse therein the like was never found*

Above all, the Earl had a unique role as steward of Mary Queen of Scots between 1569 and 1584:

> *Soe great a trust as this so long was never seene*
> *A subject for to be a keeper of a Queene.*

Mary was kept in Sheffield for most of her long captivity, either at the Castle or at the Manor Lodge; and so the Earl was also required to live there for much of that time.[5] Some local people undoubtedly benefitted from his patronage. When he died 20,000 are said to have attended his funeral, and 8000 poor received dole. Amongst other gifts, he left £200 to the poor tradesmen of Rotherham, and £500 to those of Chesterfield.[6] Joseph Hunter thought that the Tudor period was 'the age of Pericles of our little district'; and he contrasted this with the relative neglect which began in 1616 when the lordship passed to non-residents.

But, as David Hey has pointed out, there were also disadvantages in having Talbots on the doorstep, not least because they were an irascible breed, concerned to maintain their power and maximise their income.[7] The 6th Earl of Shrewsbury's attitude towards his rights as lord of the manor was shown soon after he succeeded to the title. In 1563, he demanded a sum of money on the occasion of his eldest daughter's marriage. This 'aid' had been a commonplace obligation in feudal times, but the men of Hallamshire took the view that it was now obsolete; and they refused to pay. The Earl reacted very badly and issued stern instructions to his agents:

> *I perceave by your leters the frutles and unadvised answers of my fre-*
> *holders within Hallomshire and other places . . . I have thereof no lit-*

tle mervaile, considering that at their handes I do desire no more then of right they owe, and but that which the lawes of this realme dothe bothe gyve me and will compel them to paye, as all my lerned counsaile have fully resolved withe me: Wherof throughout all Shropshire, and other places where my landes do lye, I have not beene so aunswered as most neerest home . . . Wherfore I woll you declare unto suche as you shall think most expedyent of them, that I am determyned by law to constrayne those obstynate persons to paye that which by faire meanes I have demaunded . . .

The threat was enough. Resistance collapsed. Sheffield paid £22 4s 0d, Sheffield Park £8 7s 2d, Ecclesfield £23 8s 7d, Bradfield £20 10s 8d, Rotherham £26 5s 4d and Chesterfield £11 9s 6d.[8]

This confrontation was not an isolated incident, for the Earl clashed frequently with his social inferiors. The historian of Ecclesfield records that his relations with his tenants there left much to be desired, while his treatment of Glossopdale was so rough that the Crown – fearful of a disaffected peasantry – was forced to intervene. Meanwhile, the Earl's policy towards the towns on his estates can be illustrated by an event which took place in 1567. A conference was held between Shrewsbury and the aldermen and burgesses of Chesterfield, which laid claim to corporate status. The Earl began by demanding to see the town's documents. The men of Chesterfield had to admit that they had not brought these with them, because they liked to keep them safe. The Earl took this very badly.

Why, you villain knaves,

he cried

do you misdoubt me, that I should detain or withhold your evidence if they were put into my hands?

And he vowed undying hostility:

Avaunt knaves! For I will take you as mine enemies forever, and I will charge my son upon my blessing that he shall do the same, and that me may never show you favour nor to your generation, for you have wakened a sleepy dog . . .

His parting shot was a promise to ostracise the citizens of the offending town:

You shall not come into any of my towns, neither Rotherham, Sheffield or Worksop, but as foreigners.

Shortly after this devastating interview, Chesterfield surrendered its pretensions to the status of incorporated borough. Instead of being ruled by an officer of its own choosing, it had to submit directly to the lord's bailiff, and the jurisdiction of the Earl's manor court was fully restored.[9]

Tithes and tithe disputes

Tithes were originally voluntary contributions, made by Christians for the maintenance of their minister. During the middle ages the system became formalised and the clergy claimed a tenth part of the produce of the land, as a matter of right. So far as England is concerned the voluntary offering became a legal obligation long before the Norman Conquest.

A complex body of law developed. Tithes were sometimes classified into **predial** (arising from the land itself), **mixed** (coming from the stock on land) and **personal** (from the industry of the occupiers). Another classification was into **great tithes** (those of corn, hay and wood) and **small** (those of animals, wool, eggs and so on). Tithes were originally paid in kind, and where this system survived, the resulting produce was stored in tithe barns, some of which survive; but in some places the payment in kind was converted into a monetary payment, by virtue of an agreement known as a *modus decimandi*, or *modus* for short.

The person entitled to the tithes of a parish was known as the rector, and the tithes themselves as 'the rectory'; but tithes frequently became alienated from the parish from which they derived. When a medieval lord wished to endow a monastery, one of the ways he could do it was to bestow on it the tithes of one or more parishes. The monastery then became the 'rector' while the spiritual needs of the parish were met by a 'vicar'. In general the rector kept the great tithes, while the vicar received the small; but sometimes the vicar was left with a mere salary. This system seems fundamentally unjust and did attract criticism, even in medieval times, but it was very widespread. Tithes lost their sacred character and came to be regarded as nothing more than a form of rent. Like any other item of property, they were bought and sold, assigned and leased.

Monasteries which owned tithes often employed laymen to 'farm' them. These 'farmers' were not peasants who tilled the soil, but middlemen who paid the monastery a fixed sum each year, in return for the right to collect the tithes. Thus it was not uncommon for parishioners to pay their tithes to laymen, even before the dissolution of the monasteries; but after that event the extent to which laymen became involved in the collection of tithes increased greatly, for large numbers of rectories which had belonged to the monks passed first to the Crown, and then into the hands of the aristocracy and gentry.

There were always disputes concerning tithes, once the obligation to pay them had become legally enforceable; but there was perhaps an increase in the number of lawsuits after the Reformation. This may have resulted from the fact that the new rectors were anxious to increase their profits, especially in an inflationary period; and the law responded to the changing situation. In 1536 an Act of Parliament provided that everyone should pay the amount of tithe which was customary in their parish, while in 1540 laymen who were owners or lessees of tithes were for the first time given the right to sue for them in the ecclesiastical courts. The result of these developments was that in the second half of the sixteenth century we witness the strange spectacle of laymen bringing legal proceedings in the Church courts against other laymen, for tithes, which were in origin, and were still in name, 'spiritual income'. The diocesan archives of England and of the Archbishopric of York in particular, abound with such cases.[10] The record of these tithe disputes are full of interest for the social and local historian, though they are seldom complete.

As we should expect, the 6th Earl of Shrewsbury was to the fore when it came to using these new procedures. There is fascinating evidence of this from the parish of Ecclesfield. In the 1570s the Earl brought numerous tithe cases against people living there, especially in Bradfield chapelry. He was particularly concerned to establish his right to the payment of tithes in kind, and to defeat claims that there was a *modus* in existence. The Earl argued that the customary payment alleged to exist in Bradfield was 'an arroneouse unreasonable and pernicious corruption', which was harmful to the Church – by which he meant himself. His intransigent behaviour became predictable and the inhabitants of Bradfield even set up a common fighting fund to pay for the costs of the law suits which he brought against them, since it was clearly in the interests of the community as a whole to defend these.[11]

The Lawsuit of 1584

Meadowhall was situated in the manor of Kimberworth but in the parish of Rotherham. The tithes of Rotherham had been 'alienated' at an early date, and had subsequently been split into two moieties or halves, belonging respectively to the Cistercian abbeys of Rufford (in Nottinghamshire) and Clairvaux (in France); but by the end of the thirteenth century Rufford acquired both halves. King Henry VIII's *Valor Ecclesiasticus* of 1535 shows that the tithes were then worth £67 13s 4d, though the monks paid the vicar of Rotherham a stipend of only £16 13s 4d. The tithes were farmed by the ubiquitous Robert Swift and sons, who paid £5 a year for the privilege.[12] Following the dissolution of Rufford Abbey in 1536 the tithes of Rotherham passed, with the manor, to the Earls of Shrewsbury.

Early in 1584 – the last year of his stewardship of the Queen of Scots – the 6th Earl sued Henry Swinden and Robert Parker for tithe. The proceedings were begun in the Consistory Court at York, the usual venue for this type of litigation.[13] The statement of the Earl's case has not survived, but the arguments deployed by the defendants have. These were set out in a **Libel**, containing seven **Articles**. It was said, firstly, that the disputed tithes derived from Meadowhall in the parish of Rotherham. Secondly, that it was customary for those liable to pay the tithe of hay in Meadowhall to pay a fixed sum:

> *by the space of x, xx, xxx, xl, l yers laste by paste and for tyme out of mans remembrance the owners & occupiers of Maddohaull aforsaid by custom or prescription there usyd have payd yerlye durynge the tyme aforesaid iis in money for all the tythe of hay growynge and remenynge within any the landes or groundes apperteyninge and belonginge to the said Maddohall to the persons proprietaries their farmers or deputies of the parsonage of Rotherham.*

Thirdly, it was alleged that it was not customary to pay tithe of hay in kind:

> *no tythe of hay in kynde of hay hathe bene payde of the hay growynge upon the lande and grounds aforesaide at any tyme for and durynge all the tyme aforesaide Neyther yet can the said Earle of Shrewsburye prove any one paymente of tyhe hay in kynde to have bene paide . . .*

Fourthly, that it was commonly believed that there was a customary monetary payment:

> *there hath bene and yet is a comon opinion and fame Wythin the parishe of Rotherham aforesayd that the owners or occupiers of the sayd Maddohall for tyme out of man's Remembrance have payde and oughte to pay yerlye by custome or prescription usyd the some of iis in money for the tythe hay . . .*

The defendants' fifth point was that witnesses could confirm the existence of this custom, throughout a period of at least forty years:

> *enye wytnesse in this behalf to be producyd yf he be duelye and dylygentlye examined can and wyll depose that he hathe knowne the said Custome so usyd and observyd for xl yeres before the begynnynge of this sute of his certaine syghte and knowlege And can and wyll depose that he hathe harde the sayd comon opinion and fame of the more parte of the parishioners of Rotherham And that he hathe also harde*

the same of his elders which elders have reportyd unto him that the said custome or prescription was usyd in their tyme and for tyme out of mynde of man And that they never harde the contrarye And can name some of his elders so reportynge.

Sixthly, the defendants said that the Earl had in the past actually received the monetary payment which he now sought to repudiate: *the said Earle of Shrewsburye for and durynge so longe tyme as he hathe bene supposed proprietary of farm of the parsonage of Rotherham by himself or by his fermers deputies or officers hathe had and receyved of [defendant's name] or others the owners of occupiers of the sayd Maddohall iis in money yerlye for and in the name of and Righte of all the tythe hay of the hay growynge upon the landes and grounds belongynge to Maddohaull aforesaide accordynge unto the sayd custom or prescription savynge Untyll the yere libellate* [1584].

Seventhly, the defendants had offered to pay the two shillings before the start of the court case, but the Earl had refused it: *appealed for the tythes libellat and confessyd . . . as for all other tythe hay growynge upon the lands and grounds of Maddohall aforesaid . . . he [defendant's name] . . . hathe offeryd and reallie tenderyd to the deputies of the said Earle of Shrewsbury . . . iis in money . . . Which iis he also reallye offeryd and tenderyd for the tythe hay aforesaid before this sute begane to the said Earle of Shrewsburye or his deputies or officers appoynted by the sayd Earl of Shrewsburye for the collecting of the tythes chancynge and happenynge within the sayd Rectorye who refusyd to receive the same . . .*

One can perhaps understand why the Earl's agents refused to accept the payment of two shillings: it was little enough, and clearly *a tithe farmer who one year agreed to accept a money payment in lieu of tithe . . . in kind might find that amount claimed as an ancient prescription the next year.*[14]

The reply which the Earl's proctor made to these arguments was brief. He simply stated that the more important propositions were incorrect, and that when the defendants had made the payment of two shillings which was alleged to be customary, they had done so under a misapprehension, not because there was any genuine custom in existence: 'the some arte. hathe bene offered . . . accordinge to a pretended custome or prescription'.

The best way of testing claims about the existence of customary rights was to ask the old men of the area what they thought; and so on 27 March, 1584, eight witnesses were examined upon each of the

Articles contained in the defence. The first was Edward Johns. He was quite clear that there was a custom, as alleged by Swinden and Parker in the second Article:

> *he never hard nor knewe other custom then is art. and that by ould men he hard that it was so in there tyme but he never knew it of his own knowledge but by heare say nether before the fortie years nor after.*

As to the common opinion mentioned in the fourth Article:

> *he haith hard of thre or four ould men of his owne age that there was a comon fame that iis was paid for the tieth hay of Maddo hall but of anie gretaer number he haithe not hard it.*

As to Article five:

> *he cannot of his certain sighte and knowledge depose but by heare say of anie such custom as is art. and he cannot depose that he hard it of the more part of the parishioners of Rotherham for he haithe not so hard it And he haithe hard it of men as ould as himselfe that iis was paid for the tiethe art. but not of his elders, beinge required to name of whome he hard it he saithe he haithe hard it of Ralphe Ealand (?) and of no other.*

William Waddie was 86. As to Article two he said:

> *there haithe bene suche a custom as is art. for these fiftie years laste paste for Robert Parkar and his father before him tould him so and by there Reporte he knows it and no otherwise.*

On Article four:

> *he cannot depose of anie such fame as is art. within the parish of Rotheram but he thinketh there is suche a fame as is art. within the lordship of Kimberworthe which he knoweth because he haithe hard neyhbours of the lordship so reporte.*

When asked to name names, Waddie said:

> *he haithe hard suche a fame of his elders namely John Moore Peres Lockwood Thomas Parker Roberte Dewk and he cannot say more saveinge that Moore and Lockwood were older than he and the reste was yonger . . .*

There certainly seem to have been some very old men living in this district!

Roger Ellison was a yeoman from Wurspurdale (Worsbrough Dale), in the parish of Darfield, several miles from Meadowhall. He was 55. His comments on Article four were:

> *there is now and hath bene in his tyme a comon talke that iis haithe bene paid for the tiethe hay of Maddohall which he knoweth by a*

rentall specifiying what everie man payes for tiethe hay.

This was the first time anyone had mentioned the existence of documentary evidence. One would have thought that if a rental did exist, it would have resolved the matters in dispute very quickly, for it would prove that the tithe of hay had indeed been commuted into a money payment.[15] As to Article five, Ellison said he had heard 'the common voice and fame' from his elders, but when asked to be more specific, the only name he could give was that of George Barnebroughe.

John Hill was a nailmaker, aged 50, from that part of Thorpe Hesley which was in the parish of Rotherham, and about three miles from Meadowhall.[16] On Article three, Hill confirmed that: 'he haithe not hard that anie tieth of hay of the hay art haithe bene paid in kind'.

Thomas Wainwright was a tailor, aged about 42, from the hamlet of Scholes, which is close to Thorpe Hesley and about two miles from Meadowhall.[17] Wainwright was the first witness to state how long he had known the parties to the litigation, saying that he had known them all for about ten years. This seems long enough, but in context it was probably an assertion of ignorance rather than of experience, for he was less positive in the answer which he gave with regard to Article two than other witnesses. He agreed that he had heard of the customary payment of two shillings for the tithe of hay, but he qualified this by saying that:

> he haithe hard so and otherwise he knowes not for that he is a stranger to it and dwells two myles of it and folowes his occupacion and never had the gatheringe of it.

Here is a nice phrase. When Wainwright says that he 'follows his own occupation', does he mean that he is a tailor, not a husbandman, and is not directly concerned with the tithe of hay? Or does he mean (in true Yorkshire fashion) that it is his custom to 'mind his own business'? Of course, both meanings may have been intended. On the fourth Article, Wainwright said:

> he knoweth not what the fame haithe bene in tymes paste but for this ten yeres there haithe bene such a speche as is art.

Thomas Whiteacres was a blacksmith, also aged about 42. He was from Kimberworth. He said he had known Robert Parker for 30 years, and the Earl for 20. He said that Article two was true as far as he knew. As to Article four he said:

> he haithe hard for these xx yeres a comon opinion and fame that the sum art. haithe been paid for the tiethe hay art.

Thomas Cutlove was also from Kimberworth. He was a husbandman aged about 64. He said he had known the defendant Parker from childhood, and had known the Earl of Shrewsbury some 30 years. As to Article two he stated, like Ellison before him, that he knew of documents which were relevant to the point in issue. Indeed, he went further and said that he actually had some in his possession! 'He haithe some Rentalls of the sum art. whereby the same was gathered for the tiethe hay art . . .'. (If this was really so, we may again wonder why these documents were apparently never produced to the court). As to Article four, Cutlove said:

> the article is true for these fortie yeres for he haithe hard such a fame as is art. not in Kimberworth lordship but throughout the whole parish of Rotherham.

On Article five:

> he haithe hard the same by him deposed of John Cutlove his father Robert Gilberthorpe Thomas Burlay and other ould men . . .

The eighth and last witness was William Ingle, a nailmaker from Scholes aged about 50.[18] Unusually, this witness was not sure of his ground. When addressing Article three he said 'there myghte be tiethe hay paid in kinde for him but he never hard it was paid'. As to Article four however, Ingle agreed that 'there was suche a comon voice and fame as is art. which he knoweth because he hard say so of the men where he dwells'.

Each of the eight witnesses then had to reply to a series of questions, known as Interrogatories, put to them by the Earl of Shrewsbury's proctor, in an attempt to test their credibility and their evidence. Some of these questions were of a formal nature but others referred specifically to the customs of Meadowhall. The language used has a pleasing Shakespearean ring to it:

(1) Each witness was asked to confirm that he really did have a sound knowledge of the matters he had spoken of. To this each man naturally replied *satisfactus est* – yes it was sufficient.

(2) Each witness must say how much he was worth in goods, after deducting any debts; and it is an interesting commentary on contemporary attitudes that poverty was thought to imply a lack of creditworthiness. Johns replied that he was worth £5, Waddie £10, Ellison 5 marks, Hill £3, Wainwright 40s (£2), Whiteacres £4, Cutlove £10 *et amplius* and Ingle £3. Cutlove's reply is remarkable. Men – especially farmers – usually protest that they are not as well off as others think they are; but here is Cutlove the husbandman declaring openly that he is worth £10 and more.

(3) Each witness had to say whether he was related by blood to either party to the action, or if he held an office with either, or was in service with either. If he was related, he must say in what degree. Here all the witnesses save one declared that they had no connection with the Earl or the defendants. The exception was William Waddie, who admitted *that Parker and he are cosynes*. Of course, the word 'cousin' could apply to a number of different relationships, but Waddie did not specify what he meant by the term.

(4) The witnesses were also asked which party to the litigation they favoured: how would they decide the case if it were within their power to do so? Predictably, they all replied that they had no favourites and that it was all the same to them. To have replied any differently would have discredited their evidence altogether.

(5) They were then asked

> *whether they know beleve or have hard sayd if Maddayhall and Gilberthorp Hill have been by the space of manye years last paste and yet are parte and parcell of the lordshipp of Kimberworthe within the parsh of Rotherham . . . yea or naye.*

On this point all the witnesses replied 'yea' – *respondet affirmare* – except Ingle, who could not say – *nescit deponere*. We shall see that this was to become a familiar refrain in Ingle's case.

(6) They were also asked

> *whether Robert Swyfte some tyme of Rotherham thelder was not fermor of the corne and haie of the Rectorie of Rotherham . . . before xxtie[19] yeres laste paste . . . yea or naye.*

Again, all except one of the witnesses agreed that Robert Swift had farmed the tithes of Rotherham. The exception was Ingle, who again could not say.

(7) Each witness was asked

> *whether the tennants and occupiers of the lordshipp of Kimberworthe and of the houses tenements and groundes of Maddohall & Gilberthorpp have not compounded with the fermors of the tythe corne & haie and especially with the said Robert Swyfte duringe his time of being fermor and also with the Right Honourable Francis late Lord Talbott the fermor of the said Rectorie for the tithe Corne and haie agreeing and covennanting to paie some yeres £xviii some years £xvi some yeares £xii or there abouts for the same of his or ther knowledg heresaie or belief.*

This 'Lord Talbot' was the eldest son of the 6th Earl of Shrewsbury, the same who issued the 'orders for the whole towne and Lordshipp of Rotherham', governing the occupation of the town fields there, in 1572.[20] He pre-deceased his father, dying in 1582, only two years before his father started the proceedings against Swinden and Parker. Perhaps it was his death which caused the Earl to review the level of tithe he was receiving from Meadowhall. At any rate, what the Earl's proctor was now suggesting was that various amounts had been paid by local people in times past, not only in relation to the tithe of hay, but also in relation to the tithe of corn, the implication being that there was no special *modus* concerning the tithe of hay. Some of the witnesses – Johns, Waddie, Whiteacres and Cutlove – agreed with this suggestion. Ellison agreed that what was put to him was true 'for Mr Swyftes tyme'. Hill would only say that he had heard it was true: *respondet quod audivit affirmare*. On the other hand Wainwright denied that it was true; and Ingle as usual said he could not comment.

(8) Each witness was then asked

> *whether the tennants occupiers of the grounde and lordshipp afore-said have not by covennant led home from the lordshipp of Kimberworthe unto the town of Rotherham the tyth corne chancing and growinge of the said grownd and lordshipp upon there owne cost and charge and in consideracon of the same were allowed to deteyne unto themselves ther tithe haie of the same grownde or some part of the same . . .*

This is a novel suggestion. We are beginning to realise, if it has not already become clear, how many and how various are the customs which could spring up with regard to tithe. Here again the witnesses differ from one another. Waddie, Ellison and Cutlove all agreed that what was being put to them was true. Hill and Whiteacres said it was not. Johns said he had heard it was true; and Wainwright joined Ingle in saying that he did not know.

(9) Each witness was then asked

> *whether they know beleve or have hard said yf the tennants of the said lordshipp of Kimberworth or some one or more of them did take or leasse in writing or by word of mowthe of ther tithe haie & corne chancing & growing within the said lordshipp of Kimberworth of Robert Swifte aforesaid for the space of 1 2 3 4 5 or 6 yeres and yf anie depose affirmativelie to this Interrogatorie then let enye witnes depose the names of suche persons as were leassees in yt behalf.*

Once more this question elicited differing answers. Johns and Ellison

denied that there was a lease of the tithe of corn as suggested.
Wainwright and Ingle (as ever) did not know. The other four said that
the tithe of corn had been leased, but the situation was complex.
Waddie said that:

> John Neile Thomas Boswell and Wm Banks took to farme there tiethe
> corne and hay of Robte Swifte and paid him monie for the same as
> they and he would agree.

Hill said that

> he Richard Tomlinson Robert Samson & John Brodbent took to farm
> the tithe corne and tieth hay monie of Thorpe and Scholes and
> Walkworth for ixli[21] old monie of Mr Corka[22] Steward to my lord
> Talbot.

Whiteacres said that

> Roger Ellison, George Jenkinson and John Banks tooke to farme tieth
> corne and hay of Kimberworth lordship of Mr Swifte for thre yeres
> about xvi yeres ago.

Cutlove said that

> George Jenkinson,[23] Roger Ellison and John Bankes and Thomas
> Burlay tooke to farme the tiethe corne and hay growing in the said
> lordship of the said Mr Swifte for six years or thereabouts.

(10) Each witness was asked

> whether the tenants and occupiers of Maddohall and Gilberthorp Hill
> have or ought to have anie peculier speciall or severall prescription or
> custome for paing of money for their tithe haie other than the Residue
> of the tenants of the lordshipp of Kimberworth do pretend to have . .

Here the Earl was trying to suggest that the custom which the defendants alleged to exist did not exist throughout Kimberworth. Did
they think that they were special? All the witnesses exept one said no,
there was no special custom applying to Meadowhall and
Gilberthorpe Hill. The exception was William Ingle . . . who as usual
could not say.

(11) The last Interrogatory was

> whether any tenants of occupiers of the lordship of Kimberworth have
> paid tith haie in kind within i ii or iii yeres laste paste . . . And what
> was the names of such persons.

This question, which concerned the custom existing in the Earl's
manor of Kimberworth as a whole, again produced a division of
opinion, as it was no doubt intended to do. Johns answered no,
Wainwright, Whiteacres and Cutlove all said this payment in kind

had taken place in the last year, but did not go any further. Waddie replied that

> *some of the lordship of Kimberworth have paid tieth hay in kinde as he himself and a great number more to the number of xxv to his knowledge.*

Hill said no

> *saveinge that they paid the last year and saveinge that the inhabitants of Masbrughe did all wayes pay before the last year.*

Ellison did not know. And neither, of course, did William Ingle!

The judgment in this case has unfortunately not survived, so we cannot be sure who won. However, the records at York show that in tithe cases generally the Consistory Court 'always sentenced in favour of the plaintiff – with a few exceptions'.[24] It is therefore unlikely that Swinden and Parker were successful in their attempt to limit the profits of the Earl of Shrewsbury. He probably got his way, just as we know that he did on many previous occasions. We can still visit the Earl's stupendous and vainglorious Renaissance tomb in Sheffield Cathedral, with its talbots, helmets and prolix Latin epitaph composed by John Foxe, the Protestant martyrologist; and we can still read the English eulogy which once hung nearby, in the pages of Hunter.[25] But when we read:

> *The poore mans plaint to here his eares would alwaies bend,*
> *And them in there cause against there foes defend*

we should perhaps remember the Earl's disputes with the men of Meadowhall, and wonder.

Glossary

ART: abbreviation for 'articulate', meaning 'the said'.

AVAUNT: begone!

DEMESNE: land retained by the lord of the manor for his own use and upon which tenants gave free service.

DOLES: the distribution of money or provisions to the poor.

INTERROGATORY: a question put to a witness in writing.

LIBEL: a written declaration, made by a party to litigation.

LIBELLATE: mentioned in the Libel.

MARK: 13s 4d.

PRESCRIPTION: uninterrupted use or possession from time immemorial or for period fixed by law as giving right or title.

PROCTOR: type of lawyer practising in the Church courts.

TALBOT: extinct breed of hunting dog.

VALOR: a valuation. On the dissolution of the monasteries by Henry VIII in the 1530s, a valuation of all religious property was made prior to its confiscation and acquisition by the Crown. Known as the *Valor Ecclesiasticus*, it was compiled by Royal

Commissioners whose task was to value religious houses as real estate. They were interested in land holdings, buildings and income of all kinds, including tithes.

Acknowledgments

I thank the Borthwick Institute of Historical Research for permission to reproduce extracts from the Cause Papers in the case of *Shrewsbury v Swinden & Parker*.

Note

Before 1971 there were four farthings in a penny, twelve pennies in a shilling and twenty shillings to the pound; and the abbreviations for pounds, shillings and pence were £, s and d.

Abbreviations used in references

ACM: Arundel Castle Manuscripts, held in SCL.

Aspects of Rotherham 1: *Aspects of Rotherham, Discovering Local History*, ed. by Melvyn Jones, Wharncliffe Publishing Ltd, 1995.

Aspects of Rotherham 2: *Aspects of Rotherham, Discovering Local History Vol.2*, ed. by Melvyn Jones, Wharncliffe Publishing Ltd, 1996.

Bernard: *The Power of the Early Tudor Nobility, A study of the 4th and 5th Earls of Shrewsbury* by E.W.Bernard, The Harvester Press, 1985.

Brown: *The Medieval Courts of the York Minster Peculiar,* BIHR Paper 66.

BIHR: Borthwick Institute of Historical Research, University of York, St Anthony's Hall, Peasholme Green, York YO1 2PW.

Collinson: *The English Captivity of Mary Queen of Scots* by Patrick Collinson, Sheffield History Pamphlets, Sheffield, 1987.

Complete Peerage: *The Complete Peerage* by G.E.C.Cockayne, edited by the Hon. Vicary Gibbs, 1910.

CP: Cause Papers.

Eastwood's Ecclesfield: *History of the Parish of Ecclesfield*, Rev J Eastwood, London, 1862.

Gransby: *Tithe Disputes in the Diocese of York 1540–1639*, unpublished York University M Phil dissertation, 1966, in BIHR.

Guest: *Historic Notices of Rotherham* by John Guest FSA, Robert White, Worksop, 1879.

Guy: *Tudor England* by John Guy, Oxford University Press, 1990.

Hey, *Rural Metalworkers: The Rural Metalworkers of the Sheffield Region, A Study of Rural Industry before the Industrial Revolution* by David Hey, Leicester University Press, 1972.

Hey, *South Yorkshire*: *The Making of South Yorkshire* by David Hey, Moorland Publishing, 1979.

HH: *Hallamshire, The History and Topography of the Parish of Sheffield in the County of York* by Joseph Hunter, 3rd edition, 1875, ed. by the Rev. Alfred Gatty.

HSY: *The History and Topography of the Deanery of Doncaster* by Joseph Hunter, 1828–31, republished by EP Publishing in collaboration with SCL, 1974.

Jordan: *The Charities of Rural England 1480–1660* by W.K.Jordan, George Allen & Unwin Ltd, 1961.

L & P Henry VIII: *Letters and Papers of Henry VIII in Calendar of Letters and Papers Foreign and Domestic of the Reign of Henry VIII* ed J.S.Brewer, J.Gairdner and R.H.Brodie (RP London 1862–1932).

Palliser: *The Age of Elizabeth* by D.M.Palliser, Longmans, 1983.

Ritchie: *The Ecclesiastical Courts of York*, Carson I. Ritchie, Arbroath, 1956.

SCL: Sheffield City Libraries.

Surtees: Publications of the Surtees Society.

Tate: *The Parish Chest* by W.E.Tate, Phillimore, 1983.

THAS: *Transactions of the Hunter Archaeological Society.*

Williams: *The Tudor Regime* by Penry Williams, Clarendon Press, Oxford, 1979.

YASRS: Yorkshire Archaeological Society Record Series.

Youings: *Sixteenth Century England* by Joyce Youings, Penguin, 1984 (The Pelican Social History of Britain).

Notes and References

1.   Based on the Cause Papers in *Earl of Shrewsbury* v *Swinden & Parker*, 1584; BIHR CP G 2166.

2.   Guest pp. 6, 11, 104, 615.

3.   *Complete Peerge*; THAS, vol 2 (1920–4), p. 38; Bernard pp. 53–4; HH p. 68; Hey, South Yorkshire p. 105; Bernard pp. 139–40.

4.   Guest pp. 170–1; L&P Henry VIII vol XII part II p. 350; Roger Lockyer, *Tudor and Stuart Britain*, 1471–1714, Longman, 1985; Steven G. Ellis, *Tudor Ireland*, Longman, 1985; L&P Henry VIII vol XII part II, 954; Bernard p. 142; Catalogue of the ACM in SCL 1965 p. 114 SD 268.

5.   The verses are from HH pp. 259–60. The proximity of the Castle and the Manor Lodge was the principal reason for Mary's long residence in Sheffield. Given the lack of sanitation, houses had to be vacated from time to time for cleaning purposes, and the fact that the two houses were close was very convenient: Collinson p. 2.

6.   HH p. 98; Collinson p. 21; Guy p. 309; Williams p. 430; *HH* p. 261; *Sheffield in Tudor and Stuart Times*, David Bostwick, Sheffield City Museums, 1985 p. 9; Surtees 121 (1912) p. 149; Jordan p. 292; Guest pp. 378, 394–5; HH p. 260.

7.   *Sheffield on the Eve of the Industrial Revolution*, David Hey, THAS, vol 14, 1987.

8.   HH p. 83.

9.   *Eastwood's Ecclesfield*, p. 73; E. Lodge. *Illustrations of British History*, London, 1791, vol II, p. 219 (n); Riden and Blair *History of Chesterfield*, vol V, 1985, pp. 32–3, 69–71.

10.   Palliser, chapter 5; Youings pp. 191–2; *Guy* p. 294. For the legal procedures involved see Gransby p. 166.

11.   Gransby pp. 76, 89, 92–3, 106, 110, 239. The tithe of hay was a constant source of friction throughout the diocese of York: ibid p. 110.

12.   For tithes generally, see Tate pp. 134–42; for those of Rotherham see HSY vol II p. 16; Guest p. 169; *Valor* vol V p. 173; THAS, vol 2 (1920–4) p. 37. For Swift, see *Aspects of Rotherham 1*, pp. 24–5 and *Aspects of Rotherham 2*, pp. 10, 14, 18 & 20.

13.   For the ecclesiastical courts at York see Brown; Ritchie.

14.   Gransby p. 110.

15.   Similar arguments had been deployed when the Earl sued the men of Bradfield for tithes in the 1570s: Gransby pp. 92–3.

16.   Nailmaking was a traditional cottage industry in Thorpe Hesley throughout several centuries: see the author's *A House Divided, The Life and Death of John Billam of Thorpe Hesley*, Bridge Publications, Penistone, 1987, p. 2; and HSY vol II p. 100.

17. David Hey in *Rural Metalworkers* p. 41 mentions a seventeenth century nailer in Scholes called Wainwright, and states that the name had 'long been characteristic in the area'.

18. Part of the endowment of Rotherham College, founded by Archbishop Thomas Rotherham in 1482 but dissolved by the Chantries Act of 1547 was 'a tenement and 12 acres of arable and meadow in the town and fields of Scholes . . . and an acre of wood there in the tenure of William Yngell': Guest pp. 150, 157.

19. Twenty.

20. Guest pp. 356–7.

21. £9.

22. Could this be Thomas Corker, chaplain to the Earl and vicar of Rotherham between 1567 and 1577? Thomas Corker was examined by the Archbishop of York in 1570, who reported that 'his preaching was properly maintained in the parish church, which was a fit place'; but he was in disgrace after 1573–4, when he was accused of treachery and called a 'vile wicked varlet and shameful slanderer of true religion'. In 1582 the Earl wrote to Francis Walsingham, Queen Elizabeth's spymaster: 'Now this wicked serpent Corker added, that thereuppon I should infer and say yt her Mtie thought herself a goddess, yt colde not be touched wth the handes of men; wheras I never uttered any suche thynge . . .': *HSY* vol II p. 22; Guest p. 270; *YASRS* 33 pp. 68, 74 75, 78, 80; John Strype, *Annals of the Reformation*, Oxford 1824 vol II pp. 116–7; 251–3; 288.

23. A George Jenkinson of Kimberworth was the defendant in another case relating to tithes in Rotherham parish in 1578: CP H 1896: Adams v Jenkinson.

24. Gransby p. 190.

25. HH pp. 259–60.

2. REFORMATION TO RESTORATION: EMERGING NONCONFORMITY IN SHEFFIELD 1540–1660

by Malcolm Mercer

RELIGIOUS ORTHODOXY IN MEDIEVAL SHEFFIELD was secured by the Augustinian Canons of Worksop who serviced the parish for 250 years from 1308 to 1558. The enormous transfer of ecclesiastical property into lay hands at the Dissolution of the Monasteries* in 1536 did not immediately affect the parish or people. The last Catholic incumbent, Robert Gawthorpe (1535–1558), assisted by three chantry priests, accepted the Great Bible of 1539, complied with the changes in Edwardian liturgy and was not unduly disturbed.

In 1536, Robert Ferrer, Prior of Nostell, complained to Thomas Cromwell that:

> there was almost none in those parts who sincerely, plainly and diligently, preached the Gospel though the people were hungrily desirous to hear and learn. Rodderham, Doncaster, Pontefrette, Wakefelde, Leyds, Bradforde, Halyfax, Manchester and many others had not one faithful preacher.[1]

By the same token, godly preaching was unknown in Sheffield for Gawthorpe was no reforming cleric and religious radicalism was not yet ready to emerge.

It is not surprising therefore, to find Robert Parkyn, the conservative curate of Adwick le Street near Doncaster commenting on the public rejoicing and the atmosphere of popular enthusiasm that greeted the accession of Mary Tudor and the restoration of Catholicism.[2] It is clear that the inhabitants of Sheffield dwelling in the shadow of the Catholic Earls of Shrewsbury were equally delighted and immediately petitioned the Crown for the restitution of land and income confiscated in 1548 by King Edward's Commissioners when they examined the Chantries. Supported by Francis, 5th Earl of Shrewsbury, their pleas were sympathetically received and the impropriated revenues returned. In so doing, a new body of trustees called the Twelve Capital Burgesses and the Commonality of the Town and Parish of Sheffield was created by charter dated 8 June, 1554, and hereafter referred to as the Church Burgesses.[3]

* a glossary of specialised terms is provided at the end of the article.

The creation of this influential lay body by Mary Tudor was clearly a strengthening measure in restoring Catholic orthodoxy. The reconstituted funds were designated specifically to provide for assistant clergy, maintain the fabric of the parish church and allow any surplus for approved secular purposes with particular reference to the needs of the poor and indigent inhabitants. The chantry priests dismissed and pensioned off by Edward's Commissioners were reinstated as assistant ministers, for without them the pastoral oversight of the 2000 'housling people', i.e., communicants over the age of fourteen, was almost impossible. The seven chantry priests of Doncaster complained that they 'could scarcely hear the confessions of 2000 communicants during Lent and administer the sacrament in Holy Week together with the other business of the Church'.[4] Sheffield had but three assistant clergy to care for the steadily growing population. The rites of passage alone averaged 24 marriages, 106 baptisms and 64 funerals annually in the 1560s, rising to 57 marriages, 210 baptisms and 211 funerals in the 1660s.[5]

With the accession of Mary Tudor, the Latin Mass was promptly restored. The laity were again denied the cup at Holy Communion. The wafer replaced the giving of bread and the consecration and elevation of the host was re-introduced. The Edwardian Prayer Books were set aside, the administration of extreme unction was revived as were the dirges for the newly deceased, and the references to purgatory were no longer denounced. Conservative elements within the Church Burgesses, empowered to choose, appoint and pay assistant clergy ensured that at least eleven of them appointed between 1554 and 1603 favoured the old order and retained their pre-reformation title.

However, the death of Richard Gawthorpe in 1558 coincided with the death of Mary Tudor and the accession of the Protestant Elizabeth. Richard Harvard was presented to the living of Sheffield parish by Robert Swyft, the first Capital Burgess and agent of the Earl of Shrewsbury, who had acquired the advowson on the dissolution of Worksop Priory. Old Catholic practices and ceremonies were phased out. A wooden communion table was erected in conformity with Elizabethan Injunctions but the medieval stone altars, restored during Mary's reign were not taken down until seven days after the funeral of Earl Francis in October, 1560.[6]

Succeeded by his son George, 6th Earl of Shrewsbury (Figure 1), there are clearer indications of the provision made for services in the vernacular and recognition of the Protestant Settlement. A wall plaque illuminating the Ten Commandments was fixed in 1562 and two years later, a copy of Erasmus' *Paraphrases of the New Testament* was bought, together with the Psalter in English, a copy of the Queen's Injunctions of 1559 plus the two *Books of Homilies*.[7] The second *Book of Homilies* had only recently been published and both books contained 'godly and wholesome doctrine necessary for these times' thus providing essential teaching in the absence of a preaching ministry.

On Harvard's death in 1567, Swyft's son-in-law, Richard Jessop, who had inherited the rights of patronage, invited John Atkyn, vicar of Whiston, to be vicar of Sheffield also, but he died shortly afterwards. In 1569, Richard Holland, a graduate clergyman and enthusiastic puritan, was inducted as incumbent and the process of Protestant change accelerated. All symbols of superstition were abolished. There was a general desire to remove all fears of the return of Catholicism with its implications of Papal supremacy, Spanish interference and its potential for treason – fears aggravated by the arrival in Sheffield of the Catholic Mary, Queen of Scots (Figure 2), in the custody of the Earl of Shrewsbury. The Rood Loft and Crucifix, essential elements of the Catholic faith, were destroyed and the churchyard cross was demolished. The newly revised English translation of the scriptures known as the *Geneva Bible* replaced the well worn *Great Bible* of 1539, and a copy of Bishop Jewel's *Apologia* – a defence of English Protestantism against the church of Rome, was brought from London. In an attempt to initiate congregational singing Holland ordered copies of the *Geneva Psalms*.

Evidence of Holland's leaning towards Calvinism is to be found in Edwin Sandys' (Archbishop of York, 1576–1588) recommendation

Figure 1. The tomb of the sixth Earl of Shrewsbury. *Joan Jones*

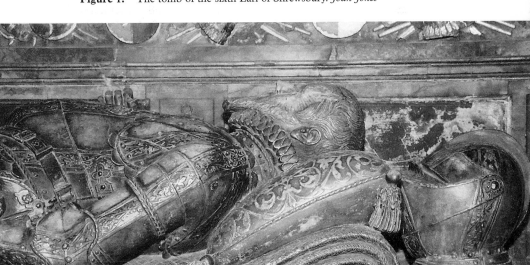

MARY, QUEEN OF SCOTS.

Figure 2. Mary, Queen of Scots. *From the original in the Earl of Morton's collection*

to Earl George that Holland should combine his living with that of the vacant benefice of Whiston. Sandys, a Marian exile and convinced Calvinist who had experienced life in a reformed Protestant Church abroad, informed the Earl that 'in myne opinion you should do a greate good to that people [Whiston] in giving them a preachinge pastor.' [8]

The Catholic laity, never entirely stifled, had hoped the accession of James I, the son of Mary, Queen of Scots, would at least inaugurate a policy of toleration. Some did attend morning and evening prayer but were not prepared to attend Communion services. Such openness led to twelve of them being charged with recusancy in 1604 including Sir William Sampson, assistant minister (1593–1603) and one time usher in the Grammar School, together with five other schoolmasters.[9]

It is clear that by the end of the sixteenth century churchmen in Sheffield were becoming increasingly independent of the national church and were prepared to ignore the discipline exercised by Bishops and Archdeacons. William Jessop clearly disregarded ecclesiastical authority and invited the excommunicate Thomas Toller to succeed as vicar on the death of Holland in 1598. Moreover, when the Grammar School (Figure 3), established by the Church Burgesses in 1565, was endowed and re-founded in 1604, a separate body of school governors was elected and the Articles of Government set out,[10] but no attempt was made to obtain a Bishop's licence for the schoolmasters in direct contravention of Elizabethan Injunctions and Canon Law.

An extreme puritan and clerical opponent of vestments, Toller had been suspended as vicar of Hayton in Nottinghamshire in 1596 for refusing to wear a surplice, being unwilling to make the sign of the cross at baptism or use the ring in marriage, and for refusing to read the Gospels and Epistles as set out in the Prayer Book.[11] Although there are indications of a fair degree of religious toleration in the Northern Province at this time under Archbishop Tobie Matthew

(1606–1628)[12], Toller was again hauled before the York Diocesan Court in 1607 and was described as a 'precisian if not a brownist' i.e., puritan and congregationalist. Ten years later he was prosecuted and charged with non-conformity and found guilty. The Commission suspended him and sequestered the benefice but when threats and persuasion failed to move him the case was eventually dropped.[13]

Enforcing regular attendance at church in accordance with Elizabethan Injunctions was proving most difficult when the parish had but one place of worship. The inhabitants of Attercliffe complained most bitterly that not only did they have to walk a considerable distance but when they arrived the church was so full they did not even have room to stand. In his enthusiasm for bible-based churches, Toller recognised the value of chapelries where congregations could worship as conscience dictated unhindered by lay or ecclesiastical patrons. He initiated the re-building of Ecclesall Chapel in 1622 (Figure 4) and the erection of Attercliffe Chapel in 1629 (Figure 5).

Figure 3. A sealing wax impression of the Sheffield Grammar School Crest. *Sheffield City Libraries, Local Studies Library*

With the support of the Church Burgesses, like-minded clergy were invited to minister there. Toller's son-in-law Edward Hunt was elected assistant minister in 1621 and the first curate of Ecclesall. He was succeeded by William Dawson, possibly the same Dawson of Bradfield who was accused of teaching without a licence in 1604.[14]

The first curate of Attercliffe was Stanley Gower, one time chaplain to the royalist puritan, Archbishop Usher. Gower later became a prominent member of the Westminster Assembly during the Commonwealth – an assembly of men 'disposed to Presbyterianism' and mostly Calvinist in point of doctrine.[15] In 1645 the Assembly authorised a *Directory for the Public Worship of God* on Presbyterian lines to replace the *Book of Common Prayer*. Another minister elected to Attercliffe was William Bagshaw who was to become known as 'the Apostle of the Peak' and ordained after the Presbyterian manner in 1651.

In the latter years of Toller's incumbency we find Thomas Rawson, master of the Grammar School (1627–1645) and assistant minister, charged by Archdeacon Easdall for not being licensed as a schoolmaster, preaching without a licence and not wearing a surplice. For conniving and not reporting the manifest defects in the performance of church services, the churchwardens were also charged with perjury. Evidence presented in the case against them in 1636 testified to the complete re-arranging of the parish church, i.e., pews, communion table, pulpit, bell ringers' loft etc., without diocesan consent and more importantly to the consistent and long standing non-conformity of the clergy in Sheffield.[16]

Toller refused to conform and, in the face of the inflexibility of Robert Neile, Archbishop of York (1631–1639), resigned from his living. Three weeks later John Bright, brother of Stephen Bright of Carbrook, principal promoter of the building of Attercliffe Chapel, exchanged priestly functions. John Bright, described as a 'conformist puritan' became vicar and the aged Toller officiated in Attercliffe but was allowed the complete freedom of the pulpit in Sheffield until he died in 1644. For 45 years Toller ministered, influenced and affected the parish and people of Sheffield with the enthusiastic support of the Church Burgesses who were now solidly protestant and puritan.

It is perhaps difficult to appreciate the effect of Godly preaching on the outlook of the parish and society at this time but the authority of the pulpit is clearly comparable to the thought control of the media today. Calvinism 'supplied a creed to the classes which was to dominate the future.'[17] Religion penetrated all secular affairs and Calvinist preachers in Sheffield addressed much of their teaching to the leading gentry families and the more industrious sort – many of whom became Church Burgesses, Town Trustees and Master Cutlers.

With the demise of manorial control after the death of Earl Gilbert, the last resident Lord of the Manor, in 1616, the cutlers pressed for self regulation and the creation of the Cutlers' Company in 1624 (Figure 6). One of their first bye laws emphasised the need to keep Sunday special and only the holidays recognised by the Church were to be celebrated. Protestantism had abolished a host of minor saints' days commemorated in the pre-reformation calendar. In 1579 the miners in Sheffield officially observed only 13 saints days

Figure 4. Ecclesall Chapel, rebuilt 1622.

Figure 5. Attercliffe Chapel, built in 1629. *Hunter's Hallamshire*

in addition to Christmas week and long weekends at Easter and Whitsun, but Candlemas, May Day, Midsummer Day, Haw Thursday and Cocking Monday were also enjoyed.[18] Fifty years later the cutlers were much more puritanical:

> *None of the Company to do or cause to be done any work concerning the said arts or trades upon the Lords Day commonly called Sunday on pain of 10 shillings nor on a day appointed by order of the Church to be kept Holyday on pain of 2 shillings.*[19]

An arbitration award in 1628 relating to a breach of the Ordinances was addressed to 'ALL XTIAN PEOPLE' and the Searchers, charged with the authority to weed out dishonest trading and 'deceiptful' wares, posted their notices in all the churches in Hallamshire throughout the seventeenth century.[20]

The impact of church teaching and the ethos of Calvinism can also be detected in the upbringing of children, the menace of pauperism and the relief of poverty. Labour was regarded as a social duty stressed most forcibly in the *Homily against Idleness* (1563):

A great part of the beggary that is among the poor can be imputed to nothing so much as idleness and the negligence of parents which do not bring up their children either in godly learning, honest labour or some commendable occupation or trade whereby when they come of age they might get their living.

On first hearing that homily

Figure 6.   The first Cutlers' Hall was built in 1638 on the site of the present hall. This nineteenth century drawing is thought by some to be the tavern in Fargate where the Company held its meetings prior to 1638. The first Cutlers' Hall was replaced in 1725 and demolished in 1822 when the present hall was built.

read in Sheffield, the Church Burgesses established a grammar school in 1565. Eight years later the Feoffees of Ecclesfield founded a petty school there. When Sheffield Grammar School was re-established in 1604, thirty pounds was bequeathed annually for the funding of 'two sufficient men to teach and bringe up the young children there in godliness and learning'. The economic advantages of a little learning were recognised throughout the neighbourhood and petty schools were created in Bradfield (1604), Bolsterstone (1622), Parson Cross (*c*.1630), Stannington (1652), Norton (1654), Attercliffe (1658) and Sharrow Moor (1668) (see Figure 7). Some were the outcome of local initiative and others by private philanthropy. The impact of these schools on literacy was quite remarkable. In 1554 only five of the Church Burgesses were able to write their names on the earliest trust deeds. A century later only 18 out of 198 churchwardens elected between 1660 and 1700 were unable to sign documents.[21]

A marginal note on Genesis XVII, v 23, in the *Geneva Bible* re-emphasised the religious and disciplinary duties of the heads of households:

> *Masters in their houses ought to be as preachers to their families that from the highest to the lowest they may obey the will of God.*

Not only were householders expected to be able to read the Bible, they were expected to send their children, servants and apprentices for instruction and examination in the Catechism to the curate of the parish Sunday by Sunday. The Orders and Articles of Sheffield Grammar School not only required the schoolmaster to attend public worship on the sabbath but also that:

> *No scholler shall be admitted or continued in the said school who shall obstinately refuse to come to divine service, sacrament, preach-*

Figure 7.   Sharrow Moor School, Bagshot Street. This petty school was built in 1668 by public subscription, encouraged by the Bright family. It was endowed in 1720 by Robert Turie and extended in 1769.

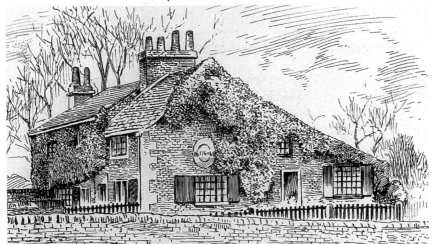

ings and catechizing.

Whilst godly learning became more accessible, the common experience of 'the poorer sort' was being set to work as soon as they were old enough.

Poor relief was widely accepted as a parochial responsibility in Elizabethan and Stuart England. In their plea to Mary Tudor in 1554 the townsfolk stressed the widespread poverty in the parish:

> w^{che} *for the moste parte are never woyd of plagis and other evell deseases by reason of the gret nomber of poore and impotent persones inhabytynge* w^{hin}. [22]

Charitable giving by the Town Trustees and the Church Burgesses increased immeasurably from the end of the sixteenth century. The combination of religious zeal and social awareness prompted a survey of the urban population in 1615 when it was found that the begging poor in the town numbered 725 and out of the 260 households within the township, only a hundred of them could relieve others. The rest 'were unable to abide the storm of one fortnights sickness but would thereby be driven to beggary.' The more wealthy inhabitants lived in the scattered hamlets outside the township. For those falling into the poverty trap a workhouse was erected in 1628 but only children not bound as pauper apprentices were clothed and boarded.

At the same time the cutlers were doing their utmost to safeguard the livelihood of the poorer craftsmen. In their Act of Incorporation (1624) they state how:

> *by their industrie and labour in the same Artes and Trades have not only gained the reputation of great skill and dexterity in the said faculty but have relieved and maintained their families and have been enabled to set on worke many poore men inhabiting there abouts who have very small means, or maintenance of living, other than by their hands and daily labour as workmen to the said Cutlers.* [23]

In addition, the fines, previously appropriated by the Earls of Shrewsbury, were now set aside for the relief of the poorest sort of cutlery workers. These measures may account for the number of poor households exempt from the Hearth Tax in 1672 recorded as 13.3 per cent, whereas the exemption rate for other urban populations was at least 33.3 per cent. [24]

It is clear that the radical nature of the Calvinistic-inspired Puritan movement appealed to the influential families in Sheffield such as the Jessops, Brights, Spencers, Staniforths and Rawsons. They took a solid parliamentary stance in the Civil War and ensured that throughout the period church and parish remained true to the puritan ideal – except for a brief Royalist intervention. When they regained control of Sheffield Castle in 1644, Edward Browne was inducted vicar of Sheffield only to discover the town was 'rebelliously affected' and he departed with the Royalist forces a few months later.

By this time Parliament had abolished the use of the Elizabethan prayer book and ordered the use of the *Directory of Public Worship* (1645) – a Calvinist form of worship consisting of general instructions on how worship should be conducted rather than set forms of liturgies. The main services consisted of prayers, two lessons, psalms and a sermon. Holy Communion was celebrated far less frequently – every seventh Sunday – following the morning sermon, with the congregation seated round the Holy Table which was no longer railed. The *Directory* made provision for baptisms, visitation of the sick and marriages but burials were to be conducted without ceremony. Feast days except Sunday were abolished.[25]

Parliament had also authorised the implementation of a Presbyterian style of church government to replace the authority of Bishops and the control of diocesan administrators. The implication of this legislation was to give the laity ultimate control in church government and the gentry families of Sheffield were free to induct to the vacant benefice whosoever they willed. The assistant minister, Thomas Birbeck, filled the role briefly on the departure of Edward Browne, but in 1646 the Revd. James Fisher, who had served in London and Rutland, was invited to accept the living.

James Fisher had married Elizabeth Hatfield of Laughton en le Morthen, whose sister was the wife of Stephen Bright of Carbrook, and brother of John, vicar of Sheffield (1635–43). Said to be 'a man of great piety and worth, an excellent preacher and an instrument of much good in the town', he veered towards the congregational view, free from episcopal or central authority. He focused on the need for a Godly fellowship of believers who worshipped enthusiastically of their own free will, and appears to have nurtured them separately whilst fulfilling his duty as vicar of Sheffield.

During the Commonwealth, Cromwell became disturbed by the welter of innovative religious practices and saw the need for some kind of organisation for the loosely structured Church. An Ordinance of March, 1654, created a national commission to approve candidates for the ministry and another body who could remove unworthy clergy from their benefices. Fisher was appointed an assistant commissioner by the Protectorate to 'eject ignorant and scandalous ministers' from their livings in the West Riding. A year earlier he had published *The Wise Virgin*, a miraculous story of the eleven year old Martha Hatfield of Laughton who had attracted people from far and wide to hear the glorious truths that she spoke in tongues even though she was normally deaf, dumb and blind.[26]

The religious reaction that set in with the Restoration of Charles II and Episcopacy created a climate whereby Fisher's conversion to Fifth Monarchy preaching, which anticipated the imminent arrival of the millennium launched by an armed uprising, led to the charge of sedition at the North Eastern Assizes in 1662.

> *The jurors presented that Fisher had 2 August 1661 in the parish church of Sheffield in open assembly, intending to promote sedition within this realm . . . uttered the seditious words following:*
>
> *We doe pray for the Conversion of our Adversaires [meaning the Lord King, the Lord Magnates and Parliament] But if our prayer cannot prevail with God for their Conversion we shall rejoyce in their Confusion . . .*[27]

Neither Fisher, nor his clergy team – Edward Prime, Rowland Hancock and Matthew Bloom – described as 'able and painefull' preachers by a parliamentary commission in 1649, were prepared to swear 'unfeigned assent' to the revised *Book of Common Prayer* (1662) and were ejected from their livings on St. Bartholomew's Day without hint of compensation. A significant proportion of the laity affected by the dispossessed ministers formed the nucleus of separate congregations and 'puritanism became dissent'.

Further accusations led to Fisher's appearance at Rotherham, Wakefield and Pontefract Sessions. The passing of the Five Mile Act of 1665 effectively prevented him from pursuing his ministry within the town and, with his health ruined by trials and privation, James Fisher died in 1666.

Residual Calvinism continued to motivate the industrious working folk of Sheffield when its theology and discipline had all but lost its grip. The unity of the Church was shattered as the sectarian congregations constituted a refuge for religious, social and political divergence. Meanwhile the Established Church in Sheffield lapsed into a quiet Anglican conformity.

Glossary

ADVOWSON: the right to present a vicar to a parish or church living.
BISHOP'S LICENCE: The royal injunctions of 1559 reinforced earlier ecclesiastical legislation ensuring that no man could teach or preach without a bishop's licence. These rules became part of Canon Law in 1571 and 1604.

CALVINISM: The religious and social doctrines of John Calvin (1509–1564), a French religious reformer who settled in Geneva and inspired the Puritan movement in the English Church.

CATHOLIC ORTHODOXY: The retention of faith, practice and devotions of the mediaeval 'One Holy Catholic and Apostolic Church' – The Church of Popes and Monks, the threefold ministry of Bishops, Priests and Deacons, the Mass, the Confessional, prayers for the dead and the adoration of Mary, the mother of Christ.

CHANTRY PRIEST: Throughout the Middle Ages wealthy people would endow a chapel called a chantry which was attached to or located within a church, and provide for a priest to sing mass for the soul of the founder.

CHURCH BURGESSES: A body of trustees created in 1554 by Queen Mary when she restored to the parish of Sheffield revenues impropriated by King Edward's commissioners in 1547. These trustees – The Twelve Capital Burgesses and Commonality of the Town and Parish of Sheffield – were empowered to: (a) provide three assistant ministers to assist the vicar of Sheffield in his parochial duties; (b) maintain the fabric of the parish church; and (c) provide for the maintenance and relief of the poor and needy inhabitants within the parish of Sheffield.

DISSOLUTION OF THE MONASTERIES: The abolition of almost all the religious houses between 1536–1540. Monastic properties and estates were transferred to the Crown but the dispossessed monks and nuns were compensated.

EDWARDIAN LITURGY: The form of public worship and administration of the Sacraments and other rites as set out in the First (1549) and Second Prayer Books (1552) of Edward VI.

ELIZABETHAN INJUNCTIONS: A sequence of directives that stemmed from the Elizabethan religious settlement of 1559.

EPISCOPACY: The government of the Church by bishops.

FIFTH MONARCHY PREACHING: Enthusiastic preaching of the imminent arrival of the Second Coming and bodily return of Christ ushered in by an armed uprising.

GODLY PREACHING: Emphasis on scriptural texts and importance of the Word of God for the salvation of mankind.

KING EDWARD'S COMMISSIONERS: The Chantries Act of 1547 required the completion of the survey of all chantries, colleges, hospitals and free chapels set in motion by Henry VIII. Edward's Commissioners were authorised to assess the usefulness of chaplains in the outlying chapels of large parishes, sanction the continuation of certain institutions (mainly grammar schools attached to the chantries) and assign pensions to the dispossessed priests.

MARY TUDOR: The only child of Henry VIII and Catherine of Aragon who became Queen Mary (1553–1558) on the death of Edward VI.

MARIAN EXILE: On the accession of Queen Mary in 1553, Catholicism was restored and many Protestant reformers fled to the continent to escape the ensuing persecution.

PRESBYTERIAN: A system of church government whereby the church was ruled by ministers and assisted by elected congregational elders. Ministers were ordained by presbyters, i.e., ministers already ordained.

PROTESTANT SETTLEMENT: The Protestant Reformation in its Anglican form was restored by parliament through the Acts of Supremacy and Uniformity in 1559. Papal authority was renounced. Queen Elizabeth was made Supreme Governor of the Church of England. The Prayer book of 1552 was re-introduced in a modified form and church attendance became compulsory under penalty of fine.

RECUSANCY: Absence from church. Catholic recusancy scarcely existed until the Papal bull of 1570 excommunicated Elizabeth.

References

1. A. G. Dickens (1959), *Lollards and Protestants in the Diocese of York 1509–1558*, p. 149.
2. Dickens, *Lollards and Protestants*, p. 211.
3. J. Hunter (1869), *Hallamshire: the History and Topography of the Parish of Sheffield in the County of York*, ed A. Gatty, pp. 239–242.
4. A. G. Dickens (1974), *The English Reformation*, Fontana edn., p. 290.
5. D. Hey (1991), *The Fiery Blades of Hallamshire: Sheffield and its Neighbourhood 1660–1740*, Appendix 2, pp. 316–319.
6. Hunter, *Hallamshire*, p. 247.
7. Hunter, *Hallamshire*, p. 248.
8. Hunter, *Hallamshire*, p. 248.
9. D. Evinson (1981), *The Lord's House: A History of Sheffield's Roman Catholic Buildings 1570–1990*, p. 21; A. C. Beales (1963), *Education under Penalty*, p. 197.
10. Sheffield City Archives, Miscellaneous Documents 456, Orders and Articles agreed upon by Sheffield Grammar School Governors, 29 Oct. James I *c.* 1610.
11. R. A. Marchant (1960), *Puritans and the Church Courts in the Diocese of York 1560–1642*, p. 285.
12. Marchant, *Puritans and the Church Courts*, p. 28.
13. Marchant, *Puritans and the Church Courts*, p. 69f.
14. Borthwick Institute, University of York, F53, Archdeacon's Court Book 1604.
15. J. W. Packer (1969), *The Transformation of Anglicanism*, p. 25.
16. Marchant, *Puritans and the Church Courts*, p. 69.
17. R. H. Tawney (1948), *Religion and the Rise of Capitalism*, Penguin edn. p. 103.
18. L. Stone, 'An Elizabethan Coalmine', *Economic History Review*, Second Series Vol.III, pp. 2–3.
19. R. E. Leader (1905–06), *History of the Company of Cutlers in Hallamshire*, Vol II, 2f.
20. Leader, *Company of Cutlers*, 2f.
21. M. Mercer (1996), *Schooling the Poorer Child: Elementary Education in Sheffield 1560–1902*, pp. 23–28; Hey, *Fiery Blades*, p. 258.
22. Hunter, *Hallamshire*, p. 239.
23. The Cutlers' Company (1972), Extracts from the Cutlers' Company, plate 13.
24. D. Hey (1987), 'Sheffield on the Eve of the Industrial Revolution', *Transactions of the Hunter Archaeological Society*, Vol.14, p. 2.
25. Packer, *Transformation of Anglicanism*, pp. 131–2.
26. W. T. Freemantle (1911), *Bibliography of Sheffield and Vicinity*, pp. 73–79.
27. A. G. Matthews (1934), *Calamay Revised*, pp. 198–9.

3.   MAHLON STACY: AN EARLY SHEFFIELD EMIGRANT

by David Hey

IN 1678 A GROUP OF YORKSHIRE QUAKERS set sail from Hull on board the Shield for a new life in America. Amongst these emigrants were Mahlon Stacy and his family, who were leaving their ancestral home in the rural hamlet of Ballifield in the parish of Handsworth. When the ship arrived in West New Jersey in December, 1678, the Stacys settled on the banks of the Delaware on a 500-acre plantation which they named Ballifield after their old home. Within a couple of years Mahlon had erected a mill near the mouth of the Assapink, the first building in what has since become the populous town of Trenton. As one of the original members of the resident Council of Proprietors and a judge of the Burlington Court, he was a prominent figure in the public affairs of the new settlement until his death in 1704. He was succeeded by his son and namesake who played an equally important role in the early history of Burlington County. The two Mahlon Stacys are well-known to local historians in that part of America.[1] The location of Trenton and Burlington County are shown in Figure 1.

Mahlon Stacy's ancestors had lived in the parish of Handsworth since at least the fourteenth century. John, Richard and Robert Stacy, and their wives, were recorded there in the poll tax returns of 1379,[2] when John was one of the two people who headed the list of tax payers in the parish, paying three times the basic rate. Perhaps the Stacys already lived in Ballifield, which stood half a mile to the east of the church, alongside the east-west road through the parish? It was certainly their home by the sixteenth century and remained so until the late eighteenth century. The place-name survives, but the Ballifield district is now much altered from the time when Mahlon Stacy knew it as a young man. The old house was demolished in 1868[3] and the rural character has been destroyed by the nineteenth- and twentieth-century houses.

Stacy, Stacey, Stacye or Stacie is a surname of multiple origins, which was derived from a diminutive form of Eustace, a personal name that was fairly common in medieval England. The origins of the unusual forename Mahlon are more problematical. This name was usually spelt Malin, but it was also recorded as Malyn, Mallin,

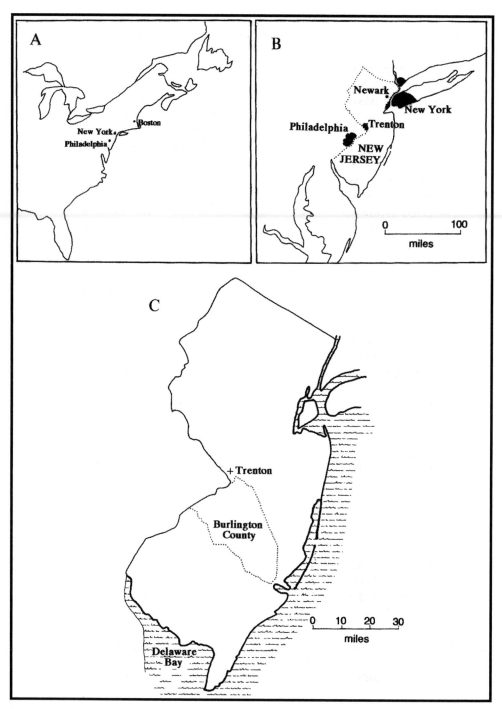

Figure 1.   A: Eastern North America; B: The State of New Jersey; C: location of the modern county of Burlington and the town of Trenton.

Mallen and Malen. In the Middle Ages Malin had been one of the many pet forms of Mary and had subsequently become a surname.[4] The use of Malin as a male Christian name seems to have been largely confined to the neighbouring parishes of Handsworth and Sheffield; only two examples are known from adjoining parishes. The Malyn Stacye who was recorded in a bequest in a Sheffield will in 1566 is the first male who is known to have borne this distinctive forename.[5] He is an early example of the new fashion for using surnames in this way, for in the *Remains Concerning Britain* (1605), William Camden commented that it was only 'in late years' that 'surnames have been given for Christian names among us.'[6] However, nobody with the surname Malin has been found who was connected in any way with the Stacys. Indeed, Malin was always an uncommon surname in South Yorkshire. It was not among the numerous names that were recorded in local deeds and manorial court rolls before the middle of the sixteenth century, and only two examples – a Mr James Malin with nine hearths at Rotherham and a Mr Maylin with six hearths at Cawthorne – were listed in the hearth tax returns of 1672 for South Yorkshire, amongst a list of nearly 8,000 householders.[7] Why the Stacys adopted this unusual forename remains a puzzle, but a connection through marriage with a family surnamed Malin seems the likeliest explanation.

Malin Bridge, a minor place-name in north Sheffield, a few miles away from Ballifield, was recorded in 1552,[8] but the person after whom it was named is unknown. The present Sheffield pronunciation of the place-name is 'May-lin', which gives us a clue as to how Mahlon Stacy pronounced his name. Numerous Malin Stacys were recorded in the parishes of Handsworth and Sheffield during the sixteenth, seventeenth and eighteenth centuries. The name was much favoured by Sheffield branches of the family; one branch there used Malin and Robert for alternate generations, another used Malin consistently. The last of the Sheffield Stacys to be christened with this name was Malin, the son of Malin Stacy, cutler, who was baptised at Sheffield in 1723, and who was himself apprenticed to a cutler in 1738. The Sheffield Stacys were a junior branch of the family at Handsworth. Thus, Malin Stacy, a Sheffield mercer who died in 1590, was the younger brother of Mahlon's great-grandfather. The Handsworth Staceys chose the name only occasionally. A Malin Stacye made his will at Ballifield in 1644, but after Mahlon's emigration the name does not appear to have been used again by the senior branch of the family.

The Stacy family seem to have been the first to use Malin as a forename, but the Sheffield parish register shows that several other families imitated them. Perhaps they were friends of the Stacys or were sometimes related? For example, in 1605 Malin Stacie was recorded as marrying Anna Slacke at Sheffield, and in 1637 Anna, the daughter of Malin Slack, was baptised there. The Sorsby family, who favoured the name Malin for much of the seventeenth century, were perhaps friends rather than relations; they were a prosperous family of cutlers and included Malin Sorsby, who was Master Cutler in 1647. The Sheffield parish register shows that the forename Malin was also used by the families of Barber, Berry, Chapman, Crookes, Gillot, Jackson, Nailor, Pye, Tailor, Topcliffe and Yates, particularly from the late 1620s to the 1640s, with a few later examples. The apprenticeship and freeman records of the Cutlers' Company indicate that the Beals, Dawsons, Habbershaws, Lillies and Wilkinsons, from the parishes of Handsworth, Ecclesfield and Rotherham also used the name Malin during the seventeenth and early eighteenth centuries. The three generations of Malin Gillatts of Sheffield, who were recorded between 1703 and 1763, were unusually late bearers of this forename.[9] No other surname was used as a Christian name by so many local families. The Stacys started the fashion and, apart from a few isolated examples in later times, continued it long after everyone else.

Mahlon Stacy was baptised at St Mary's Church, Handsworth on 1 July, 1638, the third surviving son of John Stacy of Ballifield, gentleman (1599–1658). Mahlon's grandfather, Thomas Stacy (1574–1632), had also been ranked as a gentleman, but his great-grandfather, John Stacy (died 1593), had been placed a little lower in the social scale as yeoman. All three generations had lived at Ballifield and had been substantial members of the local community. Mahlon's mother was Mary, the daughter of John Fulwood of Eastwood (Nottinghamshire), yeoman. It is notable that a John Fulwood was a plantation-holder at Trenton in 1684. Another holder was Thomas Farnsworth, who may have been connected to the Richard Farnsworth who had married Mahlon's aunt, Mary, in 1658. A Thomas Fairnsworth was taxed on a house with three hearths in Tickhill in 1672. A Susannah Fairnsworth, with her children and two servants, emigrated on the same ship as Mahlon Stacy in 1678.[10] Perhaps Mahlon's parents had met through Quaker connections? Local men usually found brides nearer home than Eastwood.

The Stacys had become Quakers in the early 1650s. George Fox is known to have preached on Cinder Hill Green, near Ballifield, in 1653 and again the following year. On the second occasion he also preached in the evening at the home of Thomas Stacy (1619–87), Mahlon's eldest brother, who was soon to inherit the family estate and style himself gentleman.[11] Mahlon would have been fifteen or sixteen years old at the time. Mahlon's other brother, Robert Stacy (baptised 11 February, 1631), also became a Quaker, probably at this time. He was to become one of the commissioners to West New Jersey who purchased lands from the Indians in 1677, the year before Mahlon emigrated.[12] The three brothers remained firm to their Quaker beliefs for the rest of their lives.

On 29 July, 1668, at the age of thirty, Mahlon married Rebecca Ely of Mansfield and set up home at Dore House (alternatively Dower House), close to Ballifield. Mansfield was another early Quaker centre. George Fox had preached there in 1647 and 1648 and the Elys were prominent members of the local society. The Joshua Ely who was constable for Delaware Falls in 1685 and Overseer of the Highways in nearby Nottingham township in 1692–3 was probably a relative of Rebecca's who had emigrated at or about the same time.[13]

Ballifield was licensed as a Quaker meeting place in 1669, during a period of temporary toleration for Nonconformists.[14] A small meeting-house was eventually built nearby at Handsworth Woodhouse. Thomas (the eldest of the three brothers) and his wife, Judith, were buried in the Quaker cemetery in a corner of their estate at Cinder Hill Green. A plan of 1795 marks it as the 'Burying Ground . . . in which several of the Stacye family were interred in the 17th century'.[15] Their descendants, however, preferred to worship at the Church of England. Thomas and Judith's son, John Stacy of Ballifield, gentleman (1656–1712), was buried in the parish churchyard and his grandson, great-grandson and great-great-grandson were all Church of England clergymen.[16] During the eighteenth century the Quakers of Handsworth declined in numbers. Only ten families met each Sunday in 1743, and by 1764 the four families that still belonged to the Society of Friends met 'very seldom'.[17]

Emigration was a major cause for the decline of the local Quaker community. In 1677 Sir John Reresby of Thrybergh, a Justice of the Peace for the West Riding of Yorkshire, reported that:

> *Severall persons with their wives and children (in all to near the number of 200) many of them Quaquers and other dissenters, inhabitants about Sheffield and the adjoining parts of Nottinghamshire and Dabyshr. (the principall of them sectaries but the rest able servants and labourers) have lately gone and are every*

day as yet going by way of Hull to transport themselves to an island in America called west Jarsey, and are dayly followed by others upon the same design.[18]

Reresby's geography was obviously sketchy when he thought of West New Jersey as an island, but his report coincides with the undoubted emigration of the Stacys and their fellow Quakers at this time.

Robert Stacy, Mahlon's elder brother, arrived in West New Jersey on board the *Kent* in August 1677 as one of the representatives of the settlers from Yorkshire, Nottinghamshire and Derbyshire. He was still there in 1681 when he was a signatory to articles of agreement, but nothing more is heard of him.[19] Mahlon Stacy arrived in December 1678 to set up permanent home with his wife, children and servants. Mahlon was one of five Yorkshiremen, all of them Quakers, who had acquired the principal holdings in the 'Yorkshire Tenth' in West New Jersey.[20] The places of origin of the other four are of interest. Thomas Hutchinson was described as a Beverley yeoman; in 1661 four Quakers had been gaoled for holding a meeting at his house.[21] George Hutchinson was possibly related to Thomas; he was described as a Sheffield distiller, but as he cannot be found in local records he had probably not been there very long before he sailed to America.[22] Joseph Helmsley was a yeoman of Great Kelk, which is a small place near Bridlington, about twenty miles north of Beverley; Kelk gave its name to a Monthly Meeting of the East Riding Quakers until Bridlington became the main Quaker centre in those parts.[23] The other principal holder was Thomas Pearson, a yeoman of Bonwick, another small settlement near Bridlington. It is clear from these places of origin why the 'county' that was laid out on the banks of the Delaware was at first called New Beverley, and then Bridlington, before it became known as Burlington.[24] The name Burlington, was simply an old alternative form of Bridlington.[25]

Another person with the surname Stacy who was prominent amongst the early settlers of Burlington County was Henry Stacy, a merchant from Stepney, east London, and a purchaser of lands in the 'Third Tenth'.[26] Perhaps the surname is a coincidence, but it is worth noting that Mahlon's uncle, Robert Stacy, had moved from Handsworth to London long before the Quaker emigration. A family connection is possible.

We are on firmer ground when we try to identify some of the other settlers who crossed the Atlantic with Mahlon Stacy on board the *Shield*. Some are named in the hearth tax returns for the parish of

Handsworth six years before the voyage, These returns list the householders and the number of chimney hearths on which they were taxed. They enable historians to judge the size of the house, and hence the wealth, of each family in the parish. Handsworth had 103 householders, nearly half of whom (50) had only one hearth; another 23 householders had two hearths, 16 had three hearths, 5 had four hearths, 4 had five hearths, 3 had six hearths, one had seven hearths, and at the top of the list was Samuel Drake, Doctor of Divinity, with eight hearths in the Rectory. Thomas Stacy had seven hearths, Mary Stacy had six hearths, and Mallin ([i.e., Mahlon] Stacy had four hearths. Mahlon was working as a tanner at this time, a trade which was pursued profitably by many yeoman families in South Yorkshire and North Derbyshire. The high social and economic standing of the Stacys within their community is made clear from these returns.[27]

The Handsworth men who emigrated to Burlington County with Mahlon Stacy, together with their families and servants, included Godfrey Hancock (five hearths), Thomas Lambert (three hearths) and Godfrey Newbold (three hearths). These men were clearly from the middling ranks of local society: solid yeomen and tradesmen. A Godfrey Newbold gave land for a Quaker burying place in the parish of Handsworth in 1686 and for a meeting-house in 1697.[28]

The surnames of some of the others on board the *Shield* – Revell, Murfin, Scholey, Dewsbury and Fretwell – are suggestive of an origin in or near South Yorkshire. (Mahlon wrote to his 'brother Revell' in England and spoke of a fellow-emigrant as 'my cousin Revell', i.e., the Thomas Revell who was elected Registrar of Burlington County in 1681).[29] The Richard Dungworth who had arrived on the *Martha* from Hull in the previous year was almost certainly from South Yorkshire, for the surname is derived from the hamlet of Dungworth on the hills north-west of Sheffield. (Between 1827 and 1842 all the Dungworths whose births were registered in England and Wales were born in the adjacent registration districts of Sheffield and Ecclesall).[30] The William Quicksall who served as Overseer of the Highways for Nottingham township in 1708 also possessed a South Yorkshire surname. He may have been connected with the William Quicksall of Sheffield, linen weaver, who was taxed on one hearth in Sheffield in 1672 and who was buried in the parish churchyard there in 1702.

William Cook, an old friend of Mahlon Stacy's and the recipient of one of his published letters, was a prominent townsman and Nonconformist (though not a Quaker). He lived from 1632 to 1694 and earned his living as a mercer or woollen draper at the junction of High Street and the Market Place. Cook was a respected member of the community who held the public offices of Church Burgess and Town Trustee.[31] Sheffield remained a stronghold of religious dissent long after the restoration of Charles II in 1660. The leading families had been puritans before the Civil War. They, and men like Cook, ensured that the dissenting tradition continued despite the laws that were passed to stamp it out. The Handsworth dissenters fared less well under the new regime. During the Civil War and Commonwealth the parish had been served by puritan rectors – William and John Cart, father and son, in succession – but John had been ejected from his living in 1662 upon his refusal to conform to the Church of England, just a few years after George Fox had established the Society of Friends in the parish. Religious toleration throughout the land was not achieved until 1689. It was against this background of repression that Mahlon Stacy and his friends decided to emigrate. Mahlon's letters show that he did not regret his decision.

Mahlon Stacy lived for twenty-five years in Ballifield, New Jersey, dying there in 1704 at the age of sixty-five. On 25 April, 1704, his personal estate was valued at £1,034, so he was obviously a substantial figure in the local community. Part of his economic success was based on slave labour, for when his widow, Rebecca, died seven years later, she left £100 to her two 'negro boys' and an annual pension to her 'nager woman', Jane, who was given her freedom. Her will also mentions her 'History of Josephus, three great bibles and other books'. Mahlon and Rebecca were succeeded by their children, Mahlon, Elizabeth, Mary, Ruth and Rebecca. The younger Mahlon quickly assumed a similar role to his father in the affairs of this Quaker stronghold in America. He also used the same unusual spelling of his family's distinctive Christian name.[32]

Notes and Reference

1.   J.E.Pomfret, 'The Proprietors of the Province of West New Jersey, 1674–1702', *The Pennsylvania Magazine of History and Biography*, LXXV (1951), pp.117–46.
2.   Printed in *The Yorkshire Archaeological and Topographical Journal*, V (1882), pp. 44–46.
3.   Revd A. Thomas, *The History of the Parishes and Churches in the Deanery of Handsworth* (London and Sheffield: Sheffield Telegraph, 1932), p. 111.
4.   P.H. Reaney and R.M. Wilson, *A Dictionary of English Surnames* (London and New York: Routledge, third edition, 1991), p. 295.
5.   T.W. Hall, *A Descriptive Catalogue of the Wheat Collection with Abstracts of Sheffield Wills Proved at York from 1560 to 1566* (Sheffield: Northend, 1920), p. 73.
6.   W. Camden, *Remains Concerning Britain* (Wakefield: EP Publishing, 1974), p. 56.
7.   Division of Adult Continuing Education, University of Sheffield, database of local medieval records; D. Hey, ed., *The Hearth Tax Returns for South Yorkshire, Ladyday 1672* (Sheffield University, 1991). At the same time, two Malins were recorded at Duffield (Derbyshire), and in 1674 six Malins were taxed in Nottinghamshire.

8. A.H. Smith, ed., *The Place-Names of the West Riding of Yorkshire* (English Place-Name Society: Cambridge University Press, 1961, part 1, p. 216). Robert Stacey held the manor of Owlerton (which included Malin Bridge) by 1640, but not before 1607.

9. C. Drury and T.W. Hall, eds, *The Parish Register of Sheffield*, 3 vols, 1560–1686 (Sheffield: Hunter Archaeological Society, 1917–21); R.E. Leader, *History of the Company of Cutlers in Hallamshire*, II (Sheffield: Pawson and Brailsford, 1906).

10. F.B. Lee, *History of Trenton, New Jersey* (Trenton: Smiley, 1895), p.19; J.O. Raum, *The History of New Jersey*, 2 vols (Philadelphia: Potter, 1877), pp. 99, 106. For Pedigrees, see J. Hunter, *Hallamshire: The History and Topography of the Parish of Sheffield in the County of York*, ed., A. Gatty (London: Nichols, 1861), p. 488; J. Hunter, *Familiae Minorum Gentium* , 5 vols (London: Harleian Society, 1895), pp. 1209–1212; Hey, *Hearth Tax*, p. 62.

11. Hunter, *Hallamshire*, p. 489, quoting George Fox's Journal.

12. Lee, p. 17.

13. Lee, pp. 19–20; W.H. Groves, *The History of Mansfield* (Nottingham: Murray, 1894), pp. 327–38.

14. West Yorkshire Archive Service, quarter sessions records.

15. Sheffield Archives, Fairbank, HAN 23L.

16. Hunter, *Hallamshire*, p. 488.

17. Borthwick Institute of Historical Research, York: Archbishop Herring's (1743) and Archbishop Drummond's (1764) visitation returns.

18. Quoted in R.E. Leader, *Sheffield in the Eighteenth Century* (Sheffield: Pawson and Brailsford, 1901), p. 287.

19. Pomfret, pp. 122–23; Raum, p. 119. The surnames of Joseph Helmsley and William Emley are each derived from a Yorkshire Settlement.

20. Pomfret, pp. 123–25.

21. K.J. Allison, ed., *The Victoria County History of York: East Riding*, VI (Oxford University Press, 1989), p. 243.

22. A George Hutchinson was taxed on four hearths in 1672, but he was most likely the barber-surgeon who was married in Sheffield 1660 and whose wife was buried there in 1681. John, the son of George Hutchinson, was baptised in 1689.

23. K.J. Allison, ed., *The Victoria County History of York: East Riding*, II (Oxford University Press, 1974), p. 189.

24. Raum, p. 99.

25. The Earls of Burlington took their title from their estate at Londesborough, near Bridlington. Their London seat was Burlington House.

26. Pomfret, pp. 128–29.

27. In the second half of the seventeenth century the Stacys mined coal on their estate and elsewhere in Handsworth and one of the earliest cementation steel furnaces was erected at Ballifield.

28. Thomas, p. 199.

29. Raum, pp. 102, 106–9; Lee, p. 18.

30. D, Hey, ed., *The Origins of One Hundred Sheffield Surnames* (Sheffield University, 1992), p. 27.

31. Raum, p. 110; D. Hey, *The Fiery Blades of Hallamshire: Sheffield and Its Neighbourhood, 1660–1740* (Leicester University Press, 1991), p. 19, and pp. 255–72 on 'The Established Church and Nonconformity.'

32. New Jersey Archives, catalogue of wills.

4. Woodland Management on the Duke of Norfolk's Sheffield Estate in the early Eighteenth Century

by Melvyn Jones

AT THE BEGINNING OF THE EIGHTEENTH CENTURY, coppice management had been the dominant form of woodland management in South-west Yorkshire for more than 300 years, having replaced the wood pasture tradition as the most important form of woodland management, from an economic point of view if not in terms of physical extent, by the mid-fifteenth century. Coppice management was to continue to occupy this premier position until the mid-nineteenth century when the conversion of coppices to high forest plantations became increasingly common.[1]

This study covers the period from 1709 to 1724. The evidence comes from the fair copies of accounts made by a succession of woodwards which were collected together in a single volume of 183 numbered and 74 un-numbered folios and entitled 'The woodwards Mr. Ashmor's, Mr. Northalls and Mr. Ibersons accounts for Sheffield cum membris' . The accounts are part of the Arundel Castle Manuscripts which are the muniments relating to the Yorkshire, Derbyshire and Nottinghamshire estates of the Dukes of Norfolk and their predecessors and which are deposited in Sheffield Archives.[2] The accounts are not just dull recitations of charges, discharges, arrears and summaries; they are full of meticulously recorded graphic descriptions of activities and transactions which are full of technical and geographical detail. Although the accounts cover only a decade and a half, a very clear picture of a sophisticated system of woodland exploitation is established, a system which had a very close relationship with other aspects of estate management and the local economy in general.

Such is the specificity of the entries in the accounts that a detailed picture is quickly built up of woodland officials riding over the countryside around Sheffield and Rotherham arranging for the felling of coppices, replanting hedges and re-building walls around recently felled woods to protect them from grazing animals, prosecuting thieves and trespassers, supervising the conversion of wood and timber into saleable products, organising their sale, and using wood and timber to maintain the fabric of the estate. In short the accounts represent an incomparable record of the details of the practice of wood-manship* as carried out on the Sheffield estate of the Duke of Norfolk during a golden age of woodland management, a practice characterised by a high degree of technical sophistication in which intensive production, where little was wasted, was matched by care-fully implemented conservation practices that guaranteed that the woods became self-renewing and inexhaustible suppliers of wood and timber.

This study, therefore, has three complementary aims. First, to identify and exemplify the characteristic features of woodmanship as practised on the Duke of Norfolk's Sheffield estate in the early eigh-teenth century; secondly, to demonstrate the close relationship between woodland management and the local economy; and, finally, to provide a glossary of technical terms associated with eighteenth century woodland management.[3] Unless otherwise stated the quota-tions are taken from the book of accounts for the years 1709–24.

The Sheffield woodland estate in the early eighteenth century

The Sheffield area in the early eighteenth century was both an important industrial district and a large landed estate. To the west of the town stretching along the middle and upper reaches of the Don and its tributaries was a rural landscape of villages, hamlets, farms, woods and moors that had once been within the bounds of the pri-vate hunting forest of the lords of Sheffield. To the east, at its great-est extent covering nearly 2,500 acres, was the site of Sheffield Park, a medieval deer park. By the early eighteenth century the park was virtually disparked and the lodge at its centre, the Manor Lodge, was being demolished in the first part of the period covered by this study. Sheffield Castle, in the town itself, was also in ruins and the 8th Duke of Norfolk (who held the title from 1701 to 1732) had his chief residence at Worksop Manor in Nottinghamshire.[4]

Coppice woods were an important component of the early eigh-teenth century landscape, encompassing more than 2,000 acres (809 ha) of ancient woodland. Many of the coppice woods lay on or near parish or township boundaries, with many woods lying on steep slopes or occupying exposed sites. This distribution pattern was the result of the clearance of land around the main settlements in parish-es and townships over thousands of years, with the surviving wood-lands occupying remote and/or unattractive sites within those terri-tories.[5]

Fifty-three separate woods are referred to in the accounts, of which 40 can be located (Figure 1). Nearly half of the woods have

---

* A glossary of woodland management terms used by the woodwards on the Sheffield estate in the early eighteenth century is provided at the end of the study.

survived to the present day. Although the woods lay outside the early eighteenth century town, some significant woodlands would have been visible from the town itself, for example Morton Bank, lying on the eastern slopes of the Sheaf valley formerly within the medieval deer park; Burngreave and Hall Carr Wood, on the northern slopes of the Don valley downstream of its confluence with the Sheaf; and most extensive, the adjacent Cook Wood, Lord's Wood, Oaken Bank and Old Park Wood, covering 230 acres (93 ha) and stretching along the northern slopes of the middle Don valley from Shirecliffe to Neepsend.

Occurring side by side with the coppice wood system was the management of holly trees as winter fodder for farm stock and for the remaining deer in Sheffield Park and Rivelin Chase.[6] The 'hollins' or 'holly hags', as they were called, were either small separate woods or compartments within woods or on wooded commons. The hollies were cut on rotation like other underwood and then allowed to grow back. John Harrison, in his survey of the Manor of Sheffield in 1637, listed 27 'hollin hagges' that were rented by farm tenants[7] and in 1696 the diarist Abraham de la Pryme made the observation that ' in the south west of Yorkshire . . . they feed all their sheep in winter with holly leaves and bark . . .'[8]

Timber and wood were also felled on a regular basis on the extensive wooded commons, usually in small parcels, and sometimes individual trees. Felled hedgerow trees produced branchwood and bark, most of the hedgerow trees being stump trees called hedgehogs, from which stithy stocks, the blocks which formed the bases on which anvils stood, were sawn. Small woods on farms ('reins' or 'shaws') were also exploited in a systematic way, as were willows and alders on river banks.

Techniques of woodland and tree management

Most of the woods on the estate in the early eighteenth century were worked as coppices and four of them, Bullas Spring, Hayfield (Highfield) Spring, Scraith Spring, and Wilkinson Spring still retained the Anglo-Saxon word for a coppice – spring – in their names. Another two, High Storth and Duxter (Duckstorth) Wood, contained the element storth, the Old Norse name for a coppice wood. The estate coppices, or spring woods as they were more usually called, had two main distinguishing characteristics: most of the trees were cut to ground level on a rotation (the coppice cycle), and the woods were protected by stockproof boundary fences.

Large woods were subdivided into compartments, locally called

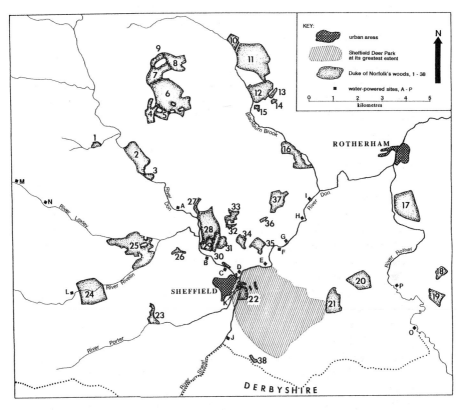

Woods:

		Water-powered Sites:
1 - Tagland Wood	20 - Highfield Spring	A- Wadsley Forge
2 - Beeley Wood	21 - Bowden Housteads Wood	B - Morton Wheel
3 - Duxter Wood	22 - Morton Bank	C - Kelham Walk Mill & Wheel
4 - Prior Royd	23 - Smith Wood	D - Wicker Tilt
5 - Wheata Wood	24 - The Coppice	E - Royds Mill
6 - Greno Wood	25 - Stannington Wood (Common)	F - Attercliffe Forge
7 - Upper Hall Wood	26 - Walkley Bank (Common)	G - Attercliffe Forge
8 - Nether Hall Wood	27 - Scraith Spring	H - Brightside Mill
9 - Little Hall Wood	28 - Old Park Wood	I - Parker Wheel
10 - Parkin Wood	29 - Lord's Wood	J - Heeley Wheel
11 - Hesley Park	30 - Oaken Bank	K - Pond Mill
12 - Smithy Wood	31 - Cook Wood	L - Rivelin Mill
13 - Clough Wood	32 - Little Roe Wood	M - Bradfield Mill
14 - Jumble Hole	33 - Far Roe Wood	N - Dam Flask Mill
15 - Starnel Bushes	34 - Burngreave	O - Woodhouse Mill
16 - Woolley Wood	35 - Hall Carr Wood	P - Treeton Mill
17 - Canklow Wood	36 - Wilkinson Spring	
18 - Burnt Wood	37 - Wincobank Wood	
19 - Treeton Wood	38 - Hang (ing) Bank Wood	

Figure 1. Fifty-three woods are mentioned in the 1709–24 accounts. Forty of these can be located with certainty and 38 are shown on the map above. A further two (Poggs Wood and Agden Wood) lay beyond the western boundary of the map area. The map also shows the 16 water-powered sites referred to in the accounts.

falls. Because falls were at different stages of growth, large woods also contained internal stockproof fences. The coppiced trees grew back as multi-stemmed trees from stumps or the root system (Figures 2 and 3). The stump was usually referred to as the stool or stowen, and the multiple stems collectively as underwood, and individually as poles or, if very young, as radlings.

The coppices of the early eighteenth century, as they had been since at least the second half of the fifteenth century, were worked as coppices with standards. Scurfield, in his study of the Sheffield area based on Harrison's survey of the Manor of Sheffield in 1637, concluded that 'evidence that the woodlands were being managed as coppice-with-standards rather than as [simple] coppice is tenuous'.[9] In fact, other near-contemporary sources show that coppice with standards was the norm in South Yorkshire in the mid-seventeenth century.[10] Moreover, it remained the principal method of woodland management in the region until well into the nineteenth century.[11]

Figure 2. A recently felled compartment in a coppice wood in early summer. In the foreground is a newly- sprouting coppice stool. In the middleground is a partially completed cord of wood – a pile of four-foot lengths of coppice poles which when completed will be four feet high, four feet wide and eight feet long. In the background is another compartment nearing the end of its coppice cycle. *Joan Jones*

Figure 3. Cutting hazel coppice with a bow saw. The photograph was taken in the Spring of 1995 in Ecclesall Woods where traditional coppicing is being re-introduced. *Ted Talbot*

The evidence in the 1709–24 accounts for the fact that coppice with standards was the normal method of woodland management in the early eighteenth century is both overwhelming and unequivocal.

In the coppices with standards, whereas the underwood was mixed, the standards were overwhelmingly of oak, though wych elm, ash and alder were locally important (Figures 4 and 5). In South Yorkshire the standards were referred to generally as reserves, though a distinction was made between wavers (invariably written as weavers in the early eighteenth century), young timber trees that had grown through only one coppice cycle, black barks, that had grown through two coppice cycles (40–50 years old) and lordings, the biggest trees in a wood that had grown through at least three coppice cycles.[12]

Coppice cycles varied in length. The internal evidence of the source employed here suggests coppice rotations of between 18–24 years in the early eighteenth century. Other near-contemporary evidence from woods on neighbouring estates suggest that this was the norm. In Ecclesall Woods, also in Sheffield, and made up of 17 contiguous woods covering nearly 370 acres, the average coppice cycle length between 1715 and 1774 was 24 years, ranging from 14 to 43 years. Ignoring the three cases where coppice cycles exceeded 35 years (suggesting that a fall had been missed for reasons that are unclear) the average completed coppice cycle was 21 years.[13] In two coppice schemes devised by Thomas Wentworth, first Marquis of Rockingham, in 1727 and 1749, covering respectively 40 and 43

Figure 4. A recently felled coppice with standards. The standards are oak. *Joan Jones*

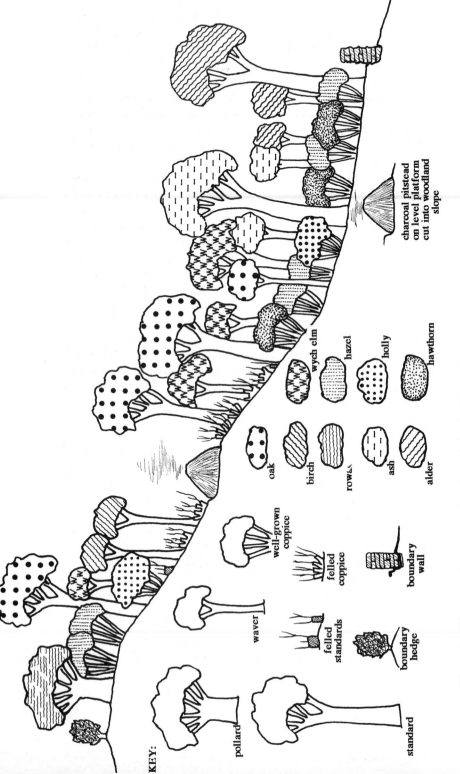

Figure 5. Diagrammatic representation of a typical early eighteenth century coppice with standards in the Sheffield area. The typical features are a steeply sloping site bounded by walls and/or hedges, mixed underwood of hazel, holly, hawthorn and oak, and standards of oak (mostly), ash, wych elm and alder.

woods or compartments in woods, 21 year cycles were used.[14]

When a wood or a compartment in a wood was ready to be felled and sold, the fall was preceded by a valuation, which involved computing an overall value for the underwood, and another for the bark. The timber trees that were to be felled ('to go down') and those to be allowed to stand had also to be selected, valued and identified in some way, usually by painting them with raddle[15] or marking them with scribe irons. The whole operation was called marking out or setting out. The process is described on a good number of occasions in the 1709–24 period. In February 1711, for example, the accounts record the money spent on food and drink when Joseph Ashmore, his son, and Abraham Ibbotson and Matthew Northall were at Smith Wood where they ' marked out ye Reserves . . . and Valued ye wood for sale.' Within a few days they were at Highfield Spring where they 'sett ye weavers out', the operations involving a charge for 'Radle for both woods'. Before felling commenced, woodland rides had to be made passable for the horse-drawn timber wagons used to carry wood, timber and bark and this involved removing the lower branches from trees and clearing the undergrowth, variously referred to as brushing or swatching. The felling of the coppice had to be organised in relation to the main rides through a wood and this was done by dividing each coppice compartment into sections or divisions. For example, in 1715, Abraham Ibbotson and Matthew Northall assisted 'Mr Stanley of Howbrook to make ye divisions in Smithy Wood' and subsequently a woodman was paid two shillings for ' cutting ye divisions in ye ffalle in Smithy Wood'.

Although most of the wood and timber felled on the estate had resulted from natural regeneration from coppice stools and naturally distributed seed, there is substantial evidence in the 1709–24 accounts that planting was a common practice by this time, both outside and inside coppice woods. In 1710, for example, 'a mett [a measure] of seed oakes yt were sown at Howden' were brought over the moors to Sheffield for planting and, in the autumn of 1718, five woodmen were paid £1-17-06 for planting 'ackhorns' in Clough Wood. In 1722 trees were planted on Park Hill (in the former deer park) and in Bowden Housteads Wood. Trees were also planted to bind river banks together and then later harvested when their growth threatened to damage the same banks. There are several references to 'pricking willows' on river banks and in 1718 Widow Hensley was paid £1-05-00 for leading brushwood from Oaken Bank Wood to Burton Dam side to protect the willows that had been planted there. In the same year ten 'stump ashes' growing beside the Blackburn

Brook 'which damaged ye waterbanks' were felled and sold for £2. The decline of the deer park, now that the Duke of Norfolk's main residence was at Worksop Manor, was reflected in the sale to Jonathan Hall 'ye Joyner in Sheffield' of '30 old walnutt trees at ye Mannor' for £4 in 1716.

Protection of coppices

The most vital element in coppice management is the protection of young growth from grazing animals. This was done by making and keeping in good repair stockproof fences in the form of hedges and walls (Figure 6). The availability of Millstone Grit and Coal Measures sandstones, from which substantial drystone walls could be built, obviated the need around many woods for the almost universal woodbanks of Eastern England, although such banks with external ditches are found around parts of some of the surviving ancient coppice woods in the Sheffield area. Whether on substantial banks or not, hedges were constantly being re-planted around newly felled woods. In 1710 William Sheppard was paid one shilling and eightpence for ' hedging at ye ffar end of Shertcliff Park new cutt' and two years later the same woodman with a partner were paid £3-03-05½ for hedging 293 roods (1470 m) 'in ye near end of Shertley Parke where ye last fall was'. Similarly, William Walker and his partner were paid £1-19-08 in 1716 for completing 136 roods (about 700 m) of 'Spring hedging betwixt Smithy Wood and Jonathan Wingfield's Close'. There are also numerous references to re-building walls that had had to be taken down in order to fell trees or cart underwood and timber out of the woods. In April 1718, for example, Jonathan Berley was paid five shillings and sixpence for 'Walling and hedging sev'all Gapps in ye ffence of Grenna Wood ye sd ffence being often Broake down by ffelling ye poles & ffalling upon it by Mr ffell's servants who cutt ye sd wood'.[16]

Even so animals got into the woods and when detected they were impounded and the owner fined. In 1718 Enoch Moor was fined one shilling when nine of his sheep were 'pounded out of Greno Wood' and in 1720 two men were paid three shillings and sixpence for their trouble in 'pounding 5 sheep belonging to Mr Watts that was trespassing in Little Hall Wood'. At the end of a coppice cycle, when the underwood was newly cut, it was particularly important to prevent animals from browsing on the young growth. In this connection the vicar of Ecclesfield was paid twopence in 1718 for giving notice to tenants and freeholders (presumably at a Sunday service) to ' take care that their goods and cattle do no longer Continue to Graise in

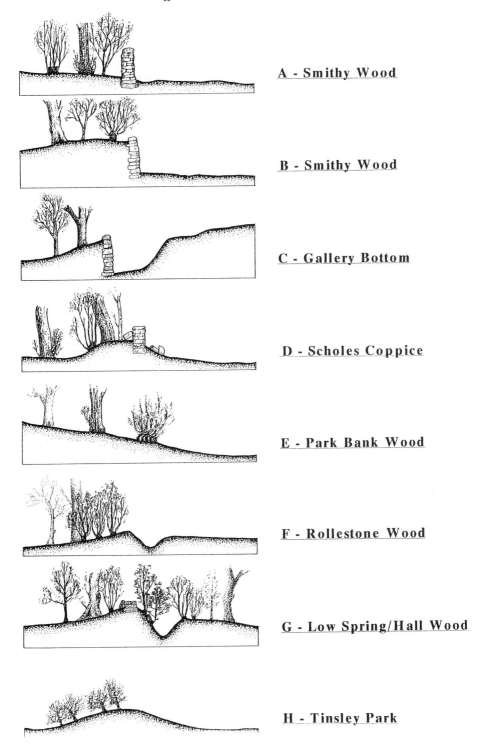

A - Smithy Wood

B - Smithy Wood

C - Gallery Bottom

D - Scholes Coppice

E - Park Bank Wood

F - Rollestone Wood

G - Low Spring/Hall Wood

H - Tinsley Park

Figure 6. Examples of surviving coppice wood boundary fences in the Sheffield area.

Greno Wood for Spoyling ye young sprouts'.

Coppice woods had also to be protected against trespassers and thieves. In 1720 Joseph Shephard and his wife were paid two shillings for 'watching to see who breaks ye Gapp open at ye upper side of Shertley Park'. The accounts duly record that 'M. Bamforth pull'd it open'. The trespass apparently continued, and in 1723, £1-06-06 was paid to two workmen for ' making Bullworks in ye Old Park to keep M. Bamforth's carrier from coming yt way'. The cutting down and taking away of wood and timber were particular irritants to the woodwards, and these offences were not restricted to building materials or firewood. Reference has already been made to the importance of holly for feeding stock in winter. It was a particularly valuable source of animal feed on the moorland fringes, and in hard weather tenants may have been tempted to cut holly grown for the Duke's deer. With this in mind, in 1710, Joseph Ashmore recorded that he had paid Henry Bromhead four shillings 'for him and horse going 2 days in ye great snow to see if any one croped Holling'.

Tracking down thieves and bringing them before magistrates consumed a considerable amount of the woodwards' time. In 1712 Joseph Ashmore claimed a shilling for time spent in searching for stolen wood in Rotherham and Kimberworth. In the next entry in the accounts he claimed further expenses for 'taking Joseph Osborn's gun and searching for wood at Blackburn'. In the same year he paid Jonathan Loy two shillings and sixpence 'for giving information yt Jonas Royston [was] felling hasles in Wooley Wood'. In 1712 and 1718 the woodwards paid for a warrant, signed by two justices of the peace, to be issued to local constables instructing them to assist in the search for stolen wood and timber. The 1718 warrant stated that 'great destruction' had taken place in the Duke of Norfolk's woods 'by being cutt downe and Carried Away by Some Idle Disorderly Persons'. Constables were to 'make diligent search . . . in the most suspitious houses' and to bring suspects before the magistrates.[17] Abraham Ibbotson Junior subsequently paid the constable of Nether Hallam five shillings for reporting 14 people to the justices of the peace for stealing birch twigs; witnesses and informers were paid £1-5-0. The next year he paid 'a constable of Rotherham' five shillings for serving a warrant on Widow Bothomly and Thomas Hugill for stealing wood out of Canklow Wood.

Felling and conversion of wood and timber

The commencement of the felling of a coppice was surrounded by a certain amount of ceremony. Crews of woodmen had to be assembled, jobs apportioned and contracts agreed. Agreements were usually concluded with the drinking of ale and sometimes with the payment of 'earnest money'. In 1710, for example at Treeton Wood, near Rotherham, two shillings and sixpence were expended by Joseph Ashmore on 'Ale when Mr Ibotson & I lett ye cutting of ye first ffall'. He also recorded that another half-crown was spent on ale at the same wood 'when we lett ye pilling [bark peeling]'. In 1715 Abraham Ibbotson paid four shillings in earnest money when he set on the bark peelers at Upper Hall Wood.

The first stage of felling involved cutting the coppice poles, felling the timber trees marked to go down, peeling the bark, removing the brushwood, and sawing up the branches. At a particular fall most of the wood, bark and timber was immediately disposed of to regular customers or to tenants or used in building projects and repairs on the estate. Long-term contracts were entered into with ironmasters but even in those cases woods were viewed prior to the commencement of felling. For example, in September 1717, Abraham Ibbotson junior spent one shilling and sixpence on himself and ' Mr Clay in going to view Agden Shroggs & Hartcliff Rocher in order to treat about them'.[18] The availability of wood and timber was also announced to the surrounding population. In 1710 Joseph Ashmore paid twopence to 'ye Cryer for crying ye sale' at Treeton Wood.

Once felled the underwood was treated in different ways depending on how it was going to be used. Tall underwood poles to be used as hop poles (1000 hop poles were cut in the first fall in Hesley Park in 1721–22 and 2,500 in the second fall in 1722–23), for scaffolding or for making ladders had their branches and the bark removed and then left as they were. Underwood to be used in charcoal making was cut into four feet lengths and stacked in cords which in South Yorkshire were piles of wood four feet wide, four feet high and eight feet long, weighing just over one and a half tons. Wood destined to be used as pit props (puncheons or punch wood) was also sold by the cord. The cording of wood was a major woodland activity every time a fall occurred, most of it destined to be made into charcoal for Chapel Furnace and Attercliffe and Wadsley Forges, collectively known as the Duke of Norfolk's ironworks.[19] In 1715, for example, 348 cords were made when the 48½ acre Upper Hall Wood was felled, amounting to nearly 550 tons of cordwood. Most of the cordwood must have been converted into charcoal at long-established charcoal making sites – level platforms, called pitsteads, dug out of the sloping woodland sites (see Figures 5 and 7). The only reference to pitsteads in the 1709–24 period was at Howden Wood where new platforms were prepared in the Spring of 1723. The accounts record a spade being bought 'to make pittsteeds att Howdyn', and then

Robert Holmes, the woodward by that time, accompanied 'Mr ffell to Howdyn to ordr places for the pittsteeds'. Two woodmen were then engaged to carry the 'cordwood together and make the pittsteeds'.

Wood was also corded to be used as whitecoal. Whitecoal was small lengths of wood, dried in a kiln until all the moisture was driven out. Mixed with charcoal it was a fuel used in lead smelting at a water-powered ore-hearth.[20] Wood for use as whitecoal was obtained from woods, but during the period in question large amounts of alder and willow from riverbanks were used for this purpose. For example in 1716 'Mr Clay'[21] paid £11-00-00 for 'all ye Owler brushwood & other wood that is fitt for makeing Whitecoal standing and being on both sides ye waterbank on ye River Sheaff from ye pond mill down to Heely Bridge'.

The smallest branches and twigs were collectively referred to as ramell[22] and were used for making besoms and faggots. Sometimes the rammel was sold to a specialist craftsman as in 1715 when all the ramell in the 48½ acre Upper Hall Wood was sold to Samuel Sykes of Anston for £10-19-00. Faggots were also made in the woods and in the period in question were referred to as kidds or long kidds, and the process as kidding up. A kidd was a bundle of ramell three feet long and a foot and a half in diameter tied with a withe at each end.[23] They were made in large quantities, for example, in 1720, 1000 were

Figure 7.   Charcoal making. The photograph was taken at Rockley, near Barnsley early this century. On the right is a completed charcoal stack and on the left a charcoal maker's hut. The hut has a framework of poles covered with turves. *C.F. Innocent (1916)*

made in Scraith Spring from the tops of trees that had been felled for the use of tenants. They were used as fuel in fires requiring high temperatures in a short period such as in bakers' ovens. In 1719 they were used to burn bad meat in Sheffield market. Long kidds were up to 10 feet long and were what are generally known as fascines and were used in river bank protection (see below).

During the 150 year period between 1680 and 1830, the production of leather and leather goods was, by value, the most important industry in England after textiles, and one of the largest employers outside agriculture.[24] Woodlands played a significant part in this important industry by supplying tree bark which, before the introduction of chemical substitutes, was the major agent used in the preparation or 'tanning' of the animal hides before their conversion into such everyday articles as boots, shoes, clogs, harnesses, saddles, breeches, aprons, gloves, mittens, bags, cases, bottles, bellows and belting. Book binders were also important consumers of leather. South Yorkshire was an important centre of the tanning industry, local tanners being able to rely upon a continuous supply of hides from the cattle farms in the Pennine foothills in the west and in the lowlands in the east, and a steady supply of oak bark from the predominantly oak-birch coppice woods in the region.[25] The best bark was that obtained from coppice poles of about 20 years of age[26] and so the bark obtained from Sheffield's coppice woods was of the best quality. The manner of peeling the bark varied from region to region. Most of the bark was peeled in pieces about two feet long and as wide as the circumference of the tree or pole from which it was removed by a first team of barkers. This was done both while trees were standing and after they had been felled. The smaller branches, even down to those of one inch in diameter, were peeled by a second team, often consisting of women and children. This was referred to as sticking bark. In 1722, for example, £1-14-04 was paid to 'seven Pillars [peelers] of bark in Hesley Park being for such Bark as Stuck to ye wood after ye first pilling thereof'. The bark was stacked to dry in the open air for a few weeks before being stacked under cover. It was then sold uncut or chopped up into small pieces ('hatched').

For Treeton Wood in 1710 the whole process from the agreement of the peeling contract to the sale of bark to tanners is meticulously recorded:

Pd for Ale when we let the pillings at ye first ffall £00-01-00
Pd Tho Lee & partners for pilling 1420 fathoms of bark £18-14-05
And for Staking the same £2-07-04
Spent at Treeton when I mett the Wath tanners £00-01-00

Pd M Turner for 104 Thack Sheaves for thatching Bark stacks
£00-4-04
Pd Jno Earnshaw for leading sods to cover 5 bark stacks £00-05-00
Pd Jno Clayton for covering 5 bark stacks with Sods
and 11 stacks Covered with Straw £00-14-00
Jno Oldam bought 100 quarts of bark from Treeton Wood £16-13-08
Lyonel Keyworth bt 62q & 2f of bark from Treeton Wood £10-09-09

Bark was chopped or ground manually and by the use of horse power and water power. The estate does not appear to have operated its own bark mills and most of the bark seems to have been sold uncut. Indeed there is only one reference to hatching bark during the whole of the period in question: in 1721 one shilling and sixpence was expended on 'six poles in Grenna [Greno Wood] to make a Hutt on to Chopp Barke'.

Large timber trees in woods, on commons, on farms, in hedgerows and along riverbanks were felled as occasion demanded. Once felled, they were treated initially like coppice poles. Oak trees were peeled and the bark sold to tanners or bark dealers. For example in 1718 the bark of '5 stump oaks . . . sett out in his own ffarm for yates and stiles' were sold to Christopher Stacy. Other tree species were also de-barked prior to their conversion. The branches were then sawn off and much of the wood sawn up again into lengths and used as cord-wood. Some large bent branches were made into 'bends', naturally bent components for water wheels. As with the underwood poles, the brushwood was made into kidds. The tree trunks were then hewn or squared with axe, adze and shave into beams and posts or sawn or riven into planks, as, for example, in 1710 when £3-00-08 were expended on two woodmen squaring and sawing 370 ware [planks two yards long and one yard wide] in Burngreave Wood.

Alongside the woodmen converting the timber trees into beams, posts and planks were others who were cleaving (usually referred to as riving) oak poles to make stakes and laths, hewing oak poles to make gate posts, cleaving and shaving ash to make tool or broom handles, and cutting hazel rods to make hurdles (fleaks or flakes), thatching spars and for basketwork (Figure 8). Transporting wood and timber and bark from the woods was also a major activity. Sledges were used for hazel rods for hurdle- and basketwork, barrows are also referred to when cordwood was being brought together, but in most cases it was the horse-drawn timber wagon that was employed both within the woods and beyond.

A minor but integral part of the management of the woods was the use that was made of the ground vegetation for grazing and bedding for stock. The pasturing of horses, called agistment ('gyst'), herbage or wood grass, in well-grown coppices, produced a regular if small income. Occasionally the woodwards were very explicit in the accounts that agistment was only taking place in woods or compartments within woods near the end of a coppice rotation when no harm would be done to new coppice growth. For example, in 1710, Joseph Ashmore noted that he had charged himself for 'My Mare & ffole in Wooley Woods this Spring a month it's old Cutt'. Similarly, the following year six shillings were charged for six horses in Burngreave 'befor ye Spring of wood'. In 1709 Nathaniel Woolas and his partner paid ten shillings for 'ye Breacken of Stanington Wood', presumably for bedding for stock. Stannington Wood was a wooded common and from 1717, Sarah Lockwood of Stannington leased the right, for ten shillings a year, to collect sap from the birch trees there. The sap, which would have been collected in Spring by cutting a slit in the trunk, was made into sugar or mixed with honey, cloves, lemon peel and ale to make a mead-like wine.[27]

Timber and wood and the maintenance of the fabric of the estate

In addition to the sales to ironmasters, coalmasters, lead smelters, tanners and sundry craftsmen, large amounts of wood and timber were used on the estate in the construction and repair of domestic buildings, barns and stables, and other wooden structures such as bridges. Buildings were blown down or burnt down and had to be rebuilt; some were in need of enlargement; others needed to be re-roofed. New buildings were also erected.

It has been estimated that there were at least 49 water-powered industrial sites on Sheffield's rivers in 1660 and that by 1740 the number had probably risen to about 90.[28] These sites included corn mills, cutlers' wheels, furnaces, forges and tilt hammers (see Figure 1). Many of the sites, together with others on the River Rother and its tributaries, were on the Duke of Norfolk's estate and a great deal of time, effort and materials (mostly wood and timber) were expended on maintaining, improving and extending them. Work consisted of repairing and maintaining riverbanks and the banks of the head and tail goits; maintaining and re-modelling the associated weirs, and making, repairing and fitting the machinery, in particular the water-wheels, in the mills themselves.

Reference has already been made to the practice of planting willows on waterbanks to bind the soil and sub-soil together. More fundamentally, squared or sawn sections of timber, or fascines ('long kidds'), held in place by stakes or hurdles, were regularly being installed to retain waterbanks. In June 1710, for example, 300 'radlins' (hurdle rods) were supplied to Mr Sylvester 'to repair his Water Banks above Neepsend', and another 100 to Mr Bamforth (of Old Park Corn Mill) 'to repair his Banks above Owlerton Bridge'. A much more substantial undertaking was carried out in 1717 when Jonathan Vintin was paid £4-03-04 for 'felling, squareing & sawing' 100 yards of timber for ' ye Water Bank near Rhodes Mill'. He was then paid a further £2-15-00 for 'staking and radling 55 yards and filling up with Brush Wood' on another part of the waterbank near Rhodes Mill.

Weirs were also regularly maintained or re-modelled. The weirs were constructed at an angle across the river to deflect water, via a floodgate (shuttle), into a channel (head goit) leading to a reservoir (mill dam). The weirs consisted of a top kerb, a slope consisting of stones set in clay, and a bottom kerb. The bottom kerb was some-times of timber. As David Crossley has pointed out, the weirs were subject to deterioration through the action of storm-water[29] , and the 1709–24 woodwards' accounts show that they were being frequently repaired and strengthened. In 1717, for example, Jonathan Sellars was paid £4-15-00 for 'felling, hewing and squareing 90 yards of

Figure 8. Coppice crafts. Against a background of cordwood in a recently-felled compartment in Ecclesall Woods are a hazel hurdle, a besom, a walking stick, hedge stakes, hazel rods for basketwork and country chairs. *Ted Talbot*

plank and ffixing them upon Kelham Ware with 25 pile shoes made therein'. The following year Thomas Ashmore was paid for three days' work 'hurrying Brushwood to ffill at ye foot of ye ware at Parker Wheele'.

Timber and wood were also used on a large scale for engineering work in the mills themselves. During the 1709–24 period one new mill was constructed – Bowden Housteads Flood Mill at Handsworth – and almost another score had timber parts rebuilt or replaced. New troughs were installed, gudgeons laid, wheel sleepers put down, horsings made, pump stocks built, shuttles repaired and trees felled and hewn for axletrees. Most frequent in the list of repairs and new constructions were water-wheels. Repairs were made to the water-wheels at Brightside and Parker Wheels and Woodhouse Mill in 1717, and new water wheels were made for Bowden Housteads Mill in 1718, Pond Mill and Woodhouse Mill in 1720, and Parker and Brightside Wheels in 1723.

From 1715, Jonathan Sellars and Jonathan Vintin or Vintaine were constantly referred to in the accounts either converting timber or working for long periods at named mills, wheels or forges. Sellars was referred to specifically in 1715 as 'ye Mill Carpinter', and the complex and comprehensive work completed by Vintin, as the following example shows, identifies him as a most experienced and skilful millwright.[30]

January 1719 Pd Jno Vintin for
makeing a New forebay at Brightside Wheele
Repareing 3 Water wheeles
making a New fall
raceing the Jack Wheele 6 yards Lower
making the Trough halfe a yard wider
Makeing New hollow Wheeles and Trough
putting New head stocks in each Wheelehouse
Makeing a new bridge ovr ye new Goyte
Staking and Raddeling above and bellow the Bridge
making a new Grate and Bridge between the said Wheelehouses
raiseing the wash and repaireing the floodgates
Laying downe 30 yards of Timber in the ware and driveing 62 piles
Stakeing and raddling the length on the foot of the sd ware
£27-01-00

Summary and conclusions

The foregoing analysis has demonstrated that woods and trees on the Duke of Norfolk's Sheffield estate in the first quarter of the eighteenth century were regarded as critically important natural resources in sustaining the local economy. There was hardly any aspect of the local economy that did not rely in some way, either directly or indirectly, on the local production of wood, timber and bark. To this end, the vast majority of the estate woodlands were managed as coppice with standards, a system in which the production of wood from the coppice, timber from the standards, and bark, from both coppice and standards, was maximised. Moreover, regrowth from the coppice stools and natural regeneration from seed guaranteed that the woods would be a largely self-renewing resource. Much effort, therefore, was expended on protecting that resource from the depredations of grazing animals and from trespassers and thieves.

The study of Sheffield's woods in the past also explodes a myth. The popular belief – and, it must be said, one held by people who ought to know better – is that many local woodlands were destroyed to make charcoal. Nothing could be further from the truth. It was not in the interests of local landowners, such as the Duke of Norfolk, the Duke of Leeds or the Marquis of Rockingham, with large acreages of profit-making woods on their estates, charcoal makers, or anyone using charcoal as a fuel, to destroy the source of supply. Just the opposite. It was the primary interest of a large number of stakeholders to sustain the supply of wood and timber. Regular annual incomes for landowners, profits for entrepreneurs and livelihoods for workers were at stake. It was because of their economic usefulness that they survived, only to be ravaged in the post-charcoal era through mining in them, through road building and the spread of urban settlement.

Glossary

Bark stack: a stack of bark, protected against the elements, built in a wood as bark peeling proceeds.

Black bark: a timber tree in a coppice with standards that has grown through two coppice cycles.

Boon (vb); boonwork (n): an unpaid service due by a tenant to his lord. In the case of woodland management this often involved the carting of wood and timber.

Brushing: clearing away undergrowth in a wood.

Coppice: multi-stemmed growth from a tree stump (stool).

Coppice cycle: rotation length in a coppice wood.

Coppice with standards: a coppice wood in which most of the trees are periodically cut to ground level from which they grow as multi-stemmed trees, and in which other single-stemmed strees are allowed to grow on through a number of coppice cycles. These are the timber trees or standards.

Cord (n): coppice poles and branchwood, cut to length and made into a stack. In South Yorkshire a cord was eight feet long, four feet wide and four feet high. Such a stack weighed about 1¹/2 tons.

Cord (vb): 'to cord' was the act of cutting coppice poles and branches into four feet lengths and making them into stacks.

Cordwood: coppice poles and branchwood cut into four feet lengths. Cordwood was the basic building block of a charcoal stack.

Crying the sale: announcement of the sale of wood and timber by the town crier.

Division: one of the sections into which a compartment in a wood was divided. This was done in relation to the rides within the wood to aid the extraction of wood and timber.

Fall: compartment in a coppice wood and the felling of coppice at a particular place at a particular time.

Go down: trees that were marked to go down were those that had been selected to be felled at the setting or marking out.

Gyst: local variant of agistment, the pasturing of animals (usually horses) in a well grown coppice wood. See also herbage.

Hedgehog: a stunted hedgerow tree.

Herbage: see gyst.

Kidd: faggot or bundle of brushwood used as fuel (eg, in bread ovens). A kid or kidd was about three feet long, double the size of an ordinary faggot, and was tied with two withes (a twisted band of ash, birch, hazel or willow), one at each end. A long kidd was up to 10 feet long.

Kidding up: the action of making kidds.

Lathwood: split timber (often oak) in the form of a strip about an inch wide used in walls and covered with plaster.

Lead (vb): to transport material, by cart or wagon.

Lording: The oldest trees (standards or reserves) in a coppice with standards. Such trees had grown through at least three coppice cycles.

Mark out: to mark with paint or by blazing(removing a slice of bark with an axe or billhook) trees which are to be felled.

Owler: local name for the alder (*Alnus glutinosa*).

Pill (vb): to peel or strip bark.

Pitstead: the place (platform) where charcoal was made.

Pole: one of the stems of a coppiced tree. Also used to describe a young timber tree.

Pound out (vb): to remove domestic animals from a coppice wood into which they had strayed and impound them in the village pound or pinfold.

Punchwood: pit timber.

Raddling (n. and vb.): a rod or stem used in making woven hurdles; raddling was the act of cutting such rods and weaving them into a hurdle.

Raddle (n): red paint used in marking out; also called ruddle.

Ramel(l): brushwood.

Rein: a narrow belt of trees.

Reserve: a single stemmed timber tree growing within a coppice with standards. A reserve was a standard.

Set out: to mark by paint or by blazing trees which are to be felled. An alternative to 'mark out'.

Shaw: a small farm woodland.

Sicklewood (siclewood): meaning unknown, possibly poles from which tool handles were made.

Snagging: the removal of branches from a tree.

Sparrpole: a rod usually of hazel or willow that was split into four for use as thatching spars.

Spring: a coppice wood, in South Yorkshire usually a coppice with standards.

Spring hedging: new hedge around a newly felled coppice; usually necessary where hedges had been removed to extract wood and timber.

Sprout: young coppice growth.

Sticking bark: bark removed by a second team of barkers which had proved obstinate to peel on the first occasion.

Stithy stock: a section of the trunk of a large tree used as the base for an anvil (stithy).

Stool: the base of a tree from which the multiple stems (poles) of coppice grew. See also stowen.

Storth: Old Norse name for a coppice.

Stowen: see stool.

Stump tree: this word has two meanings: a stool or a pollard.

Swatching: clearing the undergrowth with a bill-hook.

Underwood: collective name for coppice poles.

Ware: a plank one yard wide and two yards long.

Weaver: local spelling of waver, a young timber tree in a coppice with standards.

Whitecoal: kiln dried chopped wood used in lead smelting at a water-powered ore-hearth.

Wood grass: see gyst.

Woodmanship: the art of producing wood and timber in a wood without destroying the vegetation; usually associated with the practice of coppicing.

Woodward: a woodland officer.

References

1. Jones, M. (1997) 'The rise, decline and extinction of spring wood management in South-west Yorkshire', Proceedings of the British Ecological Society's Conference on Recent Advances in Forest and Woodland History, University of Nottingham, 2–6 September, 1996.

2. Sheffield Archives, Arundel Castle Manuscripts S 283. The title of the accounts mentions three woodwards. In fact during the 1709–24 period, there were five woodwards: Joseph Ashmore from 1709 to July 1713 when he died; Matthew Northall from May 1709 until June 1721; Abraham Ibbotson Senior from June 1710 to April 1716 when he died; Abraham Ibbotson Junior from July 1713 until October 1720 when he left Sheffield to serve the Duke of Norfolk at Arundel Castle; and Robert Holmes from October 1720.

3. The glossary contains definitions of the key terms employed by the eighteenth century woodwards on the Sheffield estate. The only dictionary of such terms is N. D. G. James's *An Historical Dictionary of Forestry & Woodland Terms*, Blackwell, 1991. The glossary contains a number of terms not found in James's dictionary.

4. For a detailed description of Sheffield and its environs in the second half of the seventeenth and the first half of the eighteenth century see David Hey (1991), *The Fiery Blades of Hallamshire: Sheffield and its neighbourhood, 1660–1740*, Leicester University Press, pp. 15–41.

5. For analyses of woodland locations and sites see Rackham, O. (1990) *Trees & Woodland in the British Landscape*, 2nd edition, Dent, pp. 112–13; Peterken, G. (1981) *Woodland Conservation and Management* , Chapman and Hall, pp. 34–37; Jones, M. (1993) *Sheffield's Woodland Heritage*, 2nd Edition, Green Tree Publications, pp. 60–62.

6. Spray, M. and Smith, D. J. (1977) 'The Rise and Fall of Holly in the Sheffield Region', *Transactions of the Hunter Archaeological Society*, 10, pp. 239–251.

7. Ronksley, J. G. (1908) John Harrison's (1637) *Exact & Perfect Survey & View of The Manor of Sheffield*, Robert White, pp. 32–33.

8. 'The Diary of Abraham de la Pryme', *Surtees Society*, Volume LIV (1870), p. 165.

9. Scurfield, G. (1986) 'Seventeenth-Century Sheffield and its Environs', *The Yorkshire Archaeological Journal*, 58, p. 154.

10. For example: Shrewsbury Papers in Lambeth Palace Library, MS 698, Fol 3, 'Estimate of Spring Woods in Co York totalling 2240 acres belonging to the Forges of the Earl of Shrewsbury . . .' (undated, late 16th or early 17th century); Sheffield Archives, WWM D778, particulars of coppices with standards on the Wentworth estate, 1657.

11. Jones, 'The rise, decline and extinction of spring wood management . . .'; Jones, *Sheffield's Woodland Heritage*, pp. 25–28; Jones, M. (1995) *Rotherham's Woodland Heritage*, Rotherwood Press, pp. 34–37; Jones. M. (1997, in the press) ' From coppice with standards to high forest: the management of Ecclesall Woods, 1715–1901', in *The Natural History and Archaeology of Ecclesall Woods, (Peak District Journal of Natural History and Archaeology, Special Publication, No 1)*.

12. Jones, 'The rise, decline and extinction of spring wood management . . .'.

13. Jones, 'From coppice with standards to high forest . . .'.

14. Sheffield Archives, Wentworth Woodhouse Muniments, A 1273.

15. The red mineral called raddle, reddle or ruddle was mined in the past at Micklebring, between Rotherham and Doncaster. See Brown, I. H. and Cowdell, F. W. (1967), 'The Mining of Ruddle in the Rotherham Area', *Bulletin of the Peak District Mines Historical Society*, 3: 3, pp. 133–42; Goodchild, J. (1996) 'The Ruddle Mines at Micklebring and the Ruddle Mill at Braithwell' in Jones. M. (Ed) *Aspects of Rotherham: Discovering Local History*, Volume 2, Wharncliffe Publishing Ltd. pp. 228–233.

16. 'Mr ffell' was John Fell Senior (1666– 1724), one of the partners in the Duke of Norfolk's Ironworks from 1716. He acted as clerk to the Ironworks Partnership, a key managerial position controlling all aspects of raw material acquisition, production and sales. See G. G. Hopkinson (1963) 'The Charcoal Iron Industry in the Sheffield Region 1500–1775', *Transactions of the Hunter Archaeological Society*, 7, pp. 125–38; Hey, *Fiery Blades* . . ., pp. 172–73.

17. Sheffield Archives, Arundel Castle Manuscripts S 541.

18. 'Mr Clay' was probably Joseph Clay, another member of Duke of Norfolk's Ironworks partnership; Hopkinson, 'Charcoal Iron industry . . .' , pp. 134.–36.

19. See Hopkinson, 'The Charcoal Iron Industry . . .'.

20. W. Linnard (1982), *Welsh Woods and Forests*, National Museum of Wales, p. 76; D. Kiernan (1989) *The Derbyshire Lead Industry in the Sixteenth Century,* Derbyshire Record Society, Volume XIV, pp. 140–43.

21. 'Mr Clay' may have been Robert Clay who acquired the lead smelting mill at Dore called the Upper Mill in 1714. For details of this lead smelting site see Crossley, D. (Ed) (1989) *Water Power on the Sheffield Rivers*, Sheffield Trades Historical Society/University of Sheffield, p. 91.

22. For a discussion of this term see James, *Historical Dictionary* . . ., p. 139. The word ramell is still used in South Yorkshire to denote rubbish.

23. James, *Historical Dictionary* . . ., p. 95.

24. Clarkson, L. A. (1974) 'The English Bark Trade 1660–1830' *Agricultural History Review*, 32, p. 136.

25. Hey, D. (1979) *The Making of South Yorkshire*, Moorland Publishing, pp. 124–25; Elliott, B (1988) 'Lime, Liquor and Leatherman: Oak-Bark Tanning – The Forgotten Rural Industry of South Yorkshire', *The Hallamshire Historian*, 2:1, pp. 12–24.

26. Clarkson, 'English Bark Trade . . .' p. 139.

27. Edlin, H. L. (1949) *Woodland Crafts in Britain*, Batsford, p. 44.

28. Hey, *Fiery Blades of Hallamshire*, p. 179.

29. Crossley, *Water Power on the Sheffield Rivers*, p. x.

30. David Crossley points out in *Water Power on the Sheffield Rivers* (p. xiii) how little is known about the millwrights who built and maintained the water-powered mills in the Sheffield area. A close scrutiny of the source used here would enable a researcher to build up a fairly comprehensive picture of the work of Vintin and Sellars in the early eighteenth century.

Acknowledgements

I wish to thank Bob Warburton for drawing Figures 1, 5 and 6.

5. Sheffield's Turnpike Roads

by Howard Smith

THE MODERN ROAD-USER IS LARGELY UNAWARE that most of the main roads in and out of Sheffield were once turnpike roads, with tollgates, standing at intervals, at which payment had to be made in order to proceed along the next stretch of road. The first toll was taken in 1756 – the last in 1884. These toll roads were planned, built, administered and maintained by turnpike trusts – legal bodies set up by private Acts of Parliament to be responsible for a precisely defined length of local highway. Each of these bodies had to be supported by trustees (sometimes well over a hundred men of property and substance – though in practice only a handful took an active role in the actual running of the road they administered). The real day-to-day work of each trust was carried out by the officers – a clerk, treasurer and surveyor, who reported to their trustees at business meetings. Tolls were collected at gates (originally wooden poles or 'pikes' which could be moved to close or open passage along a road – hence 'turnpikes'. Eventually the roads they controlled came themselves to be referred to as turnpikes.) The collectors lived in cottages at the side of their gates (see Figure 1), and were either employees of the trust, or independent operators who had bought, at auction, the rights to collect tolls on an annual basis in return for paying a lump sum to the trustees.

The first turnpike trust had been set up in 1706 to supervise a bad stretch of the ancient highway, once an important Roman road, known as Watling Street (now the A5) near Stony Stratford. The principle of the actual road-user paying towards the costs of maintaining the highways dated from 1663, when Justices of the Peace for Huntingdonshire were allowed by Parliament to charge travellers on

Figure 1. Heeley Toll Bar, on the turnpike from Sheffield to Derby via Chesterfield, in 1875.

a particularly difficult section of the Great North Road, which was regularly reduced to a disgusting and dangerous quagmire in the winter months. The existing system of road maintenance was inadequate.

This system dated back to 1555 when Parliament placed the responsibility for road repairs on each parish. The better-off villagers had to provide carts and tools, whilst the peasantry had to give four, later six, days' labour each year, all under the supervision of the annually elected overseer of the highway – an unpaid and thankless task, as the work was resented by the villagers. Any repairs would be rough and ready – the art of roadbuilding had departed with the Romans over a thousand years earlier. These bodged-up roads were adequate for merely local use, or for packhorse transport, but could not cope with long distance traffic and heavy usage, especially by the increasing number of heavy waggons and coaches – private and public. The situation was always difficult when a long-distance highway, such as the Great North Road, ran through a large and thinly populated parish with limited resources, especially over clayey soils which rapidly deteriorated to mud.

Although the idea of charging tolls for the King's highway was deeply unpopular and the practice resisted – sometimes violently in the early years – the new system soon proved to be more effective than the amateurish old parochial arrangements.

Trusts became well-established in and around London in the first quarter of the eighteenth century, with almost 900 miles (1440 km) of road turnpiked by 1730, and almost 1400 miles (2200 km), or 88 per cent of the capital's total road network, by 1750. Provincial towns gradually copied London's example, but it was not until 1756 that Sheffield built its first turnpike road.

It was the leading citizens of the town in their capacity as Burgesses and the Company of Cutlers who led the way in seeking an Act of Parliament to this end. Sheffield's poor communications had been improved by the River Don being made navigable to Aldwarke (NE of Rotherham) in 1733, and further up-river to Tinsley in 1751. This cut down the expensive land journey of twenty miles (32 km) to the old river port of Bawtry to reach navigable water to a mere three to Tinsley. Even so, better roads were urgently needed to move freight to and from Tinsley as well as further afield. The town's fathers had become aware from the experience of other parts of the kingdom that substantial economic benefits could flow from the adoption of carriageways, for the use of wheeled vehicles, to replace the packhorse bridleways. In simple terms, eight horses could now pull three tons in a waggon. The same weight carried on their backs required above thirty horses. Waggons were also more suitable carriers for heavy, bulky freight such as coal, stone, timber, lead and limestone.

The first highway to be improved was the ancient route south to Derby via Chesterfield in 1756 (see Figure 2). Two years later, other old roads – to Barnsley and Wakefield (and thus on to Leeds), Chapel-en-le-Frith (for Manchester), and Buxton via Tideswell were also turnpiked.

These improved highways totalled 100 miles (160 km) of turnpiking, with another eighteen added in 1759 when the old route from Tinsley to the river port of Bawtry was turnpiked. In 1764 Acts of Parliament set up trusts for improving two more long-established routes, Tinsley to Doncaster, via Rotherham and Attercliffe to Worksop, through Handsworth. These brought the total of turnpike roads around Sheffield to 150 miles (240 km).

After a hiatus there was another surge of road building between 1777 and 1781 when the routes linking Sheffield with Halifax via Penistone and Huddersfield and with Mansfield to the south-east, were constructed, as was the moorland road from Greenhill (Norton) to Hathersage, including two of its eventual three branches. The third, Owler Bar to Baslow was added in 1803.

Thus the turnpike network was almost completed within 25 years, with Sheffield located at the centre of a web of improved roads radiating to most points of the compass, though the north-west quadrant was only thinly served. This was remedied by the construction of the Langsett turnpike in 1805 and by the Snake road built between 1818 and 1821, though really they were only offering improved alternatives to existing parallel routes. Apart from the two roads just mentioned, most of the new road building carried out by the turnpike trusts in the nineteenth century was to by-pass some of the worst inclines on established routes. For example, the Mam Tor road offered a safer alternative to the 1:5 Winnats Pass, whilst the new Ecclesall, Halifax and Burngrave Roads all provided gentler gradients for horses, drivers and passengers.

The technical improvements of the typical eighteenth-century turnpike road must not be overstated. No body of professional surveyors, road engineers and constructors existed, so expertise was sadly lacking and progress was made by trial and error. The typical turnpike road in the Sheffield area was made from a wide variety of materials, especially stone, but there was no binding material for the road metal and no kerbs to prevent slippage. By later standards the roads remained primitive and traffic moved slowly. Freight waggons averaged two mph and could travel only up to twenty miles (32 km) a day. The first stagecoach to leave Sheffield (for London via Derby), in May 1760, took three and a half days to complete the journey to the capital: 45 miles (72 km) a day, an average speed of no more than four miles an hour.

Stories are legion about the bad, even appalling, condition of many roads. Arthur Young, noted agrarian reformer and writer, who travelled widely and recorded his views on the many roads he traversed, described the Sheffield to Rotherham road in 1770 as 'execrably bad, very stony and excessively full of holes'. And this was only six years after its turnpiking. Dyche Lane, near Little Norton, was described in 1793 as having ruts more than two feet deep, with horses or carriages unable to proceed 'at more than a foot's pace'. Sheffield Moor in 1800 was described as a 'shocking road for coaches', with the footpaths 'a good deal higher than the road' – which means that this important route south was still a deep, rutted, worn-out holloway, in spite of 'improvement'. It is not a myth that able-bodied males were expected to disembark from a stagecoach on a severe incline, such as Derbyshire Lane, and walk up the hill to save the horses.

Nonetheless, as time progressed, lessons were learned, and perhaps it would be fair to describe the network of turnpike roads round Sheffield in 1800, at the very least, as being much less bad than in pre-turnpike years. They were better administered and maintained than under the old parish system, and could all be used by wheeled vehicles, not just packhorses. Certainly, local landowners, industrialists, mine and quarry owners – and the Cutlers' Company – thought so, and were the prime movers behind new road schemes and provided many of the numerous trustees required for each new turnpike.

Overall, the turnpiking of eventually over 250 miles (400 km) of main roads round Sheffield was a key factor in the rapid industrial growth of the town in the late eighteenth and early nineteenth centuries. In the hinterland of Sheffield, enclosure of farmland and moor was stimulated, which boosted food production and raised land values. Enclosure also added many miles of new, or straightened and improved, local roads which often acted as feeders to the turnpikes. Many coal mines, iron foundries, stone quarries and lime works were made viable by improved roads, especially in areas not served by navigable water. Businessmen benefited from the more efficient links between Sheffield and its neighbouring towns and

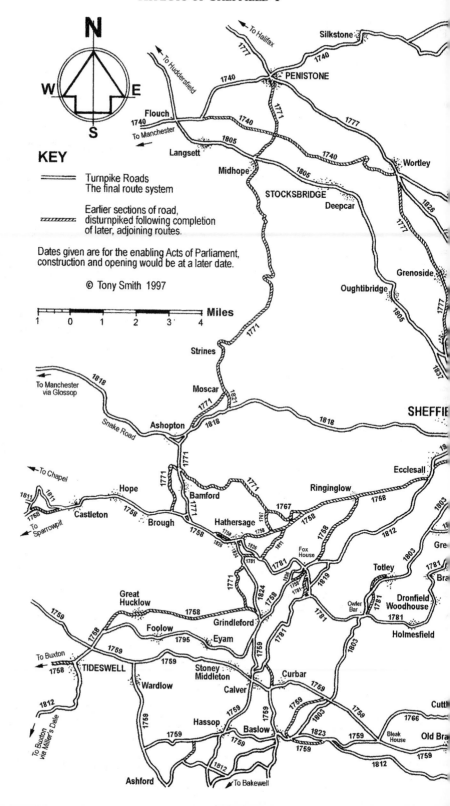

KEY

Turnpike Roads
The final route system

Earlier sections of road,
disturnpiked following completion
of later, adjoining routes.

Dates given are for the enabling Acts of Parliament,
construction and opening would be at a later date.

© Tony Smith 1997

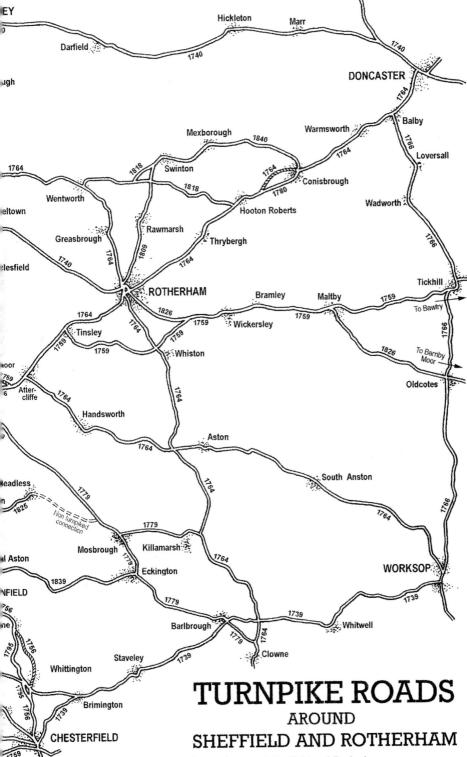

Figure 2. Turnpike roads around Sheffield and Rotherham.

other rapidly growing industrial centres like Birmingham, and London itself. By 1787 eleven coaches left Sheffield, seven on a daily basis, a figure which had risen to 36 in 1821.

Also in 1787, twenty-seven waggons were based in the town, providing a weekly or half-weekly service carrying a wide variety of cargo. The Royal Mail became vastly more efficient with its rapid adoption of specialised, speedy mailcoaches to replace the bumbling system of unreliable postboys carrying the mail on old nags – easy targets for thieves. Passenger travel became safer, cheaper, swifter and more comfortable over the decades, particularly after the great road improvements of John Loudon Macadam, Thomas Telford and their followers from around 1815. For example, London could be reached from Sheffield in 26 hours by 1787. This was down to sixteen hours in 1830 – an average speed of ten miles (16 km) per hour, unthinkable in the eighteenth century.

Quite simply, Sheffield could not have grown from a town with a population of 12,000 in 1750 to one with 35,000 in 1801, and continue to grow to 65,000 in 1821 and 110,000 in 1841, just as the Railway Age was beginning, without its network of turnpike roads.

Sheffield's experience was repeated on the national scale, of course. In 1830 England had some 22,000 miles (35,400 km) of turnpike roads, providing the infrastructure for a well organised coach and waggon industry based on hundreds of inns catering for the ever-increasing number of travellers. It is estimated that at least 100,000 people were directly and indirectly employed in keeping the coaches on the move. The 1830s were the heyday of the coaching industry, and yet it was all ended, in some cases with almost brutal suddenness, by the arrival of the steam-hauled railway.

Following the enormous success of the Liverpool & Manchester Railway in 1830, further lines were opened with astonishing speed. By 1848 there were 5,000 miles (7,700 km) of track in use, with another 3,000 (4,800 km) added in the next seven years. Rival coach services were wiped off the main roads, often within weeks of a new railway being opened.

Sheffield reflected the national trend. Its first railway – to Rotherham – opened in 1838. In 1840 the North Midland Railway linked Leeds and Derby via Rotherham which enabled passengers from Sheffield to reach London in nine hours, in almost half the journey time of the fastest coach. Travel by train was also much cheaper and more comfortable, so there was very little the coach firms could do to compete, and takings at many tollgates fell drastically, as coaches disappeared from the main roads.

In fact the competition from the railways came at a time when the finances of many of the local trusts were in poor shape. The by-passes on some of the routes had been costly to build but had generated little, if any, extra revenue. Freight traffic on some roads was quite heavy but often paid no tolls. For example, some of the nobility who had developed coal pits on their estates, were granted exemptions (as a reward for their support in getting a turnpike Act through Parliament) from tolls on the movement of their coal along a trust's road). This was true of other vested interests too, and proved a straitjacket on many a trust's finances. The decline of the Derbyshire lead mining industry caused a fall in revenue for the turnpikes crossing the Peak District. Tolls were fixed by Parliament when each Act was passed, so at inflationary periods costs rose whilst the value of receipts shrank. Some trusts suffered from competition from other trusts' roads. The Sheffield to Sparrowpit Trust of 1758 was damaged by the opening of the Greenhill Moor to Hathersage turnpike in 1781, and four decades later by the completion of the more direct route to Manchester via the Snake Pass in 1821. In turn, this latter road had hardly had chance to recoup the high costs of its construction before the Sheffield and Manchester railway via Woodhead was opened in the mid-1840s, and took most of its trade.

As receipts fell, there was less to spend on road maintenance, making the turnpikes even less attractive, so that the railways won even more traffic, creating a vicious circle from which there was no escape. For example, in the late 1840s it cost £2,900 per annum to repair the Snake Road, yet its tollgates only yielded £300–£500 each year. In desperation, Sheffield turnpike trustees tried to earn more money by erecting new tollgates to catch the greatly increased flow of traffic between the rapidly expanding suburbs and the town centre and its railway stations. Superficially, this was an attractive option, as the population of Sheffield more than doubled between 1841 and 1871 – rising from 110,000 to 240,000 in that short period. In fact, it was a short-sighted policy, because, for a time, it hindered the expansion of some suburbs, and created public resentment, adding to the growing feeling that the turnpike system was out of date, and should be done away with. Pressure groups were set up by bodies of concerned citizens, supported by the local press, and, later on, by the town council, who saw the trusts and their tollgates as a brake on the town's economic growth.

Gradually, Parliament began to repeal the Turnpike Acts, or refused to renew them at the end of their 21 year terms. The first local road to be disturnpiked by Act of Parliament was the Sheffield to Halifax road in 1867. Most of the others followed suit in the 1870s, the last being the south-westerly routes to Buxton and Chapel-en-le-Frith. The final toll-gate to close was at Hunter's Bar (Figure 3), with the last payment being taken just before midnight on 31 October, 1884. The waiting crowd celebrated the occasion by seizing the gate and tossing it into a nearby field. Thus ended 128 years of paying tolls to travel on turnpike roads in the Sheffield area.

The former turnpike roads were legally taken over by the local authority appropriate to the district through which they passed, and it was the rate-payers who provided the money to maintain the highways. The main roads within the Sheffield boundaries would be busy enough with a variety of traffic – including horse-drawn buses and trams – the former introduced in 1834, the latter in 1873. In contrast, most of the roads out-of-town would be largely deserted, as the railways had captured virtually all long distance traffic. The one exception to this were the roads of the Hope Valley, for the railway did not pass through this district until 1894 some 56 years after the first local line had been built between Sheffield and Rotherham.

The empty roads were gradually reclaimed, firstly in the 1890s by the cyclists out on pleasure rides on the new safety bicycles at weekends and bank holidays, and, secondly by the pioneer motorists in Edwardian times. The old highways were in poor condition, as so little had been spent on maintenance over the previous decades.

Figure 3.   Hunter's Bar, the last local toll bar to close, in 1884.

Pressure from the new road users forced the authorities to improve the roads. At that time most of the district's roads were surfaced with limestone chippings, which created clouds of fine, white dust every time a motor vehicle passed by on its solid rubber tyres. To combat this problem tar was sprayed on road surfaces, which solved the dust nuisance, but did not make a road suitable for motor traffic: stronger foundations, better drainage and tarmacadam did.

Following the creation of the Ministry of Transport in 1918, the country's highways were classified according to importance and geography. Most of Sheffield's former turnpikes were classified as grade 1, or A roads. Thus the Chesterfield road became A61, the Doncaster road A630 and the Snake Road A57. (All the appropriate classifications are listed in the Appendix.)

Older people continued to refer to these 'new' roads as 'turnpikes' long after the tollgates had been dismantled, in the same way that many Sheffield folk called motor coaches 'charas' for decades after the charabanc had been made obsolete by the former.

In spite of the fact that it is now well over a century since the days of the turnpikes, there is a remarkable amount of visual evidence to remind us of the old roads on our travels. Much of this legacy will be described in a sequel to this article in *Aspects of Sheffield 2*.

Figure 4.   The site of Stony Edge toll bar.

Bibliography

1.   *Transactions of the Hunter Archaeological Society*
     i)   Leader, R.E., 'Our Old Roads', pp. 7–29, Vol 1, 1917.
     ii)   Goodfellow, A.W., 'Sheffield Turnpikes in the 18th Century', pp.71–90, Vol V, 1943.
     iii) Hopkinson, G.G., 'Road Development in South Yorkshire and North Derbyshire 1700–1850'. pp.14–30, Vol X, 1971.
2.   *The Derbyshire Achaeological Journal*
     Radley and Penny, 'The Turnpike Roads of the Peak District', pp.93–109, Vol 90, 1972.
3.   Roberts, A.F., *Turnpike Roads Around Buxton*, A.F. Roberts Publications 1992.
4.   Smith, Howard, *Turnpike Trails*
     i)   *Tinsley and Bawtry*, 1988.
     ii)   *Sheffield and Buxton* (2nd ed), 1992.
     iii) *Sheffield to Chapel-en-le-Frith* (2nd ed), 1995.
     iv)   *Greenhill Moor (Norton) to Hathersage* (and Branches), 1997.
5.   Smith, Howard, *A History of Rotherham's Roads and Transport*,
     Rotherham Department of Libraries, Museum and Arts, 1992.

Appendix
Routes taken by the turnpike roads from Sheffield

Notes

1.   For each road listed the first date is of the Act of Parliament creating the Turnpike Trust responsible for first making the road, whilst the second records when the road was disturnpiked (toll gates removed).
2.   Compass directions are approximate only.
3.   Rotherham Road = street name.
     Rotherham road = road leading towards Rotherham.
4.   Street names in brackets refer to the place named immediately before the bracket e.g., Mosborough Moor (High Street, Queen Street, etc.).
5.   Street names given are those current at the time of writing.

1.   **SHEFFIELD–CHESTERFIELD (1756–1875) (33 miles/53 km)**
     South from town centre via Fargate, Barker's Pool, Cambridge Street, the Moor, through Little Sheffield and Highfields via London Road, Derbyshire Lane (through what is now the NW edge of Meersbrook Park to Four Lane Ends where Norton Lees Lane and Scarsdale Road meet). Derbyshire Lane, Cobnar Road, Bolehill Farm, through Graves Park to Little Norton Lane, Dyche Lane to Coal Aston, Green Lane down into Dronfield, Chesterfield Road (B6057) to Unstone. Then across the River Drone and uphill to Old Whittington via Church Street, and on via B6052 and B6057 through Whittington Moor and Stonegravels to Chesterfield along Sheffield Road. The turnpike continued for a further 21 miles/34 km to Duffield (5 miles north of Derby) via A61 to Clay Cross and Stretton.
     Modifications to the original route
     a) N length of Derbyshire Lane moved W away from Meersbrook House to its present line from Chesterfield Road to the top of Scarsdale Road c.1780.
     b) A by-pass was constructed to avoid the steep inclines of Derbyshire Lane and Green Lane via Chesterfield Road through Woodseats, Meadowhead, Four Lane Ends (Norton), Bowshaw and B6057 to the foot of Green Lane in 1795.
     c) B6057 from Unstone to Whittington Moor was constructed to avoid the climb to Old Whittington in 1795.
     d) Abbey Lane from the foot of Meadowhead to Beauchief was turnpiked in 1825.

2.   **SHEFFIELD–BARNSLEY & WAKEFIELD (1758–1876 (22 miles/35 km)**
     North over Lady's Bridge, Nursery Street, Pitsmoor Road over Pye Bank, Barnsley Road (A6135), High Greave, Cross Hill, Ecclesfield, (The Common, Chapeltown Road), Chapeltown (Ecclesfield Road, Station Road, White Lane),

Sheffield Road (A6135), Hoyland Common, Birdwell, (Sheffield Road, A61), then Worsbrough Road through Worsbrough Village, Park Road (A61 again) for a short way, Vernon Road, Sheffield Road, (A61 once more) and into Barnsley (12 miles/19 km). Continued to Wakefield, along A61 for a further 10 miles/16 km, whence Leeds could be reached by another turnpike road (still A61).

Modifications

a)   Steep incline at Pye Bank by-passed in 1835–36 by line of present A6135 via The Wicker, Spital Hill and Burngreave Road to its junction with Pitsmoor Road.

b)   Routes through Worsbrough Village and Worsbrough (Ward Green) were moved to the line of the present A61, in 1840 and c. 1860 respectively.

3.   **SHEFFIELD–SPARROWPIT GATE (2 miles E of Chapel-en-le-Frith) (1758–1884) (22 miles/35 km)**

Started from the Sheffield to Chesterfield turnpike at Highfields and ran W via Sharrow Lane, Psalter Lane, Banner Cross, Ringinglow Road, Bents Green, Ringinglow, Upper Burbage, Fiddlers Elbow, Callow, Mitchell Field, Dale Bottom, School Road, Hathersage main road (A625), Jaggers Lane to Hillfoot, then via the A625 through Sickleholme, Mytham Bridge (River Derwent), Hope, Castleton, the Winnats Pass and on to Sparrowpit via the present B6061 to meet the Buxton–Manchester turnpike road.

Modifications

a)   The 1:5 incline at Callow was by-passed by the road from Fiddlers Elbow past Overstones Farm to Mitchell Field c.1765.

b)   The Sharrow Lane and Psalter Lane road was by-passed by Ecclesall Road (A625) in 1811.

c)   The old route to Hathersage was superseded by a new road from Fiddlers Elbow to Hathersage Booths (this linked with the 1781 Greenhill Moor turn pike into Hathersage via N side of Leadmill Bridge and along the line of the pre sent B6001 from Grindleford).

d)   Also in 1811 a new road was made from Chapel-en-le-Frith to Castleton via Slackhall, Rushup Edge and Mam Tor in order to by-pass the 1:5 Winnats Pass.

e)   In 1825 the present main road through Hathersage village (now A625) was constructed from Hillfoot (W end of Jaggers Lane) to Hathersage Booths.

4.   **SHEFFIELD–BUXTON (1758–1884) (26 miles/42 km)**

Run by the same trust as the Sheffield–Sparrowpit Gate turnpike, and the road towards Buxton followed the same route from Sharrow Lane as far as Ringinglow. Here it turned SW along Houndkirk Road to Fox House, ran through what is now the N edge of the grounds of Longshaw Lodge, and on down to cross the Derwent at Grindleford Bridge. Next came the long climb up the Sir William Hill road to the ridgeway route to Great Hucklow and on to Tideswell. Buxton was reached via Summer Cross, Hargatewall and Fairfield Common.

Modifications

a)   In 1795 the Sir William Hill road was by-passed by the present B6001/B6521 through Eyam and Foolow to Benstor House, where it picked up the original route to Tideswell (now B6049).

b)   The road from Tideswell to Buxton was by-passed in 1812 when a new route was made to Blackwell via Millers Dale (present B6049) to join the newly opened (1810) Ashford-Buxton turnpike (now the A6).

c)   Houndkirk Road was by-passed by the present A625 Banner Cross, Whirlow, Dore Moor, Fox House road from 1812.

d)   The alignment of the road from Fox House through the grounds of Longshaw Lodge was moved NW to its present line (B6521).

NB It is interesting to think that there is no longer a direct Sheffield to Buxton road.

5.   **SHEFFIELD–TINSLEY (1759–1878) (3 miles/5 km)**

Town centre, Lady's Bridge, the Wicker, Spital Hill, Hall Carr, Royds Lane and across the Don by Washford Bridge, and then on to Tinsley along Attercliffe Road and Attercliffe Common (present A6178). This road was turnpiked to improve communications between the town and the new docks of the River Don Navigation at Tinsley (1751). It also made possible the turnpiking of the old routes to Worksop, Bawtry, Rotherham and Doncaster (see over).

Modification

The old road from the Wicker to Washford Bridge was shortened and straightened in 1806 when the present line of Savile Street (A6109)/Attercliffe Road (A6178) was built.

6. **TINSLEY–BAWTRY (1760–1878) (18 miles/29 km)**
Branched off Sheffield Road. The present A631 follows the original route all the way to Bawtry via Canklow, Whiston, Wickersley, Bramley, Hellaby, Maltby and Tickhill.

7. **TINSLEY–DONCASTER (1764–1873) (15 miles/24 km)**
Continues the Sheffield–Tinsley road running along Sheffield Road (now A6178), crossing the Rother via Bow Bridge, Old Sheffield Road, and through Rotherham, (Canklow Road, Westgate, High Street, Doncaster Gate, Doncaster Road) to Aldwarke. Then NE along the line of the present A630 through Thrybergh and Hooton Roberts to Hill Top and Conisbrough (Old Road, West Street, Old Hill), then along Doncaster Road (A630 once more), Sheffield Road to Warmsworth, High Road, Warmsworth Road, High Road, Balby Road, St Sepulchre Gate to High Street, Doncaster.
Modification
The route through Conisbrough was altered to the present A630 Sheffield Road in 1780.

8. **ATTERCLIFFE–WORKSOP (1764–1881) (16 miles/26 km)**
Branched off Attercliffe Road along Worksop Road and ran ESE towards Worksop via Darnall Road and Main Road (B6085), to Darnall, then Main Road (now B6200), Handsworth Road, Retford Road, Old Retford Road, Retford Road (A6200), Sheffield Road to Swallownest (Main Street, Worksop Road) and through Aston (The Warren, Worksop Road B6067). Then along the present A57 Worksop Road, Sheffield Road to South Anston (Sheffield Road), Worksop Road (A57 again) to Gateford Common, before turning S by present B6041 to Gateford and Worksop town centre.

9. **SHEFFIELD–HALIFAX (1777–1867) (33 miles/53 km)**
NW from town centre via West Bar, Shalesmoor, Penistone Road (A61), Penistone Road North to Wadsley Bridge, then up the steep Fox Hill Road to Grenoside village (Main Street)) and along Woodhead Road where it joins the present A629, S of Wortley. On through Thurgoland and B6462 to Penistone, via Oxspring and over the River Don at Bridge End and on to Hoyland Moor where it picks up the line of the present A629 once more all the way to Halifax via Huddersfield.
Modification
The old route through Grenoside village was replaced by a less taxing road from Wadsley Bridge to Wortley in 1826. This is now Halifax Road, Penistone Road (A61/A629).

10. **SHEFFIELD–MANSFIELD (1779–1880) (22 miles/35 km)**
SE up Duke Street, City Road and the present A616 through Intake, Mansfield Road, Birley Moor Road, Mosborough Moor into Mosborough. Here the turnpike branched:-
a)   E along Station Road, Sheffield Road (B6058) to Gander Lane to join the 1764 turnpike between Rotherham and Pleasley, where it in turn joined the Chesterfield to Mansfield turnpike (now A617). NB – the name Gander Lane has disappeared, but it was located at the three-way junction of Sheffield Road, Rotherham Road and Mansfield Road in NE Killamarsh.
b)   SE along the present A616 – High Street, Sheffield Road, Littlemoor , Station Road, Renishaw, Barlborough Hill, through Barlborough village and on to Clowne on the A616 again. Here this branch also joined the Rotherham–Pleasley turnpike in order to reach Mansfield.

11. **GREENHILL MOOR–HATHERSAGE (1781–1880) (13 miles/21 km)**
This was a spinal or ridgeway route with three arms or branches leading off. It was later back-extended to Gleadless Townend in 1825.

a)   The main turnpike branched off the original line of the Sheffield to Chesterfield turnpike at Four Lane Ends (a very common name for a cross roads) at Norton and ran W along Norton Lane, Greenhill Main Road, Hemper Lane, Bradway Road, which becomes the B6054, Tinker's Corner, Rod Moor Road, Northern Common (through W edge of Dronfield Woodhouse), Holmesfield, Holmesfield Common, Lidgate, Owler Bar, Longshaw (Wooden Pole), eastern edge Longshaw to Fox House, to join A625 route over lower Burbage Bridge, past the Surprise and down to Hathersage Booths. Here the original road ran steeply down to the N side of Leadmill Bridge, continuing into Hathersage on the line of the present B6001 from Grindleford.

This last section of road was by-passed in 1825 when the present main road through the village from Hathersage Booths to Hillfoot (W end of Jaggers Lane) was constructed.

In about 1840 the stretch of road through the edge of Longshaw was moved east to the line of the present B6055.

b)   Branch road from Longshaw to Calver Sough (1781) (3.5 miles/6 km)
This road is followed by the present B6054 past the Grouse Inn and Chequers Inn. It crossed the Derwent over New Bridge and met the Grindleford Bridge–Calver Sough road, turnpiked in 1758.

c)   Branch road from Owler Bar to Totley (1781) (1.5 miles/2.5 km)
This road ran NE to Totley via Moor Edge Farm, not on the line of the present A621 but parallel to it on the east side. Parts of the abandoned road can be seen from the modern road (constructed in 1841), itself altered and straightened in recent years. From Moor Edge Farm to Totley the original road ran on the west ern side of the present A621.

d)   Branch road from Owler Bar to Baslow (1803) 4.5 miles/7 km)
This road from the Peacock Inn to Far End (Baslow) roundabout is now fol lowed by the A621.

e)   Back extension to Gleadless (1825) (2.5 miles/4 km)
Ran NE along Norton Lane, Norton Avenue to Gleadless Townend, where it met the ancient route from Sheffield to Mosborough via Heeley Green, Newfield Green and Hurlfield Hill (now B6388, continuing SE as White lane (B6054) towards Mosborough.

12. **GOOSE GREEN–TOTLEY (1803–1880) (5 miles/8 km)**
Constructed to link London Road at Goose Green (Highfields) with the exist ing turnpike road from Totley to Owler Bar. Ran SW along Abbeydale Road, Abbeydale Road South and Baslow Road – now the A621.

13. **SHEFFIELD-LANGSETT (1805–1875) (12 miles/19 km)**
Originally started at Penistone Road in Owlerton, and followed Parkside Road, Catch Bar Lane, then ran NW along Middlewood Road and the present A6102 through Oughtibridge, Wharncliffe Side, Deepcar and Stocksbridge. To the W of Stocksbridge the road becomes the A616 and proceeds through Langsett to the Flouch crossroads. Here the new turnpike met the important cross-Pennine road running between Doncaster, Barnsley, Penistone, Saltersbrook and Woodhead on its way to Manchester, (now A628), turnpiked as early as 1740. The Langsett road was continued northwards to Huddersfield via New Mill and Honley (present A616) under a different turnpike trust.
Modification
Between 1837 and 1840 the road from Middlewood was given its own route into Sheffield along the present Middlewood Road (from Catch Bar Lane), Langsett Road and Infirmary Road (B6079) to Shalesmoor.

14. **SHEFFIELD-GLOSSOP (1818–1875) (24 miles/38 km)**
Designed to provide a more direct route to Manchester and the rapidly-grow ing industrial areas of South Lancashire and Liverpool. The road opened in 1821. The route followed was West Street, Glossop Road to Broomhill, and then what is now the A57 via Crosspool, Rivelin, Hollow Meadows, Moscar, Cutthroat Bridge, Ladybower, and the former village of Ashopton, now demol ished and inundated, Woodlands Valley, Snake Pass and Woodcock Road into Glossop.

6. THE BUTTONMAKING INDUSTRY IN SHEFFIELD

by Dennis Smith

Early Buttonmakers

BUTTONS WERE KNOWN AND USED in ancient Egypt, but arrived in Europe from the East only in the thirteenth century. A statute of 1362 limited the use of expensive cloths, jewels or buttons amongst yeomen and handicraftsmen. Early buttons, often jewelled and set in close rows upon doublets and jerkins were as much decorative as functional and amounted to something of a status symbol amongst the gentry. The button was also something of a male monopoly, playing a crucial part in the development of the close-fitting coat. Female garments retained lacing, although the royal use of buttoned skirts is noted in the sixteenth century. Eventually though, even labourers sported waistcoat buttons of wood, horn and other cheap materials.

The manufacture of buttons was established in London and Birmingham by the seventeenth century. It is therefore no surprise to find Sheffield cutlers of the seventeenth century, with their considerable metal working skills and knowledge of the uses of horn, pearl, bone and other materials, turning their hands to buttonmaking. The craft seems to have been adopted in Sheffield by *c.*1650 and may have been a 'sideline' originally or adopted when the cutlery industry was in one of its frequent recessions. That there were already buttonmakers within Yorkshire is shown by the 1669 court case of Peter Elston[1], buttonmaker of Fewston near Harrogate. Elston was selling buttons at Knaresborough market when two cards of gimp i.e., thread covered buttons, were removed from his stall by Richard Boulton, who claimed he was distracted by a lady. By the year 1720, buttons were apparently in use as gambling counters, for in June of that year Mary Mackfarlin was committed to Wakefield House of Correction 'for unlawfully following the game of thimbles and buttons'.

Block-tin buttons were used in quantity. Mr John Lord, a Rotherham mercer, had 28 pounds of them in his shop inventory dated 1728. During July, 1690, John Spencer, merchant of Cannon Hall, near Barnsley, was despatching parcels of linen and other goods for overland carriage to Hull for shipment to Stockholm, from where they were distributed to other parts of Northern Europe, including Lapland.[2] The shipment included a parcel of 'Sheffield goods', i.e., penknives, tableknives, forks, inkpots and, notably, nine gross of buttons made by Staniforth and valued at £2-18s-0d. Buttons also constituted an article of trade or barter with the inhabitants of the expanding colonies.

Details of seventeenth century Sheffield buttonmakers are sparse – due no doubt to the combination of the trade with cutlery work.[3] A lease for 88 years from the Charity Trustees of Sheffield to John Goodwin, a buttonmaker, exists, dated 1693.[4] Goodwin leased the curious property called the 'Isle of Wight' near the present Bridge Street, which property was 'encompassed round with the River Dun'. On this island were a cottage, outhouses, smithies, orchard and garden.

In 1714 Samuel Hall, a plate-buttonmaker was possessed of the parlour section of a cottage near Townhead in Sheffield. Properties were altered for industrial use. For example, in 1734 a cottage and smithy near Leavygreave in the occupation of Thomas Renshaw, buttonmaker, is described as 'formerly two tenements'. Though early buttonmakers used hand punches and other simple hand tools the craft soon utilised lathes, presses and hand-operated stamps so that the buttonmaker needed more working room than his contemporaries in the local cutlery trades (Figures 1 and 2).

The relatively few early rural buttonmakers were often smallholders. John Hall, a buttonmaker of Bradway Moor had a mare,

Figure 1. Metal button making and tools of the trade. *Pictorial Encyclopaedia of Science, Art and Technology, Diderot and D'Alembert, 1762*

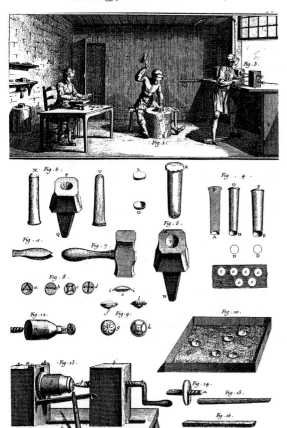

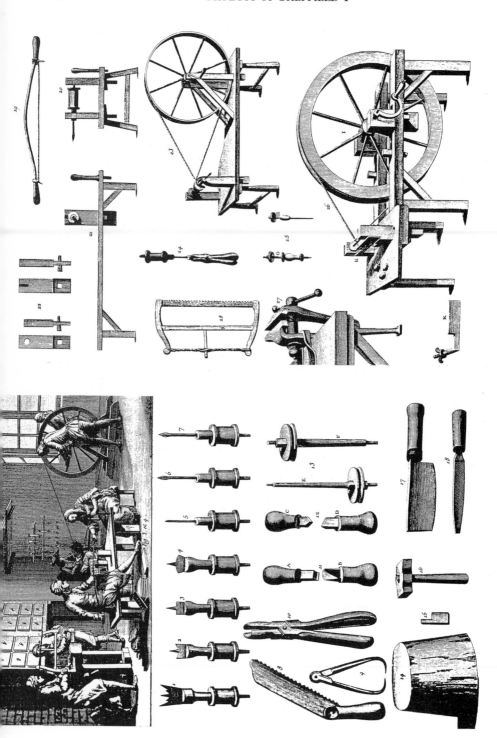

Figure 2. Button mould making and mould making tools. *Pictorial Encyclopaedia of Science, Art and Technology, Diderot and D'Alembert, 1762*

a few cattle and corn sown on the ground included in his inventory of May 1727, and in 1744 John Staniforth, buttonmaker of Hillbridge in Nether Hallam, was leasing a tenement, barns, orchard and gardens with eleven acres of land.

Like the contemporary Sheffield cutlers, the buttonmakers sold their wares through the local factors or merchants. One such merchant, Samuel Watson of Sheffield, became bankrupt in 1707.[5] Lists of his goods included cloth, gloves, socks and a stock of buttons. These included brass coat buttons, tin, glass, horn and thread buttons, as well as lacquered and silver buttons, the latter valued at eight shillings a gross. Amongst silk cloth and whalebone for stays were 'silver spangled buttons' at a penny each and five gross of 'oakarmy' (alcony) buttons valued at 7s-6d, alcony being an alloy similar to pinchbeck and having some resemblance to gold. On the list of persons owing money to Watson are the names James France, John Pearson, Samuel Bate and Thomas Allen, all names connected with the local button industry.

In May of 1720, Jeremiah Ward, a Sheffield buttonmaker, testified that some time ago he had apprehended Henry Owen and Isaac Moor with stolen goods on the road to Chesterfield. Ward had recognised cloth, knives and stockings as the goods of John Downes, a Sheffield hardware factor whose house had been robbed the night before. Four years later John Downes became a bankrupt and his large house and warehouse stock were valued.[6] Downes also had goods at Blind Lane, in five private houses and on a farm at Sheffield Park. This merchant's trade goods included hardware, paper, foodstuffs, knives, quantities of horn, tools, cloth and jewellery packed in barrels, sacks and packs. Goods sent abroad were also valued, including a basket at Mr Yeoman's in Temple Street, Bristol which contained horn and studded coat buttons. In a pack at the *White Hart* in Birmingham were razors and penknives, along with buttons of bell-metal and also glass top coat buttons, possibly not of Sheffield manufacture. His goods at Chester included files, Birmingham boxes and Welsh flannel, and 68 gross of horn coat and plain horn buttons.

From 1698 attempts were made to prohibit imports of hair buttons (covered with woven hair) and several early eighteenth century Acts were passed. Attempts were made from 1704 to protect the local horn and alcony buttonmakers against competition from makers of cloth-covered buttons. The Cutlers' Company of Sheffield gave support to the area's buttonmakers and during 1720 petitions against covered buttons were presented at Doncaster, Rotherham and Pontefract quarter sessions. During the eighteenth century tailors and also wearers of cloth covered buttons were prosecuted, but these various legal endeavours were of little use and covered buttons, often of Birmingham origin, became permanent fashion.

The Holy family

Preserved documents of the Holy family, three generations of buttonmakers, later merchants, offer a unique insight into the button trade throughout the eighteenth century. Daniel Holy, buttonmaker, was leasing an ancient subdivided dwelling at West Bar from the Capital Burgesses in the year 1734.[7] Thomas Holy, son of Daniel, acquired premises at Newfield Green in Heeley in 1750. During July and August 1751, the house at Heeley, and a smithy and workchambers there, were rebuilt. Items listed in accounts include engine wheels, a treadle board for lathes and a device made for washing metal. Thomas Holy died in 1758 leaving his wife Sarah to carry on. Premises mentioned are a 'button house' presumably a warehouse cum showroom with fittings, including shelves, a glass case, button table and drawers. Stocks of buttons valued at £233-14s-5¹/₂d included oval yellow coats, spatterdash buttons and some lacquered Birmingham coat buttons, presumably bought in, or made to a Birmingham pattern.[8] Other types of buttons were silvered, figured, pearl, brass and buttons made of yellow metal. Some had 'keyshanks'. Some are listed by number, presumably to indicate sizes, e.g., thin tens (coat), flat fours, flat sixteens (coat), flat twos (breast).

Working premises at the time of Thomas Holy's death (1758) comprised (a) smithies, where button shanks, buttons, paper, card, iron wire, moulds, etc., were stored; (b) a cellar containing quantities of brass (some in the form of sheets and wire), block-tin, spelter, coarse metal, lead and pewter; (c) a casting shop with 136 boxes of moulds, ten pairs of iron boxes, three pairs of screws, tongs, metal plates and hammers; (d) the chamber of the casting shop containing casting pots, an engine, old metal, ladles and vices and (e) a 'rubbing smithy' with a load of rubbing stone, rotten stone dust, punches, a metal plated hammer, etc.

One item listed was a quantity of Trent sand, used in the finishing of buttons. In the middle and upper work chambers were a total of eighteen 'engines' i.e., lathes, fly presses or stamps all valued at ten shillings, also vices and workboards. An engine, vice, workboard, some bad pearl, old metal and files were in the kitchen chamber.

Sarah carried on the trade, dying in 1768. In the settling of Sarah's business accounts, debts of over £3,483 were noted. Items owed to the business included local debts, others from Malton, Howden, Hull and Scarborough in Yorkshire and yet others from London, Lancashire, Newcastle, Durham and Scotland. Assets included working tools in Sheffield valued at £130, with tools in the stamp shop amounting to a further £37. Gold and silver clippings alone were valued at £130, whilst the value of Thomas Holy's old stock totalled £900. Buttons, finished and unfinished, were valued at £181-8s-4d. Despite attempts, many debtors were not found or else had failed in business. Miles Burkit of Newcastle, was 'dead 10 years ago'. Charles Cannon of Manchester had run away to Pennsylvania, whilst William Wrangham of Beverley 'ran away 9 years ago and paid nobody'.

In March of 1771 a partnership to manufacture and sell buttons was formed by Thomas Newbould, shearsmith, George Woodhead, merchant and Sarah's son, Thomas Holy, then under 21 years of age. The 14-year partnership had a joint stock of £2,400 in money and goods and employed Holy's tools and materials, though merchandise other than buttons was to be dealt in.

Attempts were made during 1771–73 to collect old debts throughout the country. Again the results were ony partially successful. Francis Glossop of Worksop who owed a debt from the year 1765 was described as 'broke and run away'. Mr Atkinson of Bradford who owed £3-9s-6d from 1760 was a prisoner in York Castle and 'never will pay'.

Holy and Company leased premises on Sheffield Moor, formerly a bowling green or skittle alley. When a 99 year lease was taken from the Marquis of Rockingham in 1776, Holy erected himself a house there and in the following year repaired and improved the warehouse, three casting shops, stamp shop and filling room.

Early in 1778 'carpenter work'[9] was being carried out on many parts of the premises, e.g., the metal and casting shops, gateway, garrets, warehouses, chambers, counting house, carding shops and packing rooms. Metal, filling and casting shops were extended and work was carried out on the burnishing room, colouring room, stamp floor, furnaces, engraving chamber, sorting room and porter's house and room. By the year 1787 the firm occupied a prominent position amongst the Sheffield makers of metal, gilt and plated buttons, and in 1790, the year of Thomas Holy's marriage to Elizabeth Beard, the firm was probably at its largest.

In 1793 the old partnership agreement expired and a new partnership was formed with Newbould, Holy and George Suckley as general merchants. It had a joint capital of £21,000 and was based

Figure 3.   Rough plan of Thomas Holy and William Newbould's Works on Sheffield Moor, 1790. *Sheffield Archives Fairbank Collection, Field Book 68, Supplement*

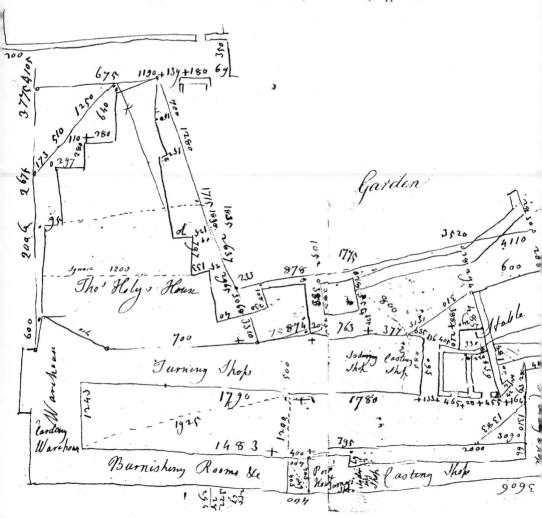

at the warehouse on Sheffield Moor (Figure 3). Suckley was to reside in America and manage that side of the trade. Goods suitable for the American markets were separated and an agreement was made to work up 'wasters' and old fashioned goods to be sold for the benefit of the partners. William Newbould now had the option of taking workshops in the backyard at the Moor premises for button manufacturing, with leave to alter the buildings. Holy for his part agreed that from 1794 onward he would no longer engage in the manufacture and sale of buttons in England, Ireland or Scotland for a 14 year period, although he retained the greatest number of shares in the business. A stockbook of the year 1797,[10] lists cutlery, files, scythes, sickles and other tools and hardware, clothing, cloth nails and tea, etc. 'Birmingham goods' such as needles, combs and candlesticks are represented, as are bar, tilted and rolled steel. Buttons listed are largely gilt and various types of striped or figured horn. The balance of the button account in 1797 was £1,735-6s-4½d. At this date however English, European and probably American debts to the partnership totalled over £19,000 owed by 190 separate customers. Letters from America tell of goods damaged in shipment. Business competition was keen and a 7½ per cent discount was allowed to some customers.

The Holy family separated to concentrate individually on merchant businesses and on silver plating during the early nineteenth century. William Newbould acquired land and coal mining interests at Intake whilst continuing the buttonmaking and merchant trades. In 1799 William Newbould was allowing his son Thomas £2,500 out of the £15,000 joint stock of the business at Sheffield Moor. By the year 1806 the elder William Newbould had died, leaving the firm to be carried on by his sons Thomas of Highfield and William and George of Broomhill. The premises on Sheffield Moor were still being rented at £70 per annum. The Newboulds combined buttonmaking with the business of merchants for a further two decades.

Eighteenth Century Heyday

The second half of the eighteenth century saw the Sheffield button industry grow to its largest extent. The invention of 'Sheffield plate' by Thomas Boulsover in the 1740s gave the local buttonmakers and silversmiths an advantage, though it was soon to be also manufactured in Birmingham. The rolled copper sheet, faced with silver was easily worked with flypresses and stamps already in use.

Boulsover himself first used Sheffield Plate in buttonmaking, noting the economy of production compared to solid silver. Premises on the local rivers were soon utilised to drive rolls used in the production of Sheffield plate, for example John Trevers Younge, 1719–1807, merchant of Sheffield, combined with John Hoyland and William Middleton, buttonmakers, in leasing Cooper Wheel on the River Sheaf in 1766. Here a former cutlers' wheel was used as a rolling mill, and a plainishing mill was also erected. Younge is also reputed to have been a co-partner with Boulsover. Active also in the manufacture of gilt buttons, Younge had extensive works at Union Street in Sheffield. The premises included plating, burnishing, casting and gilding rooms in the year 1778. The works at Union Street and Cooper Wheel were several times enlarged. In 1781 Younge was to build a substantial town house for himself near the Union Street workshop.

Another large works was established in 1766 by John Hoyland. Workshops included a casting shop, silver melting shop and refining shop. The main premises consisted of a large double storeyed building housing a box gilders' room and carding and button engine rooms. Particular provision was made to fully utilise natural light, the south front of the premises containing more than 20 windows, with 16 on the northern side.[11] In 1776 John Hoyland and others combined to establish a coach service to deliver goods to Birmingham.[12] Another partnership consisting of William Middleton, John Littlewood and William Hoyland carried on gilt and plated button making at Eyre Street in 1797. Their large workshops included a rolling shop, several warehouses, a cutting-out shop and garrets used as chasing rooms. The button and burnishing shops had barred windows.

Matthew Boulton, the Birmingham industrialist supplied goods to the Sheffield firm of Benjamin Huntsman & Co. whose founder had invented crucible-cast steel. Huntsman's firm supplied steel and dies for coining to Boulton. Correspondence between the two firms exists between 1774–97,[13] some of which concerns the making of fine rolls for rolling burnished gilt foil. Boulton also made enquiries of Huntsman for a cheaper grade of steel, suitable for the Birmingham button and buckle manufacturers. A letter of *c.*1777 refers to the considerable trade in cheap steel buttons in Birmingham, when even a penny difference in price was crucial. [14]

William, the son of Benjamin Huntsman, entered into partnership with Robert Asline, a buttonmaker, to deal in cutlery and other wares and also brass and other metals for making buttons.[15] This partnership became bankrupt in March, 1781, but was reorganised and continued in the steel and merchant businesses. An order book of 1797–1806 lists cutlery, shoe buckles, engravers' and watchmaking tools, and also cards of steel, gilt and fancy buttons despatched to London, Birmingham and France.

Although Acts of Parliament dated 1738 and 1790 exempted buttons and other items of small weight from hallmarking, small quantities of buttons were assayed at Sheffield from 1773 onwards. There was perhaps some preference by customers that they should be hall-marked.[16] Fenton and Creswick assayed coat and breast buttons in 1773 but firms such as John Winter & Co., Newbould and Holy and J. T. Younge & Co. were fairly consistent in assaying buttons. Others brought in buttons with items such as candlesticks and inkstands and Benjamin Brocklesby, a plate worker of Castle Street, assayed 16 dozen buttons in August, 1792. A further Act in 1796 attempted to discourage the making of inferior quality buttons which were being passed as gilt or silver plated, and also legislated in relation to the descriptions circulated on the cards on which buttons were mounted for sale.

We hear little of the horn buttonmakers in Sheffield though thirteen such manufacturers appear in the Directory for Central Sheffield in 1787, with a few in Heeley also mentioned. Most of the horn button pressing was done in domestic workshops, often using family labour.

In deeds connected with Pond Street during the 1770s, John Waterhouse, a Vigo horn buttonmaker, is mentioned. There were a number of buttonmakers listed under the term 'Vigo' which may have been an alloy or composition. Perhaps it was merely a pattern of button or even the source of the actual horn, i.e., Vigo in Spain. Never explained, the term disappeared by the end of the eighteenth century.

A small button industry was established at Hathersage in Derbyshire in the early eighteenth century. James Pilkington, writing in 1789, mentions the small manufactory of metal buttons employing about fourteen hands, but by 1838 the button shops had been converted into dwellings.[17]

The Workforce

Buttonmakers worked under conditions similar to those endured by their contemporaries in the cutlery industry, and had a similar lifestyle. They appeared to be no more law-abiding. Thomas Allan, a Sheffield buttonmaker, was charged with 'profane cursing and swearing' in 1701. In 1712, quarter sessions cases included John Wild, Sheffield buttonmaker, suspected of stealing cloth and Robert Hall, buttonmaker, charged with abusing Mary, wife of Thomas Cotton, a Sheffield cutler.[18] Jonathan Bullas Jnr, a local buttonmaker, and his father Jonathan, a cutler, appeared on a bastardy charge in 1763.

The buttonmaking trade did not suffer such control as did the Cutlers' Company, consequently apprenticeship was spasmodic. Casual and female labour were employed. Poor Law apprentices were sometimes bound apprentice to buttonmakers. Jonathan Fenton, bound apprentice to John Balm, metal buttonmaker, of Crookesmoor Side for seven years from August 1716, served only five years before his indentures were discharged. In June, 1721, Balm took another apprentice, Joshua, the son of Alice Bibs, a spinster of Sharrowhead. He was bound for eight years and admonished to 'keep his master's lawful commands and everywhere gladly obey'. He must not frequent alehouses, play dice, cards or other unlawful games, or marry. In return he was to be instructed in the art of buttonmaking, allowed sufficient meat, drink, lodging and washing with all linen and woollen clothes suitable, and given sixteen pence and a suit of clothes yearly. John Slater, an apprentice buttonmaker described as 'a person of ill name and fame' was charged in 1770 with taking the 'King's Shilling', i.e., seven shillings and six pence from Henry Hastley, Sergeant in the 47th Regiment of Foot, under the false pretences that he was free to serve as a soldier.[19] Leader refers to the apprentice of Thomas Renshaw, buttonmaker at Portobello, who ran away in 1755.[20] The description circulated was of a person five feet two inches tall, wearing a dark coloured kersey cloth coat, blue and white flannel waistcoat, washleather breeches and blue yarn stockings.

Elizabeth McDonald, a vagrant apprehended by the constables at Sheffield in October, 1736, told her story to the quarter sessions. Born in Canterbury and married at thirteen to a servant, they first lived at Dover. They then led a wandering existence until her husband was drowned near Gainsborough. She had come to Sheffield via Thorne on her road to Newcastle with her six year old son. She maintained herself and her child by 'sometimes making of shirt neck buttons and sometimes wandering and begging'.

Mary Owen, a town apprentice girl was bound servant to Mary Naw, spinster and property owner. After a year, in 1781, she was put apprentice to Adam Padley, a buttonmaker. After Padley's death she ran away from her mistress and was lodging in New Street in 1788, paying sixpence per week. She proceeded to torment Mary Naw, her first employer who stated that she (Owen) 'has worked at the button shops till by her conduct, somehow or other she has got a sore leg and says she will not work any more'. Naw relieved her with salve, medical help and money, but Owen continued to bring with her a saucy woman to abuse her former mistress. Naw considered Owen, then 21 years old, a 'brutish ill-disposed girl' and that 'she must have improved very much in her brutishness by her buttonshop education', and consequently was not fit to serve a woman.[21]

Many women and children were employed in processes such as

cutting out buttons, using flypresses, soldering shanks, cleaning and sorting, gilding and in sewing finished buttons onto cards. Some processes such as casting, the heavier stamping of metal buttons and the pressing of horn buttons were largely carried out by men. The expansion of the trade during the second half of the eighteenth century resulted in the evolution of hand-driven machines for some processes with some workers doing specific jobs such as burnishing, or the making of button moulds of horn, wood or bone for insertion in buttons.

Women workers employed acid in cleaning buttons, and in gilding a coating of mercury and gold was applied. Buttons were then placed in a cylindrical wire basket and rotated over a fire. None of these processes was healthy despite attempts to close in the fires and devise flues to carry away mercury vapour. Other processes such as edging the buttons in treadle lathes or the use of foot operated stamps (Figure 4) were responsible for strains and sore legs. Benchwork was dusty and monotonous, comparable with the work of local cutlers. Other hazards were flying fragments of metal, and physical deformities caused by cramped conditions.

Change in the nineteenth century

The nineteenth century opened with a retrogressive step when the local buttonmakers attempted to revive the statute on cloth-covered buttons. This proved futile for they were here to stay, although Ebenezer Hancock, a Sheffield roller, was actually fined 40 shillings for wearing twelve cloth covered buttons on his coat in March 1802, evidence being given by John Barlow, Sheffield buttonmaker (Figure 5).[22]

Specialised button manufacture had become very widespread in

Birmingham where wages were generally lower and where patented improvements to buttons and manufacturing machinery gave them commercial advantage. Richard Howlden, a Sheffielder touring Birmingham in 1835, noted a curious machine which shaped 60 button shanks per minute.[23] He also observed a machine which chased a design on a button placed in its centre. When a wheel was turned, four different patterned punches struck the button simultaneously.

Figure 4. Stamping buttons *c.*1850.

There is a telling note in the statement that the 'machine may be operated by a child'. Although many intricate and exotic buttons were now coming from Birmingham, the sole Sheffield patented button was a metal stud with a screw threaded shank fitted into the shell or disc. This was the brainchild of George Rodgers, a Sheffield merchant, and John Tatain, gardener of Hilton in Derbyshire, and was patented in 1833. However, the future of large-scale button production lay in steam driven machinery and in such machines as a rotary press for horn buttons patented in 1832. Many prominent Sheffield buttonmakers had died or ceased business by the early nineteenth century and their descendants moved into merchant trades, banking and other occupations. John Trevers Younge made his will in 1802, leaving two dwellings in Union Street to his sons Samuel and John.

Figure 5. Summons to Ebenezer Hancock to appear before a Justice of the Peace for wearing 12 cloth covered buttons on his coat. *Sheffield Archives, Wheat Collection, WC2326*

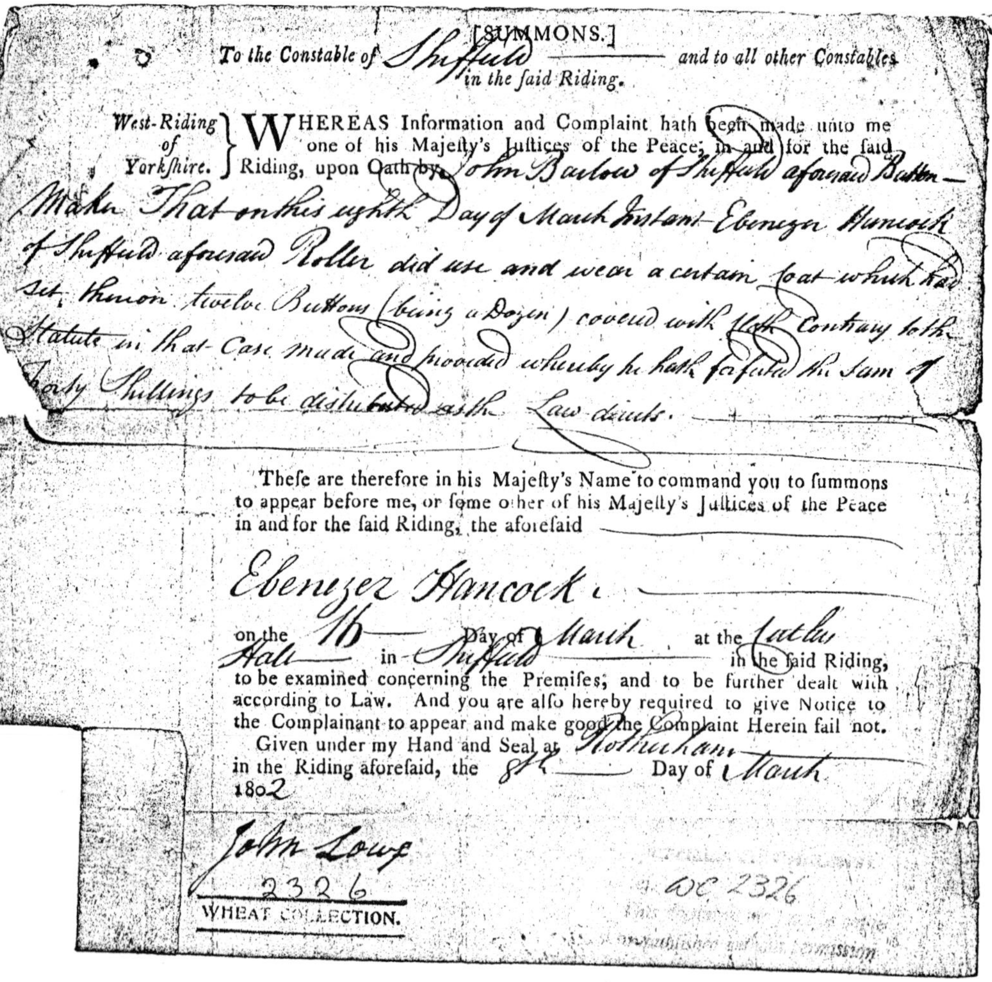

[SUMMONS.]

To the Constable of Sheffield and to all other Constables in the said Riding.

West-Riding of Yorkshire. } WHEREAS Information and Complaint hath been made unto me one of his Majesty's Justices of the Peace, in and for the said Riding, upon Oath by John Barlow of Sheffield aforesaid Button-Maker That on this eighth Day of March instant Ebenezer Hancock of Sheffield aforesaid Roller did use and wear a certain Coat which had set thereon twelve Buttons (being a Dozen) covered with Cloth Contrary to the Statute in that Case made and provided whereby he hath forfeited the Sum of Forty Shillings to be distributed as the Law directs.

These are therefore in his Majesty's Name to command you to summons to appear before me, or some other of his Majesty's Justices of the Peace in and for the said Riding, the aforesaid Ebenezer Hancock on the 16 Day of March at the Cutlers Hall in Sheffield in the said Riding, to be examined concerning the Premises; and to be further dealt with according to Law. And you are also hereby required to give Notice to the Complainant to appear and make good the Complaint Herein fail not.

Given under my Hand and Seal at Rotherham in the Riding aforesaid, the 8th Day of March 1802

John Lowe

The will makes reference to the chamber of the upper kitchen in his house 'used as part of the plated manufactory'.

John Hoole, metal buttonmaker at Sheffield Moor, occupied several warehouses, numerous workshops with garrets and chambers and a counting house in the year 1788. He made his will in 1806 when properties included premises in Blind Lane. It was stipulated that the sum of £2-10s be paid to each workman at the time of his decease.[24] The button making business was left to his nephew Samuel Hobson. John, the son of Samuel was allowed either a partnership or a payment of £1,000 out of the stock-in-trade. The firm of Hobson & Co, buttonmakers, although short lived, was the only local button manufacturer to issue a trade-token, in 1812.

In 1806 Henry Bennett, a Sheffield buttonmaker was in debt to Birmingham buttonmakers James Hancock and Thomas Bartleet. Bennett was obliged to surrender his stock-in-trade and his household goods, excepting his family's clothes to these creditors.

Another great change after 1830 affected the entire button industry. This was the decline of the fashion of wearing gilt and silver buttons on everyday dress. Although the firm of Thompson and Linley of Howard Street was making gilt buttons as late as 1832, the large firms employed in the production of gilt and silver buttons gave way to smaller concerns manufacturing pearl, bone and horn buttons. Pearl could be cut and faceted in numerous patterns, and the decoration on pressed horn buttons was limited only by the cost of producing suitable dies. Buttons of bone or ivory were turned in a 'double' lathe and a metal shank affixed, and they could also be lathe-turned to convex forms. These buttons could be coloured or varnished, or decorated in a 'scoring-engine' by the use of cording, knotting and matting tools. Buttons might also have pierced designs, be inlaid or drilled out to expose the whiteness of the bone material, coloured varnishes being applied to obtain a mottled effect. Despite these advances, the Sheffield industry never regained its late eighteenth century stature.

One of the button manufacturers' outlets was the notorious 'Tommy' shop, part of the 'truck' system whereby some large firms obliged their workmen to take some proportion of their wages in goods, or to buy goods at the company shop. During 1828, W. Horton of Rockingham Street, manufacturers of metal, pearl, livery and military buttons, supplied various types of buttons to the 'Tommy' shop of Messrs Newton Chambers Ironworks at Chapeltown.[25]

New families established in the buttonmaking trade included the

Allcard family who came from Sheldon in Derbyshire during the late
eighteenth century, establishing themselves at Scotland Street in
Sheffield. Many of the family worked at home making bone buttons
and moulds on a small scale from bone offcuts. The largest operator
in the family, Charles Allcard (1803–84) combined horn and bone
button manufacture with the making of knife handles and scales for
the cutlery trade. Utilising steam-power at Vaughan's Wheel in 1841,
presumably for bone cutting, he employed four men and seven
women two decades later. In 1867 the Allcards had a bone warehouse erected in the Soho wheelyard adjoining Bridge Street.

The firm of Samuel Meggitt & Co, bone button manufacturers,
claimed to have been established in the year 1837 (Figures 6 and 7).
This firm was investigated by the Children's Employment
Commission in 1843. The firm then employed 65 workers of whom
22 were adult, 31 were 13–21 years of age and 12 children were
under 13. Female labour predominated. The working day lasted ten
or eleven hours, a little less than that of contemporary cutlers. There
were no facilities for changing or cooking on the premises but workers were allowed two hours to go for food. The works employed a 6hp
steam engine to drive circular saws, lathes and abrasive wheels used
in finishing buttons. The machinery was 'securely fenced'.

W. & H. Guest, bone buttonmakers had shared part of a block of
workshops at Furnace Hill in Sheffield with Jepson & Co., file makers, in the year 1835. Henry Guest the surviving partner, was manufacturing bone buttons at Kelham Wheel on the Don by 1849. In
1858 Anthony Guest, former journeyman buttonmaker, was having power put into a small
workshop at Soho Steam Wheels which were
held on a weekly basis. Saws were erected for
cutting bones and pipes laid for the boiling of
them.

Compensation claims following the Sheffield
Flood of 1864 include Henry Allcard, claiming
for losses and damage at Soho Wheel. A large
quantity of buttons were lost or required refin-
ishing and £2 was also claimed for loss of wages.
William Guest, who combined buttonmaking
with the trades of cleaning and dyeing, claimed
losses of household goods plus £2 for forty gross
of lost buttons. Anthony Guest, operating at
Copper Street and Soho Wheel, claimed for the
loss of wages of 20 persons, mainly women

Figure 6.   Samuel Meggitt & Co., label. The label also carries a
            warranty to the effect that the buttons are guaranteed
            'not to change colour in washing or break in mangling'.
            Bodleian Library

employed in bone cutting and bone button manufacture. The most interesting item on the list however, is the claim for the loss of two tons of vegetable ivory valued at £15 per ton. Vegetable ivory is the nut of Corozo palm and is a substance light in weight, close grained and resembling genuine ivory in colour. It was included in patent 9058 taken out in 1841 by Birmingham buttonmaker Charles Rowley and had the properties of being easily turned in a lathe, workable in the same manner as bone, and 'as a new manufacture of buttons may be made of considerable value'. Peak production using this material occurred between 1870 and 1920, plastics having displaced it by the latter date.

Perhaps the last large-scale enterprise connected with button manufacture in Sheffield was the erection in 1871 of Messrs Guest's Neptune Works, in Watery Lane. This three-storeyed building comprised three large rooms, each 50 x 20 feet in size. Turning and boring shops were at ground level whilst the second floor housed carding and showrooms, the top floor being used as a finishing room. The works employed 60 persons working from 7.30 am until about 8.00 pm. Shortly after becoming fully operational in late June, 1872, the engine tender discovered the premises on fire. It spread quickly, gutting the front of the building and destroying the upper storey. The fire brigade managed to save half of the building and the lathes were

Figure 7. Samuel Meggitt's bone mill at Effingham Road (right) seen from the Sheffield Canal. *The Author*

undamaged but a large quantity of stock and tools were destroyed, although the property was fortunately covered by insurance.

Decline of the Industry 1870–1990

In 1876 there were thirteen button making firms in Sheffield, including William Guest's Neptune Works which was rebuilt after the fire of 1872 and operated for another two decades. Charles Allcard, who employed 20 workers in button and scale manufacture retired from business in 1881. The stock-in-trade and tools of Allcard's River Works at Granville Street were sold in September, 1884. Stock comprised 20,000 gross of buttons and knife scales. Some patterns of horn buttons bore names, e.g. 'Rosebud', possibly a component part of female underwear? Others were 'Diamond Edge', 'Bullhead', 'Shell', and 'Sugar-lump' patterns.

Census returns of 1881 show a number of young women employed in central Sheffield as 'bone button rappers', 'button borers', 'button turners', 'button sorters', and 'button carders'. Some of these women were of Irish origin but Edward Turner and Joseph Barnes, pearl button makers living in Matilda Street were of Birmingham origin. Numbers employed in the button trade in the town were small in comparison with those employed in the cutlery scale cutting and pressing, and comb making trades. Robert Myers, a pearl buttonmaker of Chester Street, employed his wife and in-laws in the trade, the females doing the sorting and carding of buttons. Other button firms were small, often sharing premises. Many were situated in small courts or yards in the backstreets of Sheffield in the 1890s. The number of buttonmakers dwindled to seven in 1903 and only two in 1916, though others were probably involved in manufacturing for the war effort. In 1925 pearl buttons were being made by one firm in Broomspring Lane. Meggitt and Co are listed as dealers in bones and horns and makers of bone buttons, rings and counters. However, as bone went out of use between the world wars they survived just long enough to become the only Sheffield buttonmakers to celebrate their centenary.

The introduction of 'press-stud', 'zip' and other fasteners for clothing caused decline in the button industry during the early twentieth century. The introduction of plastics to imitate ivory, horn, pearl and bone changed both buttonmaking and local cutlery manufacture.

Towards the end of the Second World War a small number of pearl buttonmakers were still at work in Sheffield including the Singleton family, also operating at Dale Mill in Hathersage. In post-war

Sheffield several firms were making plastic buttons, but from the 1950s the number declined until only one exists at present (1996). Buttons however remain as functional and decorative accessories to clothing and predominate in female fashions, yet considering the three centuries of button manufacture in Sheffield, effectively nothing remains and the very existence of such an industry appears to be forgotten.

References

1. West Yorkshire Record Office, Wakefield, Quarter Sessions records, QS1/10/1.
2. Sheffield Archives, Spencer-Stanhope Collection, Sp.St. 60502/60.
3. David Hey, *The Fiery Blades of Hallamshire – Sheffield and its Neighbourhood 1660–1740*, Leicester University Press, 1991, pp. 122–126.
4. Sheffield Archives, Miscellaneous Documents, MD329.
5. Sheffield Archives, Jackson Collection, JC544.
6. Sheffield Archives, Tibbitts Collection, TC1053a.
7. Sheffield Archives, Church Burgesses Collection, CB650.
8. Sheffield Archives, MD5733.
9. Sheffield Archives, Fairbank Collection, BB60.
10. Sheffield Archives, MD5734.
11. Sheffield Archives, Fairbank, BB33.
12. R. E. Leader, *Sheffield in the 18th Century*, The Sheffield Independent Press Ltd, 1901, p. 23.
13. Sheffield Archives, Photostat Collection, PhC373.
14. Sheffield Archives, Photostat Collection PhC373.
15. West Yorkshire Archives, Sheepscar Library, Leeds, Bankruptcy Assignments and Deeds of Arrangement, DB215 No. 191.
16. Sheffield Assay Office, plate books.
17. Sheffield Archives, Cammell Deeds, Cam.D78.
18. West Yorkshire Record Office, Wakefield, QS1/51/7.
19. West Yorkshire Record Office, Wakefield, QS1/109/10.
20. Leader, *Sheffield in the 18th Century*, p. 23.
21. Sheffield Archives, Tibbitts Collection, TC434/6.
22. Sheffield Archives, Wheat Collection, 2326.
23. Sheffield Archives, MD1761.
24. Sheffield Archives, MD5733/3.
25. Sheffield Archives, Thorncliffe Records, TR327,328.

Other Printed Sources

Joan Nunn, *Fashion in Costume 1200–1980*, The Herbert Press, 1984, pp. 13–53.
Diana de Marly, *Fashion for Men, an Illustrated History*, Batsford Ltd, 1985, p. 14.

Acknowledgements

Acknowledgements are due to West Yorkshire Archive Service, Sheepscar Library, Leeds for permission to use an item from the Bankruptcy Assignments and Deeds of Arrangement deposits there; to West Yorkshire Archive Service, Wakefield, for permission to use items from the Quarter Sessions records; to Sheffield Assay Office for permission to use extracts from the plate books, and particularly to Mrs J. Richardson, the Librarian, for her help; to Miss M. Platts for documents related to the Allcard family; to Tanya Schmoller for references to Newton Chambers' 'Tommy' shop records etc.; to Sheffield Archives for permission to use items from their manuscript collections and also to S. W. Fraser Esq. for permission to publish items from the Spencer-Stanhope Collection held at Sheffield Archives.

7. A Forgotten Industry: The Stove Grate and Light Castings Industry of Sheffield

by Chris Morley

Introduction

SHEFFIELD HAS BEEN ASSOCIATED with the cutlery, steel and plating industries for so long that it is not surprising to find an industry which flourished in the town for about one and a half centuries now largely forgotten, overshadowed by the histories, research, and publicity afforded to these more famous 'Sheffield Trades'. From the beginning of the nineteenth century through to the 1950s, the products of Sheffield's iron foundries were household names in the United Kingdom, gracing, as they did, the living and reception rooms, and the bedrooms and kitchens of all classes of people from the most noble to the lowest, providing heat and comfort, and the means to safely cook their foods; those products were the stove grate and the kitchen range. Figure 1 shows the earliest known illustration of a Sheffield made kitchen range.

Ironfounding had been carried out at the several blast furnaces in South Yorkshire prior to the nineteenth century, and most of the furnaces moulded and cast some products such as fire backs, fire dogs, and stove plates allied to the fireplace. With the birth of the Industrial Revolution, and the consequential rise of the urban population, housing had to be provided for the countless workers and their families attracted to the towns and cities to work in factories and mills. The close-set rows of dwellings required the provision of a safe means of heating each individual home and providing a safe cooking fire. No longer could the fire set in a fireplace opening be tolerated, it being beyond the supervision of the landlord, or his agents, to ensure the containment of the fire and the maintenance of the surrounding stone or brickwork. The stove grate, initially designed and intended as a decorative, more efficient, means of heating the stately rooms of the rich, was adapted to suit the dwellings of the artisan and labourer. As the urban centres and industrial villages expanded, both in size and number, so the demand for these cheaper stove grates and kitchen ranges grew; a growth that was to be answered by the establishment of many hundreds of foundries, large and small to make

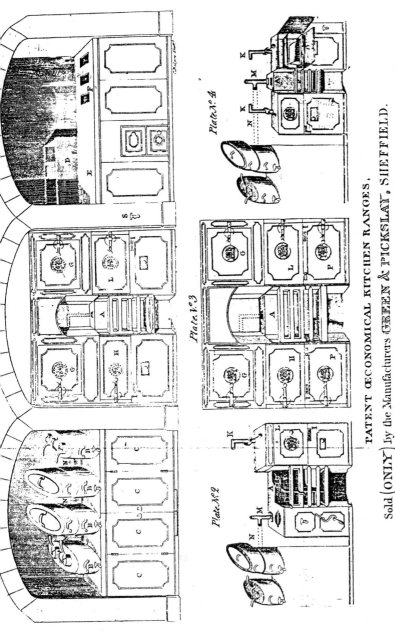

PATENT OECONOMICAL KITCHEN RANGES,

Sold (ONLY) by the Manufacturers GREEN & PICKSLAY, SHEFFIELD.

These Stoves for Oeconomy, Convenience, and Cleanliness, stand unrivalled; in them are combined all the essential parts of the best Cooking-Apparatus in use. — With one small open Fire they will Roast, Steam, and Bake; more particularly at from five to fifty Individuals, and afford a constant supply of hot Water; their Construction is so simple, that they are well understood.

Figure 1. The earliest known illustration of a Sheffield made kitchen range. Green & Pickslay made the *Patent Oeconomical Kitchen Ranges* and this illustration comes from their advertisement in Gell's *Directory of Sheffield*, 1825. The lower left-and right-hand drawings show what was typically an early 'Yorkshire Range'. The advertisement's 'blurb' states: These stoves for Oeconomy, Convenience, and Cleanliness, stand unrivalled. – With one small open Fire they will Roast, Steam, and Bake for a Family of from five to fifty Individuals, and afford a constant supply of hot Water; their Construction is so simple that they are well understood.

them and other items of domestic cast ironwork such as rainwater guttering, drain pipes, gullies, gratings and the numerous examples of other domestic utensils and machines, from that ubiquitous material, cast iron. Competition became fierce, and, as ever, cost became a foremost consideration, so that, as the second half of the eighteenth century progressed and the nineteenth century commenced, the stove grate and general light casting industry became centred in specific areas of which the West Midlands, the Falkirk and Glasgow regions of Scotland, and the Sheffield and Rotherham areas became the most important. Most towns and cities had an iron foundry, and some had several; they served the local millwrights and engineers, and among their products was the odd stove grate or range. In their cases, however, costs were high, and a landlord intent upon the development of a plot of land for workers' housing demanded cheap, mass-produced products, appliances proved to be safe, cheap to install, that protected his property, and were strong enough to withstand the misuse and neglect of the tenant. Iron foundries that specialised in such products were established and they undercut the general foundry in both price, quantity, and delivery.

It was at the Rotherham Masbrough Foundry of Samuel Walker, established in 1746, that the stove grate industry was born in South Yorkshire. At this foundry the earliest of the stove grates were produced, designed for the town houses of the professional and aristocratic classes, and methods of production were developed to enable these goods to be produced in repeated quantities at an acceptable production cost. It was also at this foundry that men, who were to carry on, and expand the trade to meet an increasing demand, were trained and who did the production development work in pattern making and moulding methods and who were to improve upon these methods in their own foundries. It was at this foundry, too, and those of Coalbrookdale in Shropshire, and of Carron in Falkirk, that stove grate products were to be 'productionised' and cheapened to enable the industry to establish itself. Famous men of scientific bent employed themselves in attempts to cure the fireplace of its troubles: smoking chimneys, excessive fuel consumption, inadequate heat radiation, and by doing so provided basic rules of design for equally famous designers and artists to produce aesthetically pleasing appliances. By 1780, the general principles of fireplace design had been established, and great use was made of cast iron both to form the safe, fire-proof container for the fireplace, and to provide a decorative encapsulation for it. In the nether regions of the kitchen, a similar scientific approach had been applied to the means for cooking.

Jedediah Strutt, of Belper, Derbyshire, a friend of the Walkers, filed a patent, No. 964, in 1770 for, 'A Machine for Roasting, Boiling, and Baking', consisting of a portable fire stove, an air jacket, and a meat screen. On the 21 October, 1780, Thomas Robinson took out Patent No. 1267 for a self-contained range, commencing the search for improvements that are seen today in the Aga and Rayburn cookers.

The Sheffield Stove Grate Makers – a selected survey

Sketchley's Sheffield Directory for 1774, lists two ironfounders: Samuel Alsop of Sheffield Moor, and John Bramah on Foundry Street. By 1787 four Sheffield foundries were listed in a national directory: Samuel Alsop's; Messrs. Appleby, Schofield & Co. on Gibraltar; Smith, Stacey & Co. of the Queen's Foundry, Paradise Square; and Booth, Binks & Hartop & Co.[1]

The above iron foundries were independent foundries relying upon their own means for melting the iron as distinct from the foundries that had previously been attached to the blast furnaces. We have no records to refer to in order to establish whether they were the first such ironfounders in Sheffield. I suspect not, but who those early operators were is unknown. Neither is it recorded whether they produced stove grates, but this fact is not surprising because at that time all such products were part and parcel of the general iron-founders' production. The first mention of stove grate makers, operating in Sheffield, is to be found in Wardle & Pratt's *The Commercial Directory* of 1816–17, in which four are listed: Barber & Genn on Bower Spring; Eyre, Ibbotson, & Henzell, on Green Lane; Shaw, Jobson & Co. on Roscoe Place; and Messrs. Proctor & Fenton, on Rockingham Place. In 1828, the number listed had risen to fourteen.[2]

Samuel Alsop was in partnership with John Smith at the Griffin Iron Furnaces, Brampton, Chesterfield. Alsop is stated to be an 'anvil smith'[3], and several members of the Smith family were to be active in the stove grate industry in Sheffield during the ensuing years.

Appleby, Schofield & Co. of Gibraltar, Sheffield, were listed in 1787 and 1797 as ironfounders.[4] Appleby, in a new partnership with a Mr Walker, established an ironworks at Renishaw in Derbyshire, whilst Edward & John Schofield continued as ironfounders on the corner of Gibraltar Street and Furnace Hill until 1825 when the firm is listed as Schofield & Loxley.[5] It was about then that they discontinued the manufacture of stove grates and concentrated upon boiler and engine making.

Smith, Stacey & Co., Queeen's Foundry, Paradise Square, Sheffield, had been established on Workhouse Croft by a member of the Smith family who, in partnership with Samuel Alsop, had a foundry on Sheffield Moor and interests in the Griffin Iron Furnaces at Brampton near Chesterfield. Like the Walkers of Masbrough, the Smiths had originally hailed from Grenoside, a small village to the north of Sheffield where they had been cutlers.[6] The building of Paradise Square was completed by Thomas Broadbent in 1771, and we know that all the houses facing onto the Square and those on Workhouse Croft, which ran northwards from the Square down to West Bar, had been built by this time. The foundry premises commenced in an alleyway at the rear of the houses on the north-east side of the Square and they stretched along to what is now Queen Street. The firm is listed in a directory for 1787.

Smith, Stacey & Co., was also involved in the operation of the Elsecar Ironworks in 1793–1794[7], but ran into financial difficulties and sold out their Sheffield and Elsecar holdings to a partnership consisting of John Darwin, Francis Frith, Joseph Ridge, and William Darwin, who began operations under the title of John Darwin & Co. It was this firm which was at the Queen's Foundry in 1795. Among the early products of the Queen's Foundry were stove grates, and also mill and engine work, and they are listed as stove grate and kitchen range makers until the early 1920s. The foundry operated until the 1950s, but as general ironfounders only under the title of Darwin, Yeardley & Co. Ltd.

Newton Chambers & Co was one of those large, multi-product manufacturing companies that grew from a small iron foundry.[8] From its earliest days two of the firm's products were stove grates and kitchen ranges, and indeed, the successors of the original company, Trianco-Redfyre Ltd., are still operating in an associated industry.

George Newton (1761–1825) served an apprenticeship to a Darlington grocer following which he went to London to be a clerk to Messrs Hetherington and Maskew who were tea merchants. After his marriage, an unfortunate affliction, that resulted in recurring bouts of deafness, caused him to join his brother-in-law, Charles Hodgson, in the latter's small iron foundry and cutlery merchant's business in Sheffield in 1790. The firm's products were then cast shovels and spades, trowels, hinges, and other small cast ware, and, in order to expand their business and premises, the partnership persuaded Mr Maskew, George's former employer, to invest in their firm which was situated in a corner of Smith Stacey's Queen's Foundry.

With Maskew's money they found new premises on Pond Hill, Sheffield. The partnership also rented part of the Nether Slack Tilt Hammer at Owlerton, to commence the manufacture of iron plate shovels and spades.

During the latter part of 1792, Thomas Chambers (1745–1817), a pattern maker who had served his apprenticeship to the Walkers' company at Masbrough, told Charles Hodgson of his intention to leave the employment of Smith Stacey and set up in business on his own account. Both Newton and Hodgson, with eyes towards further expansion, sold to Chambers the idea of them all going into business together in a blast furnace and iron ore mining venture, and so the firm of Maskew, Hodgson, Newton and Chambers proceeded to erect a new foundry, the Phoenix Foundry, at a site between Snow Hill and Furnace Hill off Gibraltar Street, and they made their first castings there in March, 1793. Shortly afterwards Maskew was forced to withdraw from the partnership due to a pressure on his capital from his tea merchant's business, and a new source of capital was found in Henry Longden, a scissor maker and ardent Methodist friend of Charles Hodgson. On the 16 January, 1793, Newton and Chambers rode out to begin negotiations for the lease of a site in the Thorncliffe valley near Chapeltown, to the north of Sheffield, upon which to build a blast furnace and commence mining for iron ore and coal. The driving of a sough to drain their intended iron ore and coalmine was commenced on 1 January, 1794, and a little later they began to build their blast furnace, a cold blast, open topped, hand charged, but coke-fired furnace which had a capacity to produce fifteen tons of pig iron a week.

Longden invested a further £12,000 into the Company in January, 1796, and a second blast furnace, this one with a weekly capacity of twenty tons of pig iron, was built. These two furnaces were to give continuous production for 78 years. The company's mining operations, however, hit an unexpected geological fault that necessitated the erection of a steam engine to aid the draining of the mine, and the brothers John Scott, a haberdasher of London, and Robert Scott, a wooldraper, invested towards this purpose. The new partnership was Longden, Newton, Chambers, & Scotts.

During these early days the Thorncliffe operations produced pig iron and coke for use at the Phoenix Foundry and for general sale, and the foundry in Sheffield produced stove grates, ranges, wheels, bushes and bearings, and machine castings – the latter especially for cotton mill equipment. By 1800, the combined works were employing about 300 men, and the capital of the Company stood at

£17,268.

During the years 1800–1802 building took place at the Thorncliffe site as a step towards the accommodation of all the firm's activities there, and the Phoenix Foundry was vacated on 24 June, 1802, and all operations were then concentrated at Thorncliffe. The move expanded the productive capacity of the foundry, and its products now included bedsteads, kitchen boilers, stoves, ranges, chimney pieces, register fronts, every kind of furniture for ovens, pans, digesters (pressure cookers), foot-scrapers, garden rakes, gopher irons, sad irons, tailors' and hatters' irons, toy irons – at 6d (2½p) each – brewing and furnace pans, plough breasts, clothes posts, railings, palisading, rain water guttering and pipes, spouts, sink-traps, spittoons, clock and sash-window weights, truck wheels, scale weights, window frames, bookcases, and anvils. During the closing years of the Napoleonic Wars, the foundry made a few cannons, possibly on sub-contract from the Walkers' ironworks at Masbrough. Following the Wars, the Company commenced to make larger castings, plates, girders, rails, and storage tanks; they also undertook some of the cast works for the Walkers' contract to make the Southwark Bridge.

Following Newton Chambers' removal to Thorncliffe, the Phoenix Foundry was taken over by Barlow & Co., a company of whom nothing is known other than that they included stove grates among their products, and that they operated from the Phoenix Foundry until 1818.[9]

Henry Longden, whose health was beginning to decline, had secured for his son, Henry, a position with Newton Chambers, but the active partners both felt that the young Henry was not of the calibre they desired, nor were they particularly keen upon the arrangements Henry, senior, had made regarding the disposal of his wealth and company holding upon his death. Longden's original capital investment of about £15,000 was, by 1811, worth £25,222, and the partners borrowed a huge sum with which to buy him out. The Longdens withdrew from the Company in about 1814, to establish a small iron foundry themselves, on Broad Lane, Sheffield, and eventually, by 1819, following the death of Henry senior, young Henry, in partnership with a Mr Walker, took over the Phoenix Foundry from Barlow & Co.

Newton Chambers had, by 1814, largely repaid the loan they had taken out to buy off the Longdens. As for stove grates, Newton Chambers had begun to produce them before the turn of the century. During the early 1830s they supplied several stoves to estate cottages for Earl Fitzwilliam in Tankersley and Wentworth, and by the 1840s they were supplying them nationally. A letter in the Company's archive shows that they were not only manufacturing a standard catalogue of products but that they were also making 'specials'. Mr Watson, of Gainsborough wrote:

> *Enclosed is the sketch of the Kitchen Range as requested for Mr F. G. Smith you must however hurry for the Gentleman says that if it exceeds 12 days he will not have it because you have had so long in hand. The Kitchen Range... must be here on Tuesday if possible...*

Watson gives a fairly detailed description of his client's specification regarding, size, the position of dampers, boiler connections, the position of flue outlets, and he attached a sketch. A Company clerk appended the following statement to the letter: 'Can not engage to make this stove and deliver in twelve days Does Mr Smith agree to pay anything for alterations? . . .'[10]

Newton Chambers reached agreements with manufacturers in other parts of the country to make, possibly with licensing arrangements, patented appliances. They were one of the first to produce the famous 'Leamington Kitchener' (Figure 2) apart from the original designer and maker, Sidney Flavel of Leamington Spa, who had introduced the model and its future many variants, during the 1790s.[11] This was to begin a relationship between the two companies that was to last until the 1960s. It is also possible that Newton Chambers were the original producers of the 'Yorkshire Range', the open fire kitchen range that almost all the Yorkshire, and many other, ironfounders were to make. Certainly, Thorncliffe catalogues carried the most comprehensive array of this popular range, in which they offered to their customers the largest variety with respect to sizes, capacities, and 'improved' models (Figure 3).

The 'Thorncliffe Range' made its first appearance in 1876, and it became a favoured choice of hoteliers and country house owners right through to the 1920s (Figure 4). The Company's draughtsman at that time was William Flower, who is listed as a designer in White's Directory for 1860 living at 168, St Philips Road. His family had been involved in the design and manufacture of stove grates and fenders for many years in Sheffield. He moved during the late 1860s to Chapeltown, which was more convenient to his work as the Company's designer under their General Manager, George Dawson.

The expansion of the Company into heavy engineering, i.e., gasworks and steelworks equipment, into chemical engineering and processing, and into the manufacture of earthmoving equipment,

Figure 2.   Improved close fire 'Leamington' Kitchen Range, made by Newton Chambers in 1890. We know that the appliance was being made during the last years of the eighteenth century, and that during the nineteenth century the manufacture was licensed to several other makers including Newton Chambers of Thorncliffe, Moorwoods of Sheffield and Yates Haywoods of Rotherham. As the years progressed many improvements to this range were introduced, and the above companies produced 'Improved Leamington Kitcheners'. *NC & Co. Catalogue 1890. Chris Morley Collection*

Figure 3.   Improved Yorkshire Cooking Range. Made by Newton Chambers & Co.Ltd. in 1890. This appliance is not much different from the Green & Pickslay Range of 1825. *NC & Co. Catalogue 1890. Chris Morley Collection*

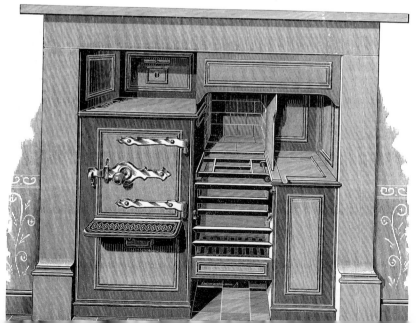

Figure 4.　The 'Thorncliffe' Patent close and open fire cooking range. (1890). *NC & Co. Catalogue 1890. Chris Morley Collection*

somewhat overshadowed light castings production. Although the stove grate and range side of the firm's business was only a minor product of a company that grew to have a very wide and diverse product range, it appears to have always been a well-supported product, and Thorncliffe's heating and cooking appliances were always abreast of, or ahead of current taste, design, and technical requirements.

During the Second World War Newton Chambers took over the patterns and trade name of **'REDFYRE'** from Swann, Garland & Co., and gradually this became their trade mark for stove grate and room heater products. The name is now carried on with Messrs. Trianco-Redfyre, the manufacturers of domestic central heating equipment who still operate from premises at Thorncliffe (Figure 5).

Henry Longden, Junior, in partnership with Walker, as **Longden, Walker & Co.**, built up a commendable business in the manufacture of stove grates and cooking appliances, in warmed air heating equipment, and in decorative and engineering ironwork at the Phoenix Foundry, Furnace Hill. The Longden Walker partnership is listed until 1834 when the firm was reorganised as Henry Longden & Co. By 1849 it was simply known as Longden & Co., the name it was to retain until 1910 whilst still in the hands of the Longden family.

At least two apprentices of the company achieved success, Isaac Ironside (1808 –1870) born at Masbrough, served his time during the 1820s, and rose to become the firm's accountant. He eventually left its employ to become a director of the Sheffield New Gas Company in 1852. George Haywood, later a partner with James Yates in Messrs. Yates, Haywood & Co., Effingham Works, Rotherham, probably one of the largest firms to specialise in stove grate manufacture, served his apprenticeship as a model maker (pattern maker) to Longdens at about the same time as Ironside.

Longden's exhibit at the 1851 Great Exhibition earned a First Council Medal. On display were a

Figure 5. The 'Redfyre' (Regd.) boiler cooker de luxe (1939 Model). This was an open or closed fire insulated cooker complete with a boiler of sufficient capability to provide background heating via several cast iron hot water radiators. Advertising leaflet, Swann Garland & Co. 1939. *Chris Morley Collection*

large cooking range, a warm-air stove heated by gas, examples of staircase balusters and newells [sic], a cast iron gallery-front for an entrance hall, and decorative enclosures for hot water heating pipes that served also as hall tables. The firm's display at the 1862 Exhibition, whilst not a medal-winning one, also attracted a great deal of attention (Figure 6).

The Longden family retained control over the Company, and its independence, until 1910 when it was purchased by the Carron

Figure 6. Longden & Co., Phoenix Foundry, Furnace Hill, Sheffield. Advert. 1862. Unfortunately there are no illustrations of Longden's exhibits at the 1851 Great Exhibition. The illustrated advertisement of 1862 shows a dining-room fireplace that formed part of their display at the 1862 Exhibition. The Official Catalogue describes it as: being an adaptation of Early Pointed art to modern requirements, consisting of register grate of cast iron electro-bronzed with copper, with brass ornaments and glass mirrors, ash pan and fender of electro-bronzed cast iron, steel fire-irons with elec-tro-bronzed handles, and mantle-piece of Devonshire and serpentine marbles, designed by Messrs. Walton & Robson, Architects, London and Durham. *Pawson & Brailsford's 'Illustrated Guide to Sheffield and Neighbourhood'*, Sheffield, 1862

LONGDEN & CO.,
MANUFACTURERS OF
ORNAMENTAL FIRE GRATES

Company, of Scotland. The Sheffield Phoenix Foundry was closed down shortly after the end of the First World War, and all pattern equipment was transferred to Scotland.

During the latter half of the nineteenth century the Company con-centrated on the design and manufacture of stove grates and fenders of high quality in reproduction and contemporary designs (Figures 7 and 8). They also designed and manufactured other quality metal work. One of their most prestigious orders came in the 1870s when His Grace the Duke of Norfolk remodelled his Yorkshire House, Carlton Towers, near Goole, and Longdens provided all the stove grates, and much of the interior and exterior metalwork; the light fit-tings are especially notable for their design and manufacture. The new Town Hall in Sheffield was one of the many public buildings that Longdens supplied with heating equipment, and several of their stove grates are still to be found in the rooms of the buildings. In St. Matthew's Church, Sheffield, and at Welbeck Abbey in Nottinghamshire, there are beautiful examples of Longdens' decora-tive metalwork.

A number of the firms who engaged in the industry commenced

Figure 7. Longden Reproduction Hob Grate. From a Carron Co. published catalogue of Longden products dated 1914. *Chris Morley Collection*

as fender makers, making sheet metal fenders from steel, wrought iron, and brass. A fender is simply a decorative obstacle placed across the front of the fire hearth to contain and prevent hot coals from falling onto the room floor and its covering. Early fenders were made from sheet metal, decorated by pierced patterns, and then polished and bent into shape. The introduction of cast iron fenders during the early decades of the nineteenth century encouraged some manufacturers to open their own foundries, and these were then used to also produce stove grates.

Joseph Shaw, of Leicester, married Sarah Hoole, and in partnership with William Hoole of Whitehouse, Sheffield, [Sarah's brother and a steel refiner] established Shaw & Co., fendermakers, Green Lane, to manufacture pierced and shaped fenders from steel and brass sheet.[12] The Company was first listed in 1787. Taking into partnership a Robert Jobson, they added a foundry onto the Green Lane site to make cast iron fenders and cast brass and ormolu decoration, and then, in 1806, in partnership with Jobson, Shaw began to build the Roscoe Place Works.

William Hoole (1763–1843), gent., of the Whitehouse, Upperthorpe, listed in the 1787 directory as a steel refiner[13], paid rates on property in Green Lane in 1811[14] thus showing that he had withdrawn from Shaw & Co. and had established a new partnership with Benjamin Boothby, as **Hoole, Boothby & Co.**, in Shaw's old premises as cast and sheet metal fendermakers. Boothby was a draper then residing at Doncaster. He was brother to Maria, the second wife of Joseph Fletcher Smith, who had been the Master Cutler in 1796, a Smith related to the Smiths of the Griffin Ironworks at Brampton, Chesterfield, and by marriage related also to the Reads, of the Sheffield Smelting Co., who held the freehold of the land in Green Lane.

By 1814, Hoole's shareholding had been eclipsed by others and a reorganisation took place with the firm becoming known as **Boothby, Eyre and Henzel**, and it was this partnership which is noted in the rate books for the years 1814–1816. By 1817 the firm had become **Eyre, Henzel, and Ibbotson**. Boothby's involvement with the firm had been a profitable one, and in 1815 he bought into the Griffin Ironworks and joined it in some managerial capacity at a salary of £200.[15] He thus withdrew from the Green Lane company.

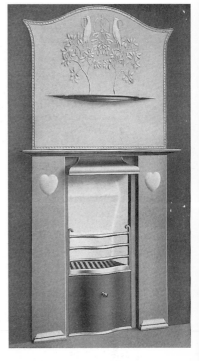

Figure 8. The very height of fashion, Longden 1914. From a Carron Co. published catalogue of Longden products dated 1914. *Chris Morley Collection*

Ibbotson, from Hathersage, joined the partnership of Eyre and Henzel in 1816, but his stay was short-lived, for he withdrew in late 1817, or early 1818 to found his own fender making business on Spring Street. Henzel also dropped out at about the same time, and his future is unknown. **Edward Eyre**, Green Lane, is listed from 1821 until 1827 in which year Eyre joined with Messrs. Hitchin & Wharton, to form **Hitchin, Wharton & Eyre**, fendermakers, in premises at 67, Carver Street, a business established in 1822. Messrs. Wharton & Eyre made a final entry in the directories in 1830 on South Street, The Moor.

Henry Elliott Hoole had been born in 1805, the son of William Hoole a steel refiner of Whitehouse, Upperthorpe, Sheffield, and formerly a partner in the Green Lane company of Hoole, Boothby & Co. Whether William Hoole had remained a partner in the Green Lane firm is unknown, but in 1827 a directory entry listed H. E. Hoole, ironfounder and stove grate manufacturer in partnership with his father at Malinda Street, Sheffield, and also concerned in Messrs. Nicholson & Hoole at Green Lane.[16] The Rate Book entry for 1828 listed **Nicholson & Hoole** at Green Lane. George Nicholson, had been a pattern maker but at which company is unknown.

In 1834, Nicholson & Hoole paid £100 rent to Reads the landlords [Reads were of the silver refiners, the Sheffield Smelting Co][17], and in 1837 Thomas Nicholson and Henry Hoole bought the land from Read for £3,400. Included were a house, workshops, gardens, counting house, warehouse, stables, grinding mill or wheel, iron foundry, steam engine house, cottages, etc., known as Green Lane Works. Nicholson & Hoole were described as merchants, steel converters, iron and brass founders, stove grate, fender, and iron candlestick manufacturers.[18]

By 1842 Nicholson had dropped out as a named partner, but he is known to have remained in active management at the works, and the firm was listed as **Henry E. Hoole**, Green Lane Works. John George Robson joined William and Henry Hoole to form a new partnership in 1846, and the firm was listed as **Hoole, Robson & Hoole**.

In 1855 the partnership was once again reorganised with H. E. Hoole becoming the prominent partner as **H. E. Hoole & Co.**, but it was still very much a three-family concern. Henry Elliott Hoole, FSA, lived at Crookesmoor House; a Joseph Hoole who was connected with the business lived at 9, Gell Street; Henry's brothers, James (gent.) and Charles, an artist, lived at 191 Western Bank; John George Robson lived at 341, Glossop Road; George Nicholson, the firm's modelmaker, lived at 7, Ellesmere Road; and his son, Vincent Nicholson, a designer, lived at 245, Lower St. Philip's Road.[19]

The preparations made for the firm's participation in the 1851 Great Exhibition, and the introduction of the designer Alfred Stevens, and others, into the works to provide the designs of the firm's intended exhibits, caused upsets to the existing workforce, and to Hoole's partners. However, the rewards and awards resulting from the Exhibition resulted in the firm becoming nationally famous, and their order books full to capacity (Figure 9).

During the mid-1850s great changes were made to the owning

partnership and to the management structure of Hoole's. Henry Hoole's father had died, as had Joseph Hoole; Henry's brothers had retired to do their own things, and both Nicholson and Robson had moved into semi-retirement. H. E. Hoole became the sole owner of the Company. New, young, and talented designers were introduced into the works adding to the prosperity of the Company and to the fine product range, so much so that the Company built an entirely new works on the Green Lane site, and in 1860 added the now famous gateway to its entrance (Figure 10).

Henry Elliot Hoole went into semi-retirement at Ravenfield Park, near Rotherham, passing control of the Company to his son, Percival F. Hoole. H. E. died, at the age of 85, on 1 February, 1891. The Green Lane Works of H. E. Hoole & Co. continued until they were taken over by the acquisitive Allied Ironfounders Ltd., who closed the Works down at the beginning of the Second World War, and transferred all the pattern equipment and designs to the Falkirk Iron Company's works in Scotland where the

Figure 9.   H.E. Hoole & Co. 1851. From the *Art-Journal Illustrated Catalogue* for the 1851 Great Exhibition, an example of a Hoole's stove grate – not designed by Alfred Stevens! The shell-shaped appliance was especially made by the firm for Messrs. Grey & Son of Edinburgh. *The Art-Journal Illustrated Catalogue – The Industry of all Nations, Virtue, 1851, p.213*

Allied Ironfounders continued to trade certain of their stove grate products under the name of H. E. Hoole & Co. Ltd., of Falkirk.[20] However, sometime during the 1950s all the pattern equipment belonging to Hoole's was scrapped, and the company sank into oblivion.

Joseph Shaw and Robert Jobson, in partnership with William Hoole, had commenced building a 'vast assemblage of workshops' at Roscoe Place by St. Philip's Church in 1805–6[21], and by 1814 the partnership, by now one of **Shaw & Jobson**, had removed completely into their new works to manufacture sheet metal fenders, and fire irons.

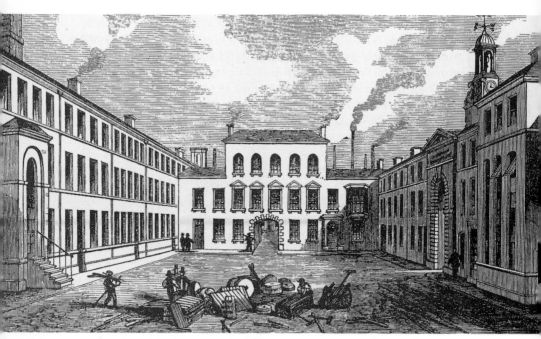

Figure 10. H. E. Hoole & Co., Green Lane Works, 1862. The interior of the yard at Green Lane Works; the entrance, through the archway, is to the right. *Pawson & Brailsford's 'Illustrated Guide to Sheffield and Neighbourhood'*, Sheffield 1862, p.175

A story told of those early days illustrates the high regard and reputation enjoyed by the company as, perhaps, one of the largest factories then in Sheffield. The Archduke Nicholas, afterwards Czar Nicholas I of Russia, accompanied by his brother and a large retinue of dignitaries, visited the works. On the morning of the visit Mr Jobson ordered his workforce to go home at lunchtime, to change and return dressed in their 'holiday attire', to receive the distinguished visitors.

Joseph Shaw went to the USA in 1818 with his son, Henry, and Jobson remained as the sole proprietor and operator.[22]

In 1825, Messrs. **Stuart & Parkin**, fendermakers, are listed in Market Street and as stove grate makers at the Savile Works on Savile Street, Sheffield. By 1828 **Parkin** joined **Ingall** at 26, Bridge Street, making stove grates and fenders, and we last hear of him, on his own, at 28, Bridge Street in 1830. The operating partnership in 1828 is listed as **Stuart & Barton**, with premises on Savile Street. Barton then appears to have discontinued his association with the company, and in 1830 the firm was listed as **Stuart & Smith**, Savile Works,

Savile Street, stove grate makers, with John Jobson Smith (1809–1878) in partnership with Stuart. John Jobson Smith was a nephew, by marriage, of Robert Jobson of the Roscoe Place Works,[23] and he was also related to the Smiths of Chesterfield, and the cutlery Smiths of Sheffield. The Company had lost the fender making side of its business when Parkin left and the Market Street premises had been vacated, and it was a business in which they very much desired to become active once again. Negotiations with Robert Jobson revealed that the Roscoe Place Works was capable of being expanded to accommodate a foundry suitable for stove grate manufacture, and it, of course, was already the foremost fender factory. Jobson agreed to a sale probably providing that he could take some of the fender patterns and tooling with him. The new foundry was built at Roscoe Place and Stuart, Smith & Co., removed from the Savile Works in 1834 to their new premises, taking over some of the workforce and fender production from Jobson who then formed a new partnership to establish **Robertson & Jobson**, fendermakers, on Love Street. Robertson & Jobson made a final appearance in the trade directories in 1849, and in that year Robert Jobson returned to the Roscoe Place Works as an independent designer of heating apparatus contracting with Stuart & Smith to have them made.[24] There does not appear to have been a connection between this Robert Jobson and a Robert Jobson of the Litchurch Foundry, Derby, which was listed in 1857 as a maker of stove grates and kitchen ranges.

At the 1851 Great Exhibition Stuart and Smith exhibited Sylvester's Patent Grate (Figure 11) and other patented register stoves, a range of fire irons and fenders, and air stoves designed for entrance halls and large rooms. For some reason they also had three miniature brass steam engines on display worked by steam and clockwork; the largest weighed two and a half ounces and the smallest but one third of an ounce! They also exhibited at the 1862 Exhibition (Figure 12).

Jobson's exhibit at the 1851 Exhibition was centred around his patented bright steel heat and light reflecting stove (Figure 13), and he included a burnished steel register-stove, a patent air-stove that appeared to be a pedestal, and a 'parlour' cooking stove.

Following the death of John Jobson Smith, on 9 September, 1878, a holding company of Messrs. Barker, Barber, & Sylvester ran the business[25], but, in 1879 they reverted to the more famous name, Stuart Smith & Co. In 1888 H. E. Hoole & Co. bought the company and transferred it to the Green Lane Works. The Roscoe Place Works was sold by auction on Tuesday, 13 November, 1888, and

Figure 11.   Stuart & Smith, Roscoe Place, Sheffield. The flamboyant decoration of this 'Sylvester's Patent Grate' was not unusual during the mid-nineteenth century. The materials used in its construction were 'dead' steel and burnished steel, with ormolu 'enrichments' with the object of its decoration being to create a style of decoration with nature *without the introduction of more conventional forms! The Art-Journal Illustrated Catalogue – The Industry of all Nations, Virtue, 1851, p. 35*

ceased to have any connection with the stove grate industry. The site is now no more, having been buried below the roadway of the junction connecting Netherthorpe Road and Infirmary Road, and the Supertram. It was for many years the site of the Roscoe Cinema and latterly the Roscoe Bingo Hall.

William Green set up his own small foundry on West Bar Green, to manufacture hammers, vices, and other small tools. He was a relative of the Green family of Ecclesfield, of which the brothers Edward and Samuel operated a corn mill on the Common, and a John Green who had a small foundry, the Ecclesfield Foundry next to the corn mill. John Green, in 1855, claimed to have been established as a maker of cooking equipment upon his filing of Patent No. 100188.[26]

Figure 12.   Stuart & Smith, 1862. This stove grate exhibited by the firm at the 1862 Exhibition
was made to a special commission. It was designed by the sculptor John Thomas,
shortly before he died, to the theme 'A Midsummer Night's Dream'. *The Art-Journal*
reported that 'the work is not only charming in design, but excellent in execution; not
overladen, as such productions often are, but simple, graceful, and most effective'. *The
Art-Journal Illustrated Catalogue of the International Exhibition 1862, Virtue 1863, p.124*

In 1860 William Green's address was given as 14, Cleveland
Place, Infirmary Road, where he was operating as a whitesmith. By
1862 he was listed as an ironfounder on Ecclesfield Common and at
4, Corporation Street, Sheffield, having inherited his relative's
Ecclesfield foundry. The 1889 directory listed William Green at
111–115, West Bar, and at the Norfolk Foundry, Ecclesfield. By that
date the small Ecclesfield Foundry had expanded into and taken
over the old cornmill, using the mill's water wheel to drive the
machinery, a practice they continued through to the 1920s.

From the days of John Green, the Company specialised in the
making of cooking equipment. They were among the first to manufacture small, compact, portable cooking ranges for emigrants who
undertook the long treks by 'covered wagons' across to America's

Figure 13. Jobson & Co., Roscoe Place, Sheffield. Jobson's Patent Heat and Light Reflecting Stove, 1851. The design of this stove, exhibited at the 1851 Great Exhibition, had, the *Art-Journal* reported, 'given Mr Jobson a peculiar reputation; the power possessed by the circular reflector which surrounds the fire-grate is very great, and more effective in throwing forward and economising heat, than any previous invention . . . it is also elegant in form, and the ornaments are judiciously connected with it'. *The Art-Journal Illustrated Catalogue- The Industry of all Nations, Virtue, 1851, p.294*

west, and they also made similar appliances for ships' galleys. In 1889 the firm was listed as, 'Manufacturers of all kinds of cooking ranges, grill stoves, hot plates, confectioners' ovens, steam closets, gas hobs and carving tables, stove grates, tile registers, dog grates, mantels, and overmantels, kerbs, fenders, ash pans, etc.[27] Later directories show them to have been makers of machine tools such as steam and hydraulic hammers and presses, and the makers of sluice and lock gate castings and equipment. William Green & Co. became a private limited liability company in 1914 registered as William Green & Co. (Ecclesfield) Ltd. with a works at the Norfolk Foundry, Ecclesfield, and showrooms at West Bar, Sheffield. The products of the Norfolk Foundry were listed as: stove grates, ranges, ships' galley and cabin stoves, general engineering products and castings, and machine tools. Green's withdrew from stove grate production during the late 1960s but continued with the manufacture of large scale catering equipment and sub-contract castings. In December, 1968, William Green & Co. (Ecclesfield) Ltd. established a new Company. Green's of Ecclesfield Ltd., to take over the manufacture and marketing of their commercial and marine catering equipment business. This enabled Brightside Engineering Holdings Ltd. (see Moorwood Vulcan Ltd.) to buy out this side of the business, and in doing so they leased part of the Norfolk Foundry for a short time while they converted part of their vast Ecclesfield Works to accommodate the combined manufacturing and administrative staffs of Moorwood Vulcan Ltd. and Green's of Ecclesfield. Moorwoods were removed from the Harleston Works in Sheffield to their new site in 1971. Green's of Ecclesfield then became a non-operational company. The engineering interests of William Green & Co. (Ecclesfield) Ltd. did not join the Brightside Group, nor did the West Bar Showroom which, by this time was a builders, ironmongers and heating and plumbing distributors and showroom, operating as a separate company, William Green & Co (Sheffield) Ltd. The latter company was closed down in 1980, and the engineering side of the business was closed in 1983–4.

Chantrey Works, on Sylvester Street, became famous as the works of Robertson, Carr & Steel. Messrs. **Carr, Woodhouse, & Carr** were listed as fender makers on Bailey Lane, Sheffield, from 1817 through to 1829. In that year they ceased to have any connection with the industry having decided to concentrate upon tool steel and tool manufacturing. The Carr family name reappeared in 1841 when Henry Smith Carr was listed in premises at 8, Sycamore Street, Sheffield. A relative, George Carr, one of the original partners in Carr, Woodhouse, & Carr, had established a fender making business on Longcroft in 1820 whilst retaining an interest in the tool company on Bailey Lane. He moved to Allen Street in 1823, then to Meadow Street in 1828. He is listed as being on Burnt Tree Lane in 1833, at Arundel Street in 1845, and, finally, on Peacroft in 1852 where, in various premises, he remained in business until 1862. He also ran a beerhouse on Broad Lane in 1859!

However, it is with H. S. Carr, at 8, Sycamore Street, that our main interest lies. By 1845 he was trading under the name of **Carr & Steel**, in partnerhsip with Henry Steel as stove grate and fender makers. By 1849 they had moved into the Union Works on Union

Street and shortly afterwards the partnership was joined by Alex. Robertson, from the Love Street partnership of Robertson & Jobson to become **Robertson, Carr, and Steel**. The Company erected a new works, the Chantrey Works, on Sylvester Street, close to St. Mary's Church, consisting of an iron and a non-ferrous foundry, smiths' shops, grinding shops, and assembly workshops. Their range of products for the fireplace encompassed a wide variety of stove grates, fenders and fire irons, and was reflected in their comprehensive exhibit at the 1851 Great Exhibition.

Steel left the partnership in 1860 to establish a new company in partnership with Richard W. Garland. From 1860 to 1880, or thereabouts, the Chantrey Works was operated by Messrs. Robertson & Carr & Co., who exhibited at the 1862 Exhibition (Figure 14). Carr Brothers, and Webster, was the name listed in 1879, and in 1885 it was Clement, Carr, & Co., Clement having joined them from Perrot, Clement & Hamill, of the Alma Works, Rotherham. Their last appearance as makers of stove grates and fenders was in the directory for 1889.

Steel & Garland, The Wharncliffe Works, Cornish Street, off Green Lane was established in 1861 by Henry Francis Steel, (from Robertson, Carr & Steel, Chantrey Works), and Richard Wheen Garland. Following the breaching of the Dale Dyke Dam, at Bradfield, in March 1864, the firm claimed losses for drawings, lithographs, five hundredweights of emery-paper, reams of tissue paper, finished ormolu, 'inside cheeks', and a lime box which had contained bright stove bars; they also suffered damage to the black leading and bronzing shop.[28] The firm exhibited stove grates and fenders at the 1862 Exhibition.

In 1865 the factory was listed as the Wharncliffe Works, Cornish Place, Green Lane. It was to operate as a stove grate maker until 1899. In 1900 the firm opened the Priory Foundry at Worksop, and in 1901 closed down the Wharncliffe Works. It was sold by auction on 19 November, 1901.

Swann, Garland, Marlborough Works, Chippinghouse Road, was established by Richard Wheen Garland, ex Steel & Garland of the Wharncliffe Works, in partnership with Swann, as stove grate makers in about 1909. They were listed in 1920, and by 1930 they had established the tradename 'REDFYRE'. During the Second World War the factory was bombed, and Newton Chambers took over their patterns and the trade name, 'REDFYRE'.

C. & J. Ellis & Co. started as an ironmongers owned by Charles and James Ellis who were also gas fitters, and hot-water warming apparatus makers on George Street, off High Street, Sheffield. They also had a small foundry and workshop on the corner of Leadmill Street and Shoreham Street in about 1860. Other partners in the business were, at that time, John Swift Ellis, and James C. Ellis, obviously relatives for they all lived at the same address, 7 George Street. They are also listed as bellhangers, and stove grate makers. By 1885 John Swift Ellis, and James C. Ellis were the principal partners in the hardware and heating business on George Street, and at the now named Norfolk Foundry on Shoreham Street where they made stove grates, ranges, gas cookers, and boilers. In 1890 they moved to the Carbrook Foundry on Bright Street financing the move by becoming J. S. & J. C. Ellis Ltd., and they vacated the Norfolk Foundry in 1893.

Ambrose Firth & Co. was never a stove and grate manufacturer, but the firm was to be very closely allied to the industry following the amalgamation of several companies that formed the Brightside Steel & Engineering Co. Ltd. Frederick Firth had a small foundry on Bailey Street off Trippet Lane in 1860, where he cast small ware and cast iron cutlery. His brother, Robert, owned an ironmongery, on Matthew Street, off Shalesmoor. Frederick's son, Ambrose, opened his own foundry on Brightside Lane in 1864 to manufacture cast iron products for the local steelworks, especially

Figure 14. Robertson & Carr, Chantry Works, Sheffield. Among the contributions of this company to the 1862 Exhibition was this basket grate with dogs made to a design by R. W. Billings of London, for Dalziel Castle, Scotland. It was said that no particular style of architecture predominated in this grate: 'it may be considered suitable to the period when Elizabethan architecture became established in the sixteenth century. In some respects the present design differs from fire-grates in general – it has not a particle of foliation about it, nor any vegetable or animal feature'. *The Art-Journal Illustrated Catalogue of the International Exhibition 1862, Virtue 1863, p.83*

steel-ingot moulds. During the 1870s he moved into larger premises, the Newhall Works on Newhall Street, Attercliffe. The Company was reformed as a limited liability company in 1899, and the influx of capital enabled it to expand. By taking over the firm of J. S. & J. C. Ellis and its Carbrook Foundry and George Street business, the new company was reorganised and the Brightside Foundry & Engineering Co. Ltd. was formed. Stove grate production in the Brightside factories, other than that of Moorwoods, ceased in 1906.

The **Eagle Foundry**, on the corner of Duke Street and Norwich Street in the Park district of Sheffield, was established by Messrs Taylor & Co. in 1818 as a general ironfounders catering for the requirements of local coal mines, smithies, and forges. By 1828 Wilson & Fowler formed the operating partnership, manufacturing general iron castings and stove grates. John Fowler severed his connection during the early 1830s to commence business on his own account eventually based at the **Sheaf Foundry** on Furnival Road. Thomas Wilson was a relative of the Thomas Wilson who operated the Kilnhurst Forge, and by 1841 he had taken over the Forge and was running the Eagle Foundry. William Wilson, the son of Thomas, was running the Eagle Foundry in 1850.

John Robinson, of Attercliffe, and Samuel Biggin, of Cemetery Road, Sheffield, joined William Wilson in 1852, and this partnership ran the Foundry until 1858 when it was sold to Messrs Walker, Heaton & Co. William Wilson then joined his father at the Kilnhurst Forge, and Robinson & Biggin set up the **Royd's Foundry**, in Attercliffe, as a general iron foundry and stove grate makers which joined the Brightside Group in 1916. It was then transferred to the Group's foundry at Ecclesfield.

Walker, Heaton & Co., the Wicker Iron and Steel Works, had been established by a partnership of William Hughill Walker of Burngreave, a Mr Eaton, and others in 1832 to make stove grates and as a general jobbing foundry. Within a short time they had expanded into steel converting and refining, and the manufacture of steam engines and mill machinery. The building of the Wicker Arches in 1847–8, took away from the factory quite a large area, and the firm purchased the lease on the Eagle Foundry in 1858 and transferred to it the heavy castings side of their business, keeping their stove grate manufacture at the Wicker Works. Walker, Heaton operated at the Eagle Foundry until 1877–88, when the lease ran out. It was then taken over by **Lockwood & Carlisle & Co.**, to manufacture stove grates. Walker, Heaton & Co. became part of the Brightside Group of companies just before World War I, and they stopped the production of stove grates in 1916.

Marshall, Watson, Moorwood, & Co. was a partnership started by Henry Watson, an ironfounder and stove grate maker at the Alma Works, Masbrough, who was looking for larger premises and the means with which to expand. He found these by going into partnership, in 1864, with William Marshall, a Sheffield ironmonger, and Henry Moorwood. A site had been cleared and laid out on rising land on property belonging to the Duke of Norfolk to the north of the town and 99-year leases drawn up on it in 1858. The partnership took over a lease on what was to be known as the Harleston Ironworks and moved into the newly-built factory in 1865 as stove grate, kitchen range, and ornamental and decorative castings makers. The letter heads of the later companies of Moorwoods Ltd. claim that they had been established in 1847, but this is true only for the business of William Marshall. In 1868 they were described as 'General ironfounders, and manufacturers of stove grates, Leamington Kitcheners, cooking apparatus, ovens, boilers, and kitchen ranges of every description, gates and palisades, and plain and fancy castings'. During the 1870s a 'Heavy Side' was introduced to manufacture chilled and grained rolls for steel works, and ingot moulds for the Bessemer process of steelmaking.

William Marshall died in 1881, and his son withdrew his father's capital from the Company, forcing it to go into liquidation. A new partnership was drawn up and the firm became Watson, Moorwood & Co. Henry Watson died in 1888, and his son, Thomas, withdrew from the firm and, in partnership with his own sons, commenced in business at the Wheathill Foundry, Rotherham. The Sheffield company was then registered as Moorwood, Sons, & Co. Ltd. in 1889. Another reorganisation took place in 1913 when they became Moorwoods Ltd., Harleston Works, and in 1917 the company became a wholly owned subsidiary of Brightside Foundry & Engineering Ltd. Moorwoods withdrew from the stove grate and allied trades in the late 1950s, and closed down their foundry in September, 1960, but continued to manufacture commercial and marine catering equipment at the Harleston Works. In 1961 they entered an agreement with the American company, Vulcan Hart Corporation of Baltimore, to manufacture under licence some of that firm's catering equipment, and the name of Moorwoods was changed to Moorwood Vulcan Ltd., Vulcan Hart having acquired a one-third share in the British Company. This share was re-acquired by Brightside in 1965, and although the firm retained the name, Moorwood Vulcan, it was once again a wholly owned subsidiary of the Brightside Group.

During the late 1960s the steelworks equipment side of the Brightside Group was acquired by Davy & United Engineering Ltd., and the Brightside foundries in Ecclesfield and Sheffield were closed. A complex move then took place. Brightside bought Green's of Ecclesfield from William Green and moved Moorwood Vulcan from Harleston Works to part of the Ecclesfield Norfolk Foundry while part of Brightside's Ecclesfield Foundry was cleared and adapted to accommodate the land and marine catering equipment manufacturing operations. Moorwood Vulcan Ltd. and the now defunct Green's of Ecclesfield moved into their new home on Green Lane, Ecclesfield in 1971.

In June, 1971, the whole of Brightside's holdings was taken over by Jessel Securities Ltd., and was asset-stripped. Moorwood Vulcan was amalgamated with other Jessel holdings into Newhome Veritas Ltd., comprising Stoves Ltd. of Rainhill, Liverpool, makers of Newhome gas cookers; Moorwood Vulcan Ltd.; and Falks, Veritas, the makers of gas light mantles and gas fittings. A launch on the Stock Exchange resulted in Newhome Veritas becoming part of Valor Company in 1973. Following the takeover of the Valor Company by Williams Holdings in 1990, Moorwood Vulcan Ltd. was subject to a management buyout that included Jackson Water Heaters of Leeds and Sadia Refrigeration of West Drayton, London. The new company became Viscount Catering Equipment Ltd., with the name Moorwood Vulcan retained as a brand name. Viscount went into receivership in 1992, and was purchased by Hallamshire Investments. In December, 1993, Viscount Catering Equipment Ltd. was purchased from Hallamshire Investments by Mr Gordon Shepherd, a former chief executive of Hallamshire. It continues to operate, now quite successfully, on the Green Lane site in Ecclesfield, being one of the foremost wholly UK-owned manufacturers of catering equipment.

Frederick Bagnall, 168 Shalesmoor, commenced as a fendermaker in 1842, the firm opening a foundry, the Shalesmoor Foundry of William Henry Bagnall, in 1881 to make stove grates. They continued in the trade until 1920 when they became jobbing founders.

John Fowler, Exchange Inn Lane, 34, Furnival Road, commenced in business as a fendermaker in 1841. By 1860 Mrs Fowler and her son, John, were ironfounders and stove grate makers at the Sheaf Foundry on Furnival Road. They were bought out by Thomas Simmons in 1867. Simmons had commenced his stove grate factory in 1856 having left his family's business of Norton, Simmons & Co.

He continued in the trade until 1889.

Norton, Simmons & Co. was at the Union Foundry, Furnace Hill, off West Bar, in 1852, making stove grates. The partnership was William Shield Norton and William Simmons, and it lasted until 1862. W S. Norton & Co. was last listed in the trade in 1865 on Mowbray Street.

Hydes & Wigfull, 88, Market Place & Stanley Street, Wicker, started in 1872 as stove grate makers and general ironfounders. They became a limited liability company in 1914 continuing to make stove grates and heating stoves until 1930. In 1975 they were at Carlisle Street where they made heating stoves.

Oxley & Staniforth, Willey Street, were first listed as stove grate makers in 1856. The following year the firm was George and William Oxley, operating as Oxley Brothers. They were listed at the Queen's Foundry, Mowbray Street in 1872, and then, in 1920, at the Union Foundry when they were ironfounders.

Goodhall, Bellamy & Co., of Norfolk Lane, Sheffield, and the **Grenoside Foundry**, Middleton Green, Grenoside, were listed in 1854 as stove grate, fender, and fire iron makers. The Grenoside Foundry had been established during the 1820s by Jonathan Tingle as a successor to the Walkers' Grenoside Iron Foundry established in 1741. Messrs. Bellamy, Booth & Stanley took over in 1851. Joseph Bellamy and William Booth were both residents in Ecclesfield, and Stanley was an ironmonger in Sheffield. Booth and Stanley had withdrawn from the partnership by 1854 when Bellamy was listed in partnership with William Anderson Goodhall who had businesses of his own as Goodhall & Co., fender and fire iron maker, at 101, Norfolk Street, and **W. A. Goodhall**, stove grate maker at 12 Norfolk Lane. He became a dealer in these items in 1856 on South Street in partnership with John G. Porter; the business closed in 1862.

Stanley rejoined Bellamy in 1855 and they took over the Midland Works on Savile Street East. However, in 1858, the firm was listed as owned by George Bellamy, Joseph's son. Its final listing was in 1862 at the Midland Works, and it was about this time that the Grenoside Foundry closed, to become a nut and bolt factory owned by a Mr Beal. This site was sold in August 1869. **John Stanley**, of the **Midland Works**, Sheffield, exhibited air stoves, kitchen ranges, and stove grates at the 1862 Exhibition.

Many older residents of Sheffield will remember **Wilks Brothers**, the hardware merchants on Norfolk Street which closed during the 1960s. They sprang from Joseph Wilks who commenced to make stove grates in about 1820 on the Wicker.

Outside Sheffield was the **Greenside Foundry** at Chapeltown, established in about 1899 and which made stove grates until 1920. At Charlton Brook near High Green, was **Charlton Brook Ironworks**, established by Rebecca Ogden as a brass and iron founders and first listed in 1879.[29] Mrs Ogden also kept a beerhouse, and operated the Brook Valley Blacking Mills at Charlton Brook. Jabez Stanley, of Stanley Street, Newhall, Sheffield, and Edward Aston of Burncross, Chapeltown, also ran the Charlton Brook Malleable Ironworks in 1879. By 1881 Rebecca Ogden was listed, but Jabez Stanley was an ironfounder in Wincobank.[30] However, in a directory for 1884 Stanley was, once again, at the Charlton Brook Malleable Ironworks, although he lived at Wincobank.[31] This was his final listing. Rebecca Ogden went through to 1896, and in 1898–99 the firm was listed as G. Harvey & Co., ironfounders, makers of cooking ranges, mantels, etc.[32] They were also coal merchants. In 1934 George Harvey & Co., of the Charlton Ironworks, (established 1896) were making the Harvey Patent Adjustable Ranges (Patent No. 13479).[33] By 1947 the firm had become the Charlton Ironworks Ltd., and while they still made cooking ranges, they had begun to specialise in the products for which they were to become more famous, street gulley drain covers and frames, and manhole covers. The Charlton Ironworks closed down during the late 1980s and the works were demolished in the early 1990s.

Postscript

At the height of the popularity of the stove grate in the middle of the nineteenth century Sheffield had more than 20 stove grate makers and as many fine iron and fender manufacturers. By 1965 only three firms engaged in stove grate and kitchen range manufacture were listed in the Sheffield and Rotherham area: William Green & Co., (Ecclesfield) Ltd.; W. H. Micklethwaite & Co. Ltd., of Rotherham; and Yates, Haywood & Co. Ltd., also of Rotherham.[34] All three firms were to withdraw from the industry shortly afterwards. The demise of stove grate manufacture cannot be attributed to any one cause. The introduction of the 'Clean Air Acts', the availability of cheaper fuels in the way of gas and oil and the consequential introduction of relatively cheap but well-designed and attractive gas and oil-fired appliances, all served to make the labour-intensive solid fuel-fired grate and cooker outmoded. Only recently has there been a reawakening of interest in the aesthetic attraction of a stove grate in the domestic living room, although these contemporary installations favour gas rather than a solid fuel and, as in the early years of the industry, we now see numerous small foundries using the products of the specialised, albeit now defunct foundries, as patterns from which to mould and cast the modern 'fireplace'. Indeed, we are once again witnessing the popularity of 'those inexhaustible mines of bad taste, Birmingham and Sheffield.[35]

Notes and References

1. Gale & Martin's *Directory*, Sheffield, 1787.
2. Piggot & Co., *National Commercial Directory 1828–1829*, pub. London & Manchester.
3. P. Robinson, *The Smiths of Chesterfield – A History of the Griffin Foundry Brampton 1775–1833*, Chesterfield, 1957, p.11.
4. 1787 – Gale & Martin's *Directory*; 1797 – A Directory of Sheffield.
5. *A Directory of Sheffield, etc., 1825*, R. Gell, Manchester.
6. P. Robinson, *The Smiths of Chesterfield*.
7. A. K. Clayton, *The Story of the Elsecar & Milton Ironworks*.
8. For a comprehensive history of Newton Chambers & Co. Ltd., see H. E. Elliot, *Thorncliffe, a short history, etc.*, published in parts by the Company, c.1958.
9. *The Commercial Directory*, 1814–15, Wardle & Bentham.
10. Sheffield Archives, Thorncliffe Records.
11. *How We Build*, Sidney Flavel & Co. Ltd., Leamington, not dated but c.1937.
12. For details of the Green Lane Works site see: R. E. Wilson, 'Green Lane Works', *Transactions of the Hunter Archaeological Society*, 9(4), 1969. Details of Henry Shaw are given in Charles Drury, *A Sheaf of Essays by a Sheffield Antiquary*, p.72 et seq.
13. R. E. Wilson, 'Green Lane Works', p.225.
14. Sheffield Archives, Rate Books.
15. P. Robinson, *The Smiths of Chesterfield*.
16. R. E. Wilson, 'Green Lane Works', p.226.
17. R. E. Wilson, 'Green Lane Works', p.226.
18. R. E. Wilson, 'Green Lane Works', p.226.
19. *White's Directory of Sheffield*, 1860.
20. Basil H. Tripp, *Grand Alliance*, published for Allied Ironfounders Ltd., 1951.
21. R. E Leader, *Reminiscences of Old Sheffield*, 1876, p.144.
22. Charles Drury, *A Sheaf of Essays by a Sheffield Antiquary*, p.72 et seq.
23. J. H. Stainton, *The Making of Sheffield*, p. 248.
24. Robert Jobson exhibited an example of his patent light and heat reflecting stove at the 1851 Great Exhibition, as Jobson & Co., Sheffield. Stuart & Smith exhibits were displayed under their own name. See Catalogue, Class 22, Section III.
25. Pawson & Brailsford, *Illustrated Guide to Sheffield, 1879*.
26. Catalogue of products, William Green & Co., 1937. Author's collection.
27. Advertisement in *White's Directory*, 1889.
28. Transactions of the *Hunter Archaeological Society*, vol. 15, 1989, p.30.
29. *White's Directory*, 1879.
30. *Kelly's Directory*, 1881.
31. *White's Directory*, 1884.
32. *White's Directory*, 1898.
33. *Sheffield Commercial Handbook*, 1934.
34. *Kelly's Directory of Sheffield, Rotherham & Suburbs*, 1965.
35. Augustus Welby Pugh, lecture given at St. Marie's, Oscott, in 1843.

8.   THE ELECTRO-PLATE CONTROVERSY

by Geoffrey Tweedale

SHEFFIELD HISTORIANS HAVE SELDOM paid much atten-
tion to the city's great silver and electro-plate industry, particularly in
its nineteenth-century heyday. To be sure, Frederick Bradbury's
History of Old Sheffield Plate (published in 1912) provides a detailed
account of the first product to establish the town as a world-ranking
silver manufacturer, but this sector was a spent force by 1850, and of
the subsequent period Bradbury had little to say. No historian has
followed up his work. Most books on Sheffield give the distinct
impression that the silver and electro-plate industry took second
place to cutlery in the late Victorian and Edwardian era.

Nothing could be further from the truth. On the eve of the Great
War, the precious metals sector of the Sheffield light trades employed
about 10,000 workers – almost as many as the traditional cutlery
wing of the industry. Almost all the leading firms in the light trades
– such as Wm. Hutton, Mappin & Webb, James Dixon & Sons, and
Martin, Hall – were makers of silver and electro-plate. From their
factories poured a huge variety of silverware for the Victorian and
Edwardian middle and upper class dining table: trays, meat dishes
and covers, table gongs, tea sets, jugs, cruet sets, biscuit tins, egg
cups, fruit bowls, celery stands, crumb collectors and fish knives.
This was aside from the demand for presentation trophies, trowels
and cups. Even some of the largest knifemakers, such as Joseph
Rodgers and Harrison Bros and Howson, did not neglect silver and
electro-plate. They would have been foolish to have done so: it was
one of the fastest growing areas in the cutlery industry, as the rising
demand was boosted by the abolition of the silver tax in 1890 and the
steady fall in the price of silver.

Largest of all the silver and electro-plate firms was Walker & Hall,
which by the early 1900s had assumed the leadership of the silver
trade. Its Electro Works on Howard Street (Figure 1) was a city land-
mark – a massive, multi-storey block, with two clock towers above
which Walker & Hall's pennants always 'flew' (they were, after all,
made of metal!). A contemporary trade publication, *The Century's
Progress* (1893), described the factory as 'one of the sights of
Sheffield, particularly at night time, when its hundreds of close-set
windows, emitting a ray of light from within, present a very brilliant

ELECTRO WORKS, 1845, AND AS THEY APPEAR TO-DAY

Figure 1.   Walker & Hall's Electro Works – reputedly the largest cutlery factory in Sheffield by 1914. *Courtesy Sheffield City Libraries*

and striking scene indeed.' In the ground floor windows were displayed examples of the firm's craftsmanship: some were made in traditional sterling silver (in other words, 'solid' silver, an alloy with over 92.5 per cent silver); others were in Britannia or 'white' metal – much cheaper metals, which were shiny enough to be sold as imitation silver at the lower end of the market. But Walker & Hall's speciality and the basis of its fortune were objects made in electro-plate (Figures 2 & 3). By this process a layer of silver was deposited on a base metal (usually nickel-silver) – a technique that, because of its many advantages in mass production, had destroyed the Sheffield

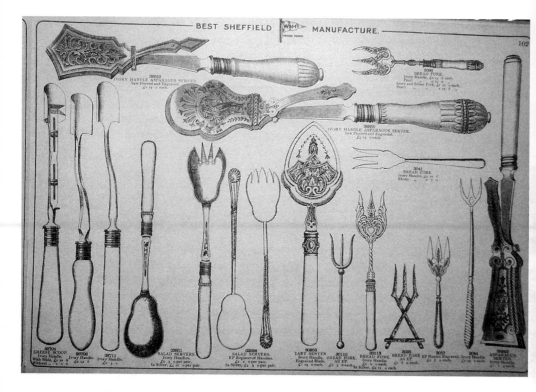

Figure 2. Electro-plate products from a Walker & Hall catalogue, 1906.

Figure 3. A Walker & Hall electro-plated crumb collector.

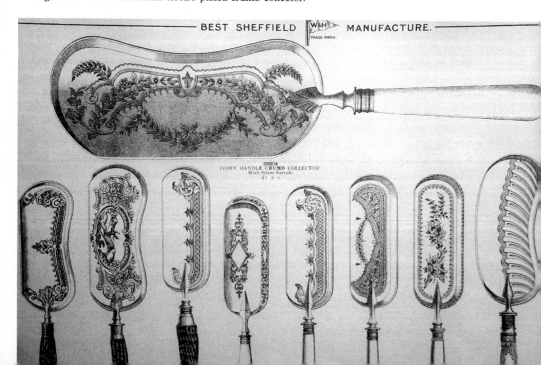

Plate industry after 1840. Whereas old Sheffield Plate needed highly developed craft skills in rolling and die-stamping, electro-plate items (even the most ornate) could be cast in one piece. Skilled workers were no longer needed; silver could be plated thinly; and production runs could be fast and flexible (Figure 4). Electro-plating could even be used to rejuvenate old Sheffield Plate with a fresh layer of silver. Electro-plate filled the large middle ground in the market between costly sterling silver and cheaper Britannia ware.

Figure 4. Electro-plating tanks at Walker & Hall.

Who had brought this great industry into being? Walker & Hall had their own story of the main events, which appeared in *The Century's Progress*. The extensive profile of Walker & Hall, in the best Victorian tradition, told an uplifting tale of local business enterprise. The leading protagonist was George Walker, a poor working cutler, who in the 1840s was supporting his mother and two children on fifteen shillings per week. His industry, application and indomitable resolution, however, soon marked him out for greater things:

After preparing his mind by reading such books as he could obtain, George Walker sought in earnest for the acquirement of practical knowledge, and to this end he petitioned to be admitted to the electrical classes then conducted by Mr Branson, a surgeon . . . This request was acceded to, and Walker's instruction was to be paid for by his personal services in cleaning and keeping in order the various apparatus used for the class experiments. Mr Wright, surgeon, of Attercliffe (then a suburb, now a part, of Sheffield), who was ultimately the inventor of electro-plating, selected George Walker to assist him in his development of the discovery . . . These two laboured so successfully together that eventually they brought into practicable condition the great invention which was to add beauty and durability to countless articles of daily use, and to provide a means of livelihood for thousands of people.

This was not the first time that it had been implied that Sheffield had introduced electro-plate. Pawson and Brailsford's *Illustrated Guide to*

Sheffield and Neighbourhood (1862) had credited 'Mr Wright, of Norton, near Sheffield' as the inventor. The revised edition of Joseph Hunter's *Hallamshire,* published in 1869, had also mentioned Mr Wright as the discoverer of electro-plate – a man connected with the Wrights of Anston, near Sheffield, whose widow had married the well-known steelmaker Charles Cammell. This information was repeated in a detailed article on the electro-plate trades in *The Ironmonger* on 12 November, 1887. This trade journal gave 'Mr Wright, of Norton,' the credit for the discovery of electro-plate, the rights later being purchased by Birmingham manufacturers. George Walker was described as the first electro-plate manufacturer in Sheffield, though *The Ironmonger* noted that there was a rival claimant in the town – John Harrison – who had aided Walker on a fact-finding mission to Birmingham. The journal added, intriguingly, that Walker & Hall still had the original apparatus that George Walker had used to plate two teaspoons – 'the first electro-plated articles on record.' Wright's widow, it was said, still resided near Sheffield, drawing an annuity from her husband's invention.

Running through all these accounts was a simple idea: whatever the claims of rival cities, it was Sheffield that was really responsible for the start of the electro-plate industry.

To what extent contemporary readers accepted these pronouncements is open to conjecture; certainly some would have been aware that the Sheffield version of events sat precariously on some uncomfortable facts. First, it was Birmingham that was the capital of the silver trade in the late nineteenth century: although its reputation for quality was not as high as Sheffield's, Birmingham employed more workers in the precious metal trades than Sheffield and its consumption of silver was far higher. Second, whatever Walker & Hall's ranking as an industry leader and pioneer in Sheffield, Elkington & Co, founded by the Birmingham industrialist George Richards Elkington (1801–1865), was the dominant electro-plate firm in the country before 1900. It was this company which many credited as the pioneer in the patenting and introduction of electro-plate.

Given the long-standing rivalry between Sheffield and Birmingham, a dispute over the origins of electro-plate was perhaps inevitable. Unlike the invention of Sheffield Plate, which was invariably credited to Thomas Boulsover, the development of electro-plate was a complex affair. From the vantage point of the twentieth century, we can see that several individuals were involved, numerous patents were registered, and various improvements were made to the original ideas. But a large industry had grown up on the back of electro-plate and a firm or individual who could prove that they had pioneered the process alone stood to gain considerable prestige.

The controversy got fully under way in the Sheffield press in the 1880s. In Spring 1887, *The Sheffield & Rotherham Independent* had reported on a Manchester trade exhibition, and had stated that George Walker was the founder of the electro-plate industry in Sheffield. On 4 May, an anonymous correspondent wrote to the newspaper questioning this attribution and reminding the newspaper that several years previously strong claims had been made on behalf of John Harrison. The claims had been made by Samuel Coulson in a letter to *The Independent* on 26 July, 1881. Coulson had been closely involved with the birth of electro-plate in Sheffield: he was said to have been a schoolteacher, but he had also been one of George Walker's first partners before the firm had become Walker & Hall. Coulson's letter offered a detailed account of the early electro-plate industry, which clearly stated that John Wright was a Birmingham surgeon (though he had trained in Rotherham), who had discovered the art of electro-plating and had then sold the process to Elkington. Sheffield had licenced the product from Elkington, with John Harrison of Scotland Street becoming the first licencee in 1843 (Figure 5). George Walker was recruited to help on the technical aspects and Harrison sent him, at his own expense, to learn electro-plating at the Elkington factory. In Coulson's view:

> George Walker was . . . the first <u>operative</u> electro-plater in [Sheffield], and Mr John Harrison was the first <u>manufacturer</u> of electro-plate goods, and the introducer of the process for his own private business.

According to Coulson, an argument had soon developed between Walker and his employer, over Harrison's demand that Walker educate his son. Walker, fearing that his long-term job prospects were in jeopardy, refused and then resigned. On leaving Harrison, he took out a licence from Elkington and set up his own electro-plate business in Howard Street, with Coulson as his partner (who provided much-needed capital).

John Harrison had died in 1863: however, his son, William Wheatcroft Harrison, was still in business as an electro-plate manufacturer in 1887 and on 10 May of that year he wrote to *The Independent* underlining Coulson's account and describing George Walker as an 'amateur,' who 'had experimented with a small battery, and had a little knowledge of chemistry.' William Harrison confirmed Coulson's view that Walker had been sent (twice) to Birmingham to learn electro-plating from Elkington, before launching his own enterprise in 1845.

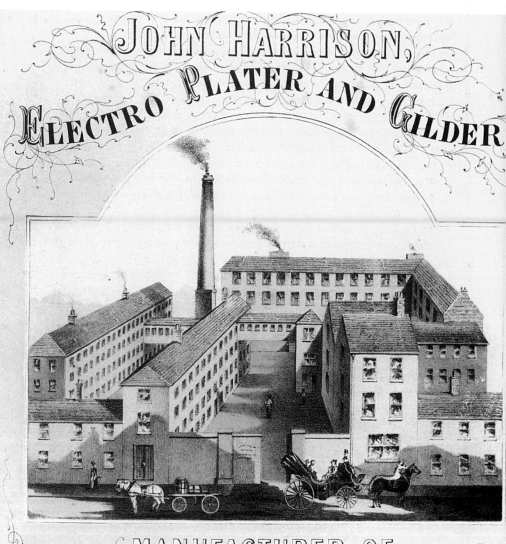

Figure 5. Frontispiece from the catalogue of John Harrison – the first Sheffield licencee of Elkingtons' electro-plate process. *Courtesy Sheffield City Libraries*

These press statements directly contradicted the Walker & Hall version and so, not surprisingly, a letter from that company soon followed. It was written by Sir John E. Bingham, Walker & Hall's senior partner, and one of the leading figures in the Sheffield cutlery trade (Figure 6). He had been born on 27 July, 1839, into a well-known Chesterfield family. His uncle was Henry Hall (d. 1889), who had joined George Walker as a partner at the Electro Works in 1848. When Coulson retired in 1853, the firm was re-named as Walker & Hall and began a period of steady expansion. Walker (who died in 1881, aged 65) was the technical man; Hall was the traveller and provider of capital. It was Hall who brought his nephew into the business in 1856, when John Bingham was aged 16. Hall retired in 1873 and Bingham gradually assumed control of the business, with his brother Charles Bingham (1848–1900) as his partner.

Figure 6. Sir John Bingham (1839–1915), the senior partner at Walker & Hall.

In the 1880s, John Bingham made his fortune and his reputation. He is 'a man of inexhaustible energy', declared one trade journal, 'of fine business tact, and of universal popularity. He is what the Americans call a "live man," and is bound to make any concern move in which he has an interest.' Under the Binghams, Walker & Hall began expanding rapidly: a concern that had only employed tens of workers in the 1850s, now had hundreds on the payroll. By 1890, the firm was probably amongst the top six cutlery firms in Sheffield, competing with other famous names such as Wm. Hutton, Mappin & Webb, James Dixon and Martin, Hall. The firm had acquired an excellent reputation for its quality and high output, with its business split between the home market and the colonies. A string of lavishly stocked Walker & Hall retail outlets appeared around the country (and overseas), where customers were allowed to shop only after a suitable introduction. Acceptance as a Walker & Hall 'customer' was regarded as a great privilege, especially since goods were then offered at wholesale price – the famous Walker & Hall 50 per cent discount.

Such a patronising attitude matched the personal philosophy of the firm's head, who was rapidly ascending the social ladder. In the 1880s, Bingham transformed himself into a typical Victorian 'man of mark,' whose business and public activity was – in the words of one local biographical tome – as 'of so comprehensive a character as to touch almost every department of local life.' He was Master Cutler twice, in 1881 and 1884 (the year he was knighted); and a JP in 1885. By 1887 he was a city councillor and was to serve again in the late 1890s – a position that gave him a platform to further several personal crusades. Contemporaries described him as a man of 'strong antipathies,' and two of the strongest were against granite and smoke. The first stemmed from the city's use of granite setts on Sheffield roads, which had once caused Sir John's horse to slip and pitch him head first onto the road. The result was Bingham's implacable opposition to granite paving slabs, which he furthered by his presidency of the Sheffield Street Pitching Defence Association. He also greatly disliked one of Sheffield's most infamous trade marks – the black smoke that belched from its hundreds of chimneys – and therefore took an active part in the formation of the Smoke Abatement League.

In the economic sphere, Bingham was a free-trader, who through organisations such as the Fair Trade League campaigned for tariffs to help the local cutlery industry. In politics, he was a die-hard Conservative, but it was religion that seemed to have held a greater fascination for him. He was a Churchman of the most zealous kind, with a 'profound dread' of Roman Catholicism, which meant that he was ever alert to the introduction of Ritualism into Protestant services. 'Nothing,' it was said, 'roused so quickly the combativeness of his nature as the action of those clergy who, openly flouting authority, have introduced into their churches Roman practices and doctrines.' However, the absurd rituals of freemasonry bothered him less, and he was one of the city's most prominent members of the brotherhood.

When he was not running the great Electro Works, castigating Popery or holding forth on the dangers of granite setts, Bingham was likely to be drilling the local Volunteers. Organisations for these non-regular troops enjoyed something of a vogue amongst the Victorian upper and middle classes in the years before the outbreak of the Great War and several Sheffield industrialists, such as Tom Vickers and Edward Tozer, were keen supporters of the Volunteers. Bingham, who took over the Sheffield Engineers Volunteers, seems to have been more enthusiastic than most. Now a Colonel (a title he was happy to use, even though he was not a soldier and had never been to war), Bingham was able to indulge his patriotism, his love of uniforms and deference, and his fondness for shooting (Figure 7). A rifle range was even installed at the Electro Works, where ambitious male employees could sharpen their sights and keep well in with the boss. 'A nation in arms' was Bingham's motto and he was a supporter of national service.

Some described him as pig-headed; certainly, he was uncompromising. A contemporary recalled:

> *Once Sir John Bingham had made up his mind on any subject nothing could move him. The explanation was that he thought things out for himself, and having hammered out his own views he was confident that they were right. They might seem peculiar to other people. He could not help that. A fact of that kind did not worry him. He had to be true to himself. That was a natural habit that could not be overcome.*

Figure 7. Sir John Bingham (founder of the Sheffield Society for the Encouragement of Bravery) ready for action in his Volunteers uniform. *Courtesy Sheffield City Libraries*

Bingham had evidently thought long and hard about electro-plate and on 11 May, 1887, *The Independent* published his own views on the matter. He accused Harrison of attacking the memory of George Walker and of being envious of the latter's success. In a spiteful aside, Bingham informed the newspaper's readers that Walker & Hall had plated 'wheelbarrow loads' of articles for William Harrison. Bingham admitted that Walker had been employed by John Harrison, but claimed that Walker had been the assistant of the 'late Mr Wright, who resided at Attercliffe or Rotherham.' It was Walker, therefore, who was the founder of electro-plate in Sheffield, which gave his firm 'this great priority in the trade.'

Harrison replied to this attack on 13 May, 1887, with a tactful letter, which remarked that he and George Walker had been friends, though he had never heard Walker in his lifetime make the claims that had appeared since his death.

The matter rested there for over a decade. But in 1900 the battleground switched to the letters-page of *The Sheffield Daily Telegraph*. The controversy was rekindled by the death of the wife of the steelmaker Charles Cammell, whom we may recall was said to have once been the widow of the mysterious Wright. The argument over priority was once more rehearsed by W. Shirley in a letter headed, 'The Truth about Electro-Plating.' Wright was again described as the inventor, with Walker as very much a minor character who had been sent to Elkington at John Harrison's expense. This was too much for Bingham, who fired off another letter (printed in the same newspaper on 25 April), which added further details to the career of George Walker. According to Bingham, Walker, a table knife hafter, had visited the home of Dr Branson (whose surgery later became part of Walker & Hall in Howard Street) and offered his services during the evenings to keep in order the equipment Branson used to train his surgeons in chemistry. After a time, Wright of Attercliffe, who was one of the students, employed Walker as an assistant in his trials with electro-plating. Bingham stated he had a letter from Branson as evidence; and, anyway, George Walker had never told him (Bingham) that he had been to Birmingham to learn electro-plating – a trip that Bingham thought unlikely and unnecessary, as Walker understood the process 'better than anyone else.'

A flurry of letters followed in *The Sheffield Daily Telegraph* on 30 April, and on 5 and 9 May. Some contested Bingham's version; others supported him. New facts appeared to emerge. One novel suggestion was that Walker had gone to Birmingham to teach Elkington! Another correspondent identified the elusive Wright as being definitely a Norton man and the brother of a celebrated surgeon of Greenhill.

It was all very confusing for the ordinary reader, but a little more light (and heat) was to be shed on the identity of Mr Wright in the pages of the leading London hardware trade journal *The Ironmonger* three years later. On 5 December, 1903, in a brief article describing a Birmingham silver-plate works, the electro-plate process was credited to John Wright, a Birmingham surgeon, in 1840. Sir John's predictable response, rebutting this claim, appeared in a subsequent edition of the journal on 19 December. Immediately below Bingham's letter, however, was a comment from the editor of *The Ironmonger*, who mentioned some awkward facts: namely, an advertisement in the *Sheffield Mercury* on 30 August, 1845, which announced Walker's new venture and stated he had a licence from Elkington and had gained his experience with Harrison. As the editor pointed out, this would suggest that Walker had started his business some five years after Elkington – hardly the action of a pioneer. The editor did admit, though, that he might have later settled in Attercliffe – after all, his widow had married Charles Cammell.

Bingham returned to the subject with another letter on 2 January,

1904, in which he refused to give ground, arguing – as ever – that Wright was from Attercliffe and that he had a letter from Branson as proof. He continued:

Of course, I am well aware that the invention was sold by Dr Wright to a Birmingham house, who patented it, and I am also well aware that Mr George Walker laid down vats and apparatus for Mr John Harrison, of Sheffield, before he himself commenced business. I also know that Mr George Walker was sent to Birmingham by Dr Wright to educate others in the then new art of electro-plating, and to perfect himself. All this proves that, wherever Dr Wright originally came from, he was the inventor, and invented electro-plating in Sheffield.

With its national circulation, *The Ironmonger* made a wider readership aware of the controversy, and some interested parties began to report on some historical digging of their own. On 9 January and 6 February, 1904, two correspondents (one the writer of the original article; the other a man from Rotherham) reported on their research into John Wright. Although neither was able to prove that he had never lived in Sheffield, the weight of the evidence from local directories and rate books suggested that Wright was indeed a Birmingham man, though he had spent some of his life in Rotherham and attended classes in Sheffield.

The debate in *The Ironmonger* was reported in detail in *The Sheffield Daily Telegraph*, which sent one of its journalists to interview Sir John (who was now a baronet). Bingham reiterated his statements and displayed his various letters on the subject – documents that the overrawed journalist clearly felt proved that Wright's (and, of course, Walker's) experimental work had been done in Sheffield. Moreover, the newspaper reported the existence of Walker's vat – still at the Electro Works – alongside the residue of the first pint of electro-plating solution ever used in Sheffield (Figure 8). This was the firm's treasured possession, which the newspaper took as evidence that Wright and Walker had discovered the secret and successfully plated articles before Birmingham entered the picture.

Whatever the general public thought (if they were interested) is anybody's guess, but certainly Bingham himself refused to alter any of his opinions. In 1906, a Walker & Hall catalogue carried an illustration of George Walker's original vat. In 1907 Bingham chaired a lecture at the Royal Society of Arts on 'Sheffield Plate and Electro-Plate,' that was subsequently published in the Society's journal. The speaker (Sherard Cowper-Coles) was, not surprisingly, favourable to Sheffield, stating that the Yorkshire town now had 170 electro-platers compared with a hundred in Birmingham. In the subsequent dis-

Figure 8. The vat said to have been used by George Walker. *Courtesy Sheffield City Libraries*

cussion, Bingham told the audience that Wright of Attercliffe and Walker had 'really discovered electro-plating.' Another round of controversy followed.

The arguments then appear to have subsided. Bingham returned to the running of his great Electro Works. Sales of silver and electroplate in the country were now reaching their peak (the weight of silver marked by the Sheffield Assay Office hit a record level in 1912) and Walker & Hall and its dynamic head were at the height of their powers (Figures 9 & 10). Sir John was now into his seventies, but he had not loosened his hold on the business. In vigorous old age, with his venerable beard and skull cap, tail-coat and flower in his button hole, he was said to combine the 'solidity of the old school with the alertness of the younger generation.' One story has him at the age of 74 crossing the Atlantic on business and returning to Liverpool late one night; but he was still back in his Electro Works office by 10 o'clock the next morning.

Unknown to Bingham, however, the electro-plate controversy was about to resurface. In early 1913, Frederick Bradbury, the authority on Sheffield Plate and a silver and electro-plate manufacturer himself, had corresponded with one of George Elkington's surviving sons, Hyla. Perhaps Bradbury was following up the research that had stemmed from his recently published book. Whatever the reason for the initial contact, Bradbury was invited by Hyla Elkington to Birmingham to inspect the company's records at the Newhall Street premises. Bradbury took up the offer, but when he travelled to Birmingham he decided to take with him a friend – none other than Sheffield's foremost local historian, Robert E. Leader (Figure 11).

Figure 9. Casting nickel-silver ingots at Walker & Hall.

Figure 10. Stamping nickel-silver articles at Walker & Hall.

Leader, too, had written extensively on the cutlery trade and per-haps it was this interest that made him offer Bradbury his assistance in inspecting the Elkington records. Certainly Leader would have been aware of the electro-plate controversy and may have wished to conduct his own research into the matter. Either way, when the records were made available to the two Sheffielders, they proved of sufficient interest and volume for Leader to offer to catalogue them. Subsequently, all these records were sent to Leader's private resi-dence in London, where, according to Bradbury, Leader worked incessantly for twelve months in sorting and cataloguing them. While he picked his way through the dusty documents, Leader began to assemble the jig-saw puzzle that was the history of elec-tro-plate.

The task was very much to Leader's liking. As it happened, his ancestors had operated a prominent Sheffield Plate firm (Tudor, Leader & Nicolson, situated in Tudor Place), though his immediate forebears had bought *The Sheffield Independent*. Leader's grandfather became owner of the news-paper in 1830, and Robert was the younger son of the next owner, Robert Leader (1809–1885). Robert E. Leader himself was born in Charlotte Street on 2 January, 1839 – the same year as Bingham. Educated at New College, London (where he graduated with a BA degree), he joined *The Independent* as a partner in 1860, alongside his elder brother, John Daniel Leader (1835–1899). The pace at the newspaper was beginning to quick-en at this time, as it was about to become a daily like its rival, *The Sheffield Daily Telegraph*. Robert Leader eventually became the editor, with his brother as the commercial manager.

Figure 11. Robert E. Leader (1839–1922), who was Bingham's main protagonist in the electro-plate controversy. *Courtesy Sheffield City Libraries*

The Leaders were closely involved with Sheffield's political and public life and were one of the most promi-nent Liberal families in the town. Robert Leader Snr had been an Alderman and a JP; Robert Jnr later gave up his work as a full-time journalist and tried to enter Parliament twice in the 1890s as a Liberal, but was defeated on each occasion. Nevertheless, he was successful in his election to the town council in 1886 and he served as the representative for the Ecclesall ward until 1892.

Leader's métier, however, proved to be local history. He had two good qualifications for the job: one was a talent for research and writing; the other was a private income, always so essential in the pursuit of what most of the population have always regarded as rather a waste of time. According to his friends, Leader 'was an antiquary to his finger-tips, with an infinite relish for patiently searching among old records . . .' His bent towards local history, which he shared with his brother John (another well-known antiquarian) had developed during his running of the family newspaper: a weekly column devoted to literature and antiquities was a feature of *The Independent* after 1874. Soon afterwards, in 1875, Leader published his first major work on his home town. Entitled *Reminiscences of Old Sheffield*, the book was an extended dialogue among five speakers, mulling over their memories of Sheffield in the early years of the eighteenth century.

This was completed while Leader was the active editor of *The Independent*, but in 1892 he resigned from the post and in the following year moved permanently to London. After the failure of his parliamentary ambitions, he now became a full-time writer, specialising in Sheffield history. Like the town's other great antiquarian, Joseph Hunter, Leader built up a formidable reputation in this sphere, while never actually living in Sheffield. His publications included a biography of the well-known radical Sheffield MP, John A. Roebuck, and a sequel to his reminiscences of old Sheffield, titled *Sheffield in the Eighteenth Century* (1901), in which interestingly he briefly mentions a Mr Wright at Rotherham and emphasises Birmingham's debt to Sheffield in electro-plate. Leader then dedicated himself to writing the history of the Company of Cutlers, a massive undertaking that was eventually published in two volumes by 1906.

Most of these works are now little read. His book of old Sheffield Reminiscences is occasionally picked over by local historians, or by the small minority who still share his antiquarian tastes, but mostly it is forgotten. Similarly, his two-volume history of the Cutlers' Company – as heavy as a tombstone and often as readable – is rarely consulted. However, we should be wary of scoffing: this is the common fate of every historian, no matter how famous or prolific. Judged by the standards of his day, when historical research amongst original records was not very widespread, Leader appears in a more favourable light. As his work on the cutlery industry shows, Leader was an accomplished historian, with a talent for interpreting old records.

Leader's qualities were to be deployed to good effect as he began sifting through the Elkington records. He did so systematically, arranging the documents into ten large folders. As the letters, patents and cuttings were sorted and glued onto sheets, he wrote marginalia to explain the significance and date of a particular record. As any historian and archivist will know, the intimate knowledge gained through arranging and reading a group of old records often results in the cataloguer becoming an expert in the area. By the time he had finished working on the Elkington papers, Leader felt that he had solved the question at the heart of the electro-plate controversy.

Leader decided to publicise his findings by returning to Sheffield: it was to be his last visit to his native city. On 7 January, 1914, he gave a lecture on 'Sheffield and Silver – My Story of Electro-platers and Electro-plate' at the University's Mappin Hall. Frederick Bradbury chaired the lecture, which was delivered before the distinguished audience of the Sheffield Society of Applied Metallurgy.

Leader began by positively identifying the inventor of electro-plate as John Wright, a Birmingham surgeon, who had discovered the process while living in Bordesley in 1839. Wright later combined his knowledge with the Elkingtons (who had also been conducting experiments in gilding) in a master patent, registered in 1840, which was to be the basis of the future electro-plate industry. Having sketched the facts, Leader then provided a detailed biography of Wright. He had been born in 1808 on the Isle of Sheppey in Kent. Intriguingly, he did have distant relatives in the Yorkshire region and had briefly attended the medical classes of Dr Sherman of Rotherham. But by 1833 he had established his medical practice in Bordesley, where he began pursuing his experiments in chemical metallurgy. As to his subsequent career, Wright remained in Birmingham throughout his life, which proved to be a short one. In 1843 he became ill (apparently from having fallen from a gig) and died in May of the following year from his injuries. His interest in the Elkington patent had not yet made him wealthy, though Elkington agreed to pay his widow (Mary Annie Rollason, whom he had married in 1835) a lump sum and an annuity. In 1845, she married the steelmaker Charles Cammell, who lived at Norton.

Leader then turned to analyse the Sheffield legend of electro-plate and began demolishing it, pointing out discrepancies in the dates and poking fun at the idea of Wright living at Attercliffe either in the 1830s and 1840s, or later in his life. As to sightings of the elusive Wright in Sheffield (one of which was by the eminent scientist H. Clifton Sorby, who had said he met Wright in a local smelting factory), Leader had an explanation: John Wright had three brothers who did live in the Sheffield area. He believed that these brothers accounted for some of the confusion, especially the one named Charles, who was a surgeon at Greenhill, near Norton.

Having greatly diminished George Walker's role in the discovery of electro-plate, Leader proceeded to cast doubt on his part in its commercial development. His research of Elkington's correspondence and patents had shown that far from pioneering electro-plate, Sheffield makers were reluctant to exploit the new process. Affronted by Elkington's high licence fee and convinced that Sheffield Plate would never be superseded by 'Brummagem wash,' the Sheffield silver platers, such as Roberts, Smith & Co and Creswick, initially spurned electro-plate. It was not until 1843 – when the Britannia ware manufacturer John Harrison took out a licence – that electro-plate arrived in the town. Even then, George Walker was not at the forefront. When Walker and Coulson purchased their licence they had neither the works nor the articles of partnership to begin production. When they eventually did start, it was already some two years after Harrison and Hutton, and some five years after Elkington and Wright had filed their master patent.

Leader denied he was being disloyal to his great city, but felt that Sheffield's claim to the discovery of electro-plate was 'a bogus honour which had no foundation.' He told his audience: 'We are not, surely, so poverty-stricken as to want pinchbeck decorations for our city: if we have not honour enough without that, then we won't have any.'

Bingham hit back in *The Sheffield Daily Telegraph* on 10 January, 1914, after the newspaper had solicited his response. Predictably, Bingham questioned Leader's motives in presenting the lecture and wondered why he had spent a year of his valuable time in investigating a Birmingham firm (in Bingham's eyes the ultimate sin). He cast doubts on Leader's consistency, pointing to the page in *Sheffield in the Eighteenth Century*, where Leader had supported Sheffield. Quite simply, stated Bingham, he knew more than Leader about the origin of electro-plate – after all, he had had over sixty years' experience of the subject. A man of the world, Bingham was not about to take a lesson in the history of manufacturing from a Liberal nonconformist (the Leaders were Congregationalists), a man whom he clearly felt was a dilettante.

For *The Telegraph's* journalist, Bingham produced his file of letters, which proved (according to Bingham) the truthfulness of Walker's account. In particular, Bingham flourished two letters that he had received from Clifton Sorby in 1904, when the subject had been in the news. Sorby stated that he had met Mr Wright, the surgeon and inventor of electro-plate, at an Attercliffe silver refinery 'about sixty years' before. This did not impress Leader, who elaborated his arguments in *The Telegraph* on 13 January, 1913, in an attempt to force Bingham to swallow some more 'bitter medicine.' Bingham countered again on January 14, refusing to give ground and arguing that Sorby's testimony was 'indisputable.'

Leader still had plenty to say. On 19 January, 1914, *The Telegraph* published, under the heading 'Electroplating: "The First Useful Article in the World"', his account of electro-plate technology before 1840. It was a detailed article, which demonstrated Leader's mastery of the subject. He described George Walker, somewhat insultingly, as Dr Branson's 'cleaner-up' and 'caretaker.' In the face of this onslaught, Bingham still stuck to his guns and repeated the content of Sorby's letters in a communication to *The Telegraph*, published on 21 January, 1914. It was to be his final riposte. He declared loftily – in a dig at the bookish Leader and his supposed treachery – that as a manufacturer keen to keep Sheffield at the forefront, he had 'no more time to spend in answering attacks against Sheffield and its interests.'

It was Leader, though, who was to have the last word in this duel of words. When he had catalogued the Elkington papers, Leader had set aside several pages in volume two for 'An Analysis of the Various Statements, Claims and Fictions Relating to the Claims made for Sheffield.' In two columns, Leader weighed up the evidence and the claims and counter-claims. In *The Telegraph* on 24 January, 1914, he refined and repeated the exercise. Here in précis, Leader gave the results of his research, reproducing extracts from letters, establishing definite dates, and carefully apportioning credit. The article, which filled three densely packed columns in the newspaper, remains an important source on the introduction of electro-plating.

There the controversy rested. Within months, the country was at war and events were about to sweep away some of the protagonists. Sir John Bingham did not long survive the heyday of the silver and electro-plate trade: he died unexpectedly on a business trip to London on 18 March, 1915, aged 75. His townsmen lamented the loss of a 'keen fighter' and doughty defender of Sheffield's business interests. Leader continued his literary career during the War, publishing histories of Sheffield banks and continuing writing up his work on electro-plate. There are hints that he intended to write a book on the subject. This was never realised, but he did produce a detailed history of Elkington as a companion to the records, though it was never published. He also completed a referenced article for the

Journal of the Institute of Metals in 1919. It is the standard work on the subject, and amongst the best things Leader ever wrote.

Walker & Hall ignored it. In 1919, the company, now under the direction of Sir John's son, Albert E. Bingham, published a souvenir booklet, which reiterated the saga of how Wright of Attercliffe and George Walker had discovered electro-plate and founded Walker & Hall. A copy of this booklet in Sheffield Local Studies Library has scribbled comments in Leader's hand, denouncing the booklet's 'lies.' Pasted inside is a letter, dated 12 December, 1919, in which Frederick Bradbury had alerted Robert Leader to the booklet, suggesting that perhaps some sort of published refutation was again in order. Leader never appears to have done so. Somehow the whole subject appeared less important. The mighty silver and electro-plate firms had been seriously hit by the War, as demand for luxury goods fell and the price of silver rose. Walker & Hall, James Dixon, and Elkington were past their peak. Stainless steel had appeared, which was largely to supersede electro-plate later in the century. The electro-plate controversy was as old-fashioned as the style of many of the old Victorian and Edwardian electro-plate articles. On 18 April, 1922, Robert Leader himself died at his residence in London, the dispute with Bingham now very much a fading memory (though an obituarist in *The Independent* did mention Leader's role in the affair).

All told, Leader had had much the better of the argument. Retracing his path is now probably not worth the effort of a present-day historian. However, the Elkington papers still survive at the Victoria & Albert Museum and appear to confirm Leader's careful conclusions. Sir John Bingham's case, on the other hand, looks weak and unconvincing. It was based largely on hearsay and none of the documents he cited have survived. One is struck in his numerous pronouncements on the subject by his complete refusal to ever mention the dread name of Elkington, let alone accord the Birmingham makers any credit. Ultimately, one feels, Bingham was driven by commercial and not historical considerations. In which case, his obstinancy did have a certain logic, even if it shows he lacked a generosity of spirit. Leader was right: Walker & Hall's and Bingham's achievements were impressive enough, without claiming false honours.

Does it matter now? To a certain extent, the answer must be yes. Faint echoes of the controversy continue to be felt. Walker & Hall were still peddling their version of events in their trade literature even after the Second World War. For example, a Walker & Hall commemorative booklet, *On War Service 1939–1945* (1945), repeated the

Wright/Walker story. These accounts lie in wait to trap the unwary historian and collectors' books and articles on electro-plate still contain elements of the Sheffield legend. The Sheffield versus Birmingham debate therefore endures: but even if it did not, the story of Wright of Attercliffe, George Walker and Elkington would still have interest. It teaches us the value of regarding all historical traditions and published 'facts' with scepticism. Above all, it shows how vested interests, rumour, and dim memories can combine with germs of the truth, to produce what Leader described as a 'fantastic fabric . . . based on foundations as unstable as sand.'

Notes and References

The Elkington papers were eventually deposited (still as Leader arranged them) at the Victoria & Albert Museum, in the Archive of Art and Design. Leader's unpublished typescript 'History of Elkington & Co' (1913), can be consulted at the British Library. It appears to be the only extant copy.

As regards published sources: the electro-plate controversy can be followed in the newspaper and trade journal sources cited in this article. Also useful from the local press are the obituaries of Sir John Bingham and Robert E. Leader. Interested readers can also consult:

S. O. Addy, 'Robert Eadon Leader: An Appreciation,' *Transactions of the Hunter Archaeological Society*, 2, 1922–4, pp. 213–19.

Gay Booth, 'The Manufacturing Silversmiths of Sheffield,' Royal College of Art Master of Arts thesis, 1991. Copy at the Sheffield Assay Office.

Shirley Bury, *Victorian Electro-plate*, 1971.

The Century's Progress, 1893.

Sherard Cowper-Coles, 'Sheffield Plate and Electro-Plate,' *Journal of the Society of Arts* 55, 12, 19 July 1907, pp. 853–66, 873–86.

John Culme, *The Directory of Gold and Silversmiths, Jewellers and Allied Traders 1838–1914*, 1987.

D. Higgins and G. Tweedale, 'The Commercial Development of the Sheffield Silver and Electro-plate Industry, *1840–1914*,' *Transactions of the Hunter Archaeological Society* (forthcoming, 1997).

R. E. Leader, 'The Early History of Electro-Silver Plating,' *Journal of the Institute of Metals*, 22, 1919, pp. 305–26.

R. Vander, 'Some Sheffield Silversmiths,' *Proceedings of the Silver Society*, 11, Spring 1979, pp. 118–25.

Walker & Hall, *Trade Catalogue*, 1906.

Walker & Hall, *Souvenir Booklet* [The Flag Known to the World], 1919.

Walker & Hall, *On War Service 1939–1945*, 1945.

Acknowledgements

I am grateful to the following for their help: Sheffield City Library Local Studies Department; Sheffield Assay Office (Jackie Richardson); and the Archive of Art & Design, Victoria & Albert Museum (Elizabeth Salmon); and the Rural History Centre, University of Reading.

9. THE WROUGHT IRON ERA – WITH RECOLLECTIONS OF SHEFFIELD'S LAST PUDDLER

by Trevor Lodge

It was just answer of Solon to Croesus, who showed him all his treasures. 'Yes, sir, but if another should come with better iron than you, he would be master of all this gold'. Francis Bacon

THE PRODUCTION OF WROUGHT, or malleable, iron in the South Yorkshire region is an industry stretching back into antiquity. Comparison with Sheffield's long-standing cast steel industry – which started with Huntsman's crucible process – will serve to make the point. Huntsman's process is just over 250 years old; man has produced wrought iron locally, on the other hand, by one means or another for at least two thousand years.

The earlier means of making wrought iron date back to the so-called Iron Age, and employed crude direct reduction techniques in which the iron ore was reduced to the metal using charcoal fuel in variously modified open fires, or bowl hearths.

By the Middle Ages these direct reduction hearths had evolved into stone shaft furnaces known as bloomeries. The product of the bloomery was a pasty mass of crude wrought iron, suitable for direct forging. From the late fifteenth century even bigger shaft furnaces, so-called blast furnaces, were introduced into Britain from mainland Europe. The size of these structures, coupled with their more efficient draughting arrangements – hence the use of the word 'blast', signifying air blast – resulted in higher furnace temperatures and a molten iron product.

Blast furnace iron contained much chemically dissolved carbon (typically 4 per cent) from its reaction with the charcoal; as a result the product, also known as pig iron, was brittle and although suitable for the production of castings, pig iron was unsuitable for forging. Following the introduction of the blast furnace a second process was now needed to produce a malleable type of iron. In this second process the blast furnace pig iron was remelted and excess carbon removed by oxidation (decarburization) to leave a purer, more malleable iron. This second process was known as puddling. Initially, this second process was effected in a finery furnace, but from the late eighteenth century the finery process was replaced by the more efficient puddling process.

In 1988 I interviewed Frank Barraclough, a former iron puddler, about his working life. At that time Mr Barraclough was probably the last ex-puddler still alive in the South Yorkshire region so his recollections – incorporated here – have particular significance. Never again will the opportunity arise for us to learn the 'how and why' of making wrought iron from someone with first hand local puddling experience.

Mention wrought iron to the average person and he or she will almost certainly relate it to the decorative scroll metal work used in fabricating the better class of garden gates. The fact is, however, that many people below the age of 50 have never seen real wrought iron, for so-called wrought iron gates made nowadays are actually mild steel. And, sadly, whilst these are just as decorative as real wrought iron gates, they have nothing like the corrosion resistance of the latter.

True, wrought iron was once used for light decorative metalwork fashioned by smithing, but essentially it was only put to this mundane use in the twilight years of its production. To put the metal in true perspective we have to realise that, prior to about 1870, wrought iron was the metal that designers and architects used – to the virtual exclusion of all others – for engineering and constructional purposes where strength and resistance to shock and corrosion were essential.

Wrought iron was the metal on which the Industrial Revolution thrived. It enabled agriculture to mechanise and increase output, thereby feeding an exploding population; it transformed cottage spinning 'jennys' into a mechanised factory textile industry to clothe the growing population; and it made possible a national transport network (railways) which was needed to sustain the industrial transformation by cheap efficient movement of goods – raw materials, coal, agricultural produce and finished goods.

It also gave us the world's first commercial metal-hulled ocean going vessels (in place of wooden ships), a significant step forward in the growth of international trade. Indeed, the Wonder of the Age – Brunel's 19,000 ton *Great Eastern* steamship of 1858 – used almost exclusively wrought iron plates from Park Gate Iron Works, Rotherham, for her 12,000 ton hull. Such was her magnitude that she was still the world's heaviest vessel in 1900, fully forty years later!

For the Sheffield region the expansion of the country's railway network was of particular significance. Victorian railways, the arteries of our industrialising nation, were quite literally 'iron roads'. By 1870 some 15,000 miles of such railways laid with wrought iron rails existed in Great Britain and Ireland and, as if this were not enough, the bulk of the ferrous metalwork on the locomotives and rolling stock (coaches, wagons, etc.) was also fashioned from the same metal. According to a number of economic historians, the demand for wrought iron rails in the 1830–1860 period was probably the largest single stimulus which affected the growth of the British iron industry. Quite a claim, especially when one remembers that there was no bulk steelmaking at that time.

By the middle of the last century, South Yorkshire housed several wrought iron producers, notably around Barnsley and Rotherham, but also in Sheffield. Size of works, and diversity of product, were quite wide. At one end of the scale was the Stocksbridge Works of Samuel Fox, which employed four puddling furnaces as a mere preliminary in the production of steel wire. A nearby contemporary, Wortley Forges, operated 16 puddling furnaces, with a high proportion of output going to 'heavy engineering', i.e., wrought iron railway axle production. Finally, at the other end of the scale came Yorkshire's largest producer, the Park Gate Iron and Steel Company Ltd, near Rotherham which puddled iron in over eighty furnaces and rolled a high proportion of it to railway rails and ships' armour plate.

The significance of South Yorkshire's wrought iron producers went far beyond their own industry, for they gave local engineers the first practical material from which to construct large capital items such as locomotives, boilers, mill engines and the like. In reality they laid the foundation for the so-called Heavy Trades of the Sheffield region, which in turn ensured the vigorous growth of the infant Bessemer steelmaking industry locally, and in the 1860s established Sheffield as the world's first bulk steelmaking centre. We do well to remember this, and not simply dismiss the wrought iron industry as an anachronism.

So much for the significance of wrought iron in the Victorian era. What of its production? Methods varied from area to area, and to some extent were governed by quality of raw material, intended end use and – not surprisingly – local tradition. Our account is based on the practice employed at the Tinsley Works, Sheffield, of William Cooke & Co Ltd, where Frank Barraclough began work about 1922, (Figure 1). The firm, established in 1866, was un-typical of Sheffield's emerging Heavy Trades insofar as it continued to work largely in iron, rather than Bessemer steel, which soon came to dominate the scene.[1] Cooke's produced pig iron using two blast furnaces fed with Frodingham ironstone from Scunthorpe brought by barge via the South Yorkshire Navigation (Figure 2). The firm was

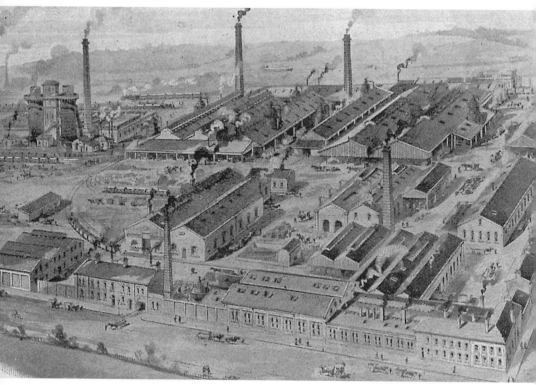

Figure 1.   General view of the Tinsley Works of William Cooke & Co Ltd, about 1890.

Figure 2.   The two blast furnaces at Cooke's Tinsley Works, taken from the canal side.

actually one of the first to run trials on iron ore from this source, indirectly helping to establish the iron and steel town of Scunthorpe in the process.

This pig or cast iron was brittle and not capable of being forged directly, so had to be converted to wrought iron by puddling. A high proportion of the malleable product of puddling was subsequently rolled through one or other of two mills into various sections – large rounds, flats and bars. Bessemer and Siemens Martin steel bars were also rolled at Cooke's, using bought-in steel billets as feedstock. Shortly following the turn of the present century the blast furnaces were closed down, making it necessary thereafter also to buy in the pig iron for puddling.

Well known speciality products were steel vehicle springs, wire ropes, 'Best Yorkshire' iron axles for traction engines and wrought iron horseshoes. Springs seem to have been made from the firm's earliest days, together with wrought iron wire ropes, though the latter were eventually (*c*.1880 onwards) superseded by superior steel wire ropes, (Figure 3). Mass horseshoe production did not begin until the closing year of the last century, and was carried out in a specially designed manufactory. Mr Barraclough and his colleagues at Billy Cooke's used to call this, somewhat disrespectfully, the Donkey Shop!

I was a product of Sheffield's East End

recalled Mr Barraclough.

I was born at Darnall in 1905 but the family moved to Attercliffe when I was about six years old. Father was a puddler by trade, and by the time I was ready to start work he had just returned to his old job at Billy Cooke's following an enforced spell working at Bilston in South Staffordshire. [He had been directed to Bilston by the Government on being demobbed from the army after service in

Figure 3.   Cooke's advertisement of 1899 showing a list of the company's products.

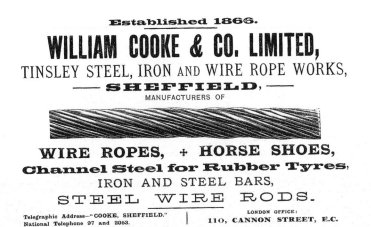

Established 1866.

WILLIAM COOKE & CO. LIMITED,

TINSLEY STEEL, IRON AND WIRE ROPE WORKS,

— SHEFFIELD, —

MANUFACTURERS OF

WIRE ROPES, ✦ HORSE SHOES,

Channel Steel for Rubber Tyres,

IRON AND STEEL BARS,

STEEL WIRE RODS.

Telegraphic Address—"COOKE, SHEFFIELD."
National Telephone 97 and 2053.

LONDON OFFICE:
110, CANNON STREET, E.C.

the Great War.]

After leaving school I worked briefly hammer driving for £1 per week at Benjamin Huntsman's works on Coleridge Road then moved to Kayser Ellison's for more money. However, orders soon became scarce and they found they had no need for me. My father spoke up for me at Cooke's and after a short initial spell as a 'bogie lad' – of which more later – I joined my father on the puddling furnaces.

For the uninitiated, a puddling furnace is simply a coal fired metal box structure lined with firebrick in which pig iron, placed on a shallow hearth, is converted into wrought iron, [Figure 4]. Such a simple description, however, gives no impression whatsoever of the enormous amount of manual labour involved in the job. Puddling was acknowledged to be one of the hardest manual jobs, and I would certainly endorse that view from my personal experiences.

Cooke's had some 24 puddling furnaces in two banks, each of a dozen or so. There were referred to as the Outside Forge and Inside Forge, respectively, indicating their proximity to the main rolling mill buildings. An individual furnace was about 11 feet 6 inches long, 6 feet 6 inches wide and 5 feet 6 inches high, tapering to 4 feet 6 inches high at the back. Each furnace was manned by a crew of two – the puddler, or forehand, and his underhand. Both had quite clearly defined jobs, which to some extent were dictated by where they worked on the furnace.

We started the week on Monday morning at 4.00am after walking to work. Many is the time we have been stopped by the local bobby on

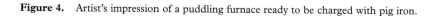

Figure 4. Artist's impression of a puddling furnace ready to be charged with pig iron.

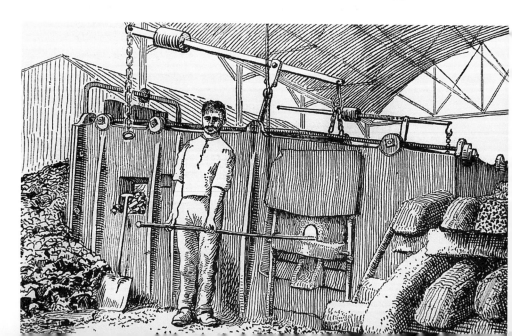

the night beat, curious to know what we were about at that ungodly time!

During the night the works' boilerman lit fires in the furnaces to warm them in readiness for their crews, and my first job was to fettle the fire and get our furnace up to full working temperature. Coal was fired through a stoking hole at the back of the furnace. Once it was hot enough, we manually charged the furnace with five or six iron pigs – approximately 5 hundredweight (250 kilograms) in total – through the main door on the furnace front, or foreplate. This door, which moved up and down on a counterbalance, was then wedged down in place and the furnace damper opened to raise the temperature.

As the pigs began to melt we robbled, or stirred, them continuously using a long 'raking' tool – a robble[2] – through a slot in the charging door to prevent them sticking to the furnace hearth. After an hour or so, the charge had melted and begun to boil, whereupon the surface of the molten iron became covered in tiny dancing blue flames.[3]

We left the charge boiling for about ten minutes then brought a cinder wagon -a low slung iron-bodied four wheel truck – alongside the furnace taphole, [Figure 5]. The furnace damper was shut and a clay plug wedged in the taphole was driven out with a bar and hammer, allowing the molten slag of impurities – called cinder – to flow into the truck, almost filling it. Left behind in the furnace was a hot pasty mass or wrought iron, which the forehand gathered into three lumps of about 1½ hundredweight (50 kilograms) each, using a broad bladed tool called a paddle.

At this point the puddler sounded a gong to call the bogie lad, who brought to the furnace front a flat topped two wheel bogie fitted with a metal shield which protected the user from the heat. The puddler used a large pair of tongs to drag one of the puddled iron balls on to the trolley, with the underhand using the paddle to help with the operation. It could be quite a tricky operation; the knack was to get the barrow as near the furnace foreplate as possible, and anticipate the ball of iron landing on the bogie so that it didn't upset the balance. The barrow had to be at just the right angle – if too high the ball rolled back into the furnace; if too low the weight of the ball tipped up the barrow handle.

We on the furnace did not have the comfort of a heat shield like the bogie lad, and used to keep the furnace door down as much as possible to avoid a scorching at this point, though having it down too far could interfere with getting the balled iron out of the furnace.

The bogie lad then took the puddled iron – one ball at a time – to

Figure 5.   Artist's impression of cinder wagons.

a large (five ton) steam hammer. Here it was fashioned by a shingler, whose job it was to hold the metal in tongs and turn it as necessary whilst it was squeezed gently under the hammer initially (to remove excess molten slag pockets), then hammered more firmly to weld the mass into a sound forging, often referred to as a billet or bloom.[4] The still hot bloom was then taken directly to the Forge Mill for rolling.[5]

Because of the very real danger of being showered with molten slag during hammering, the shingler wore a 'uniform' of tin leggings (including spats over his clogs) a gauze face mask similar to that worn by a fencer, and a large leather apron. The apron was often soaked in water prior to shingling to give some relief from the heat experienced during the hammering, [Figure 6].

The forehand and his underhand did not wear such protective clothing, and on more than one occasion I remember my hair being singed by the hot slag which shot out during shingling, despite the fact that we were a good thirty feet away from the hammers! The only concession we made to safety was to cover our boot lacings with a makeshift flap of leather to prevent slag splashes or sparks entering our boots, particularly when taking iron out of the furnace.

Shinglers were usually tall, well built men, since they were required to manipulate the heavy ball of iron on the hammer anvil quickly. They used tongs with lengthy handles to position the puddled ball while it was being squeezed into shape, although during the later, heavy, forging operations the bloom was left 'free-standing' on the anvil, [Figure 7]. As can be imagined, both puddlers (in particular) and shinglers had prodigious appetites for ale to replace body fluids lost as sweat during working periods.

One of the shinglers we worked with, Ralph Cliff (or Cliffe), created a lasting impression in my youthful mind. He seemed to have something of a technical bent, and this was enhanced by the 'pince-nez' spectacles he wore. He was certainly not all brawn and no brain and I was told he had once become quite deeply involved in an experiment at Cooke's to introduce an 'iron man' into puddling. By 'iron man' was implied a mechanical device capable of stirring round the charge during puddling to eliminate the back-breaking manual labour. Unfortunately there were too many problems and the idea never really got off the ground. Other shinglers I remember were Tom Perry and a Mr Driver.

If, for whatever reason, a puddler's heat was not ready for shingling as his turn came due, he forfeited his position in the rota for the rest of the shift, effectively going to the back of the queue. He still got in his four heats during the day, but naturally was last away at the end of the shift.

Figure 6. A shingler at work forging a ball of puddled iron into a bloom at the works of the Midland Iron Co Ltd, Rotherham. Note the face mask, leather apron and leggings, 'a uniform' designed to protect him from the molten slag which showered out during shingling.

As can be imagined, this practice caused a great deal of trouble at times. I remember, in particular, one Saturday incident when an ardent Sheffield Wednesday supporter missed his turn for the hammer bogie and in desperation – so he wouldn't leave work late for the football match – he tried to get his charge to the hammer himself on a metal barrow unsuitable for the job. He came a real cropper, however, because he didn't get many yards before his face blistered with the intense heat. No match for him that Saturday afternoon – he spent it in the Ambulance Room having his burns treated.

On odd occasions I remember us producing Best Yorkshire Iron – or B.Y. Iron as we called it. This was a premium grade which demanded a portion of Swedish pig iron in the charge and took longer in the puddling. We could only manage three heats of B.Y. per shift and by tradition were allowed a pint of beer each as a consolation or sweetener at such times! There was something of a special air about making B.Y. Iron, and this was emphasised during the puddling operation, when one of the gaffers would come over to the furnace and add two scoops of 'physic' – a chemical powder – to improve the melt.[6]

Cooke's also employed two ball furnaces in the manufacture of 'Best Scrap' wrought iron.[7] Items of scrap wrought iron were built into large square piles and these piles were heated individually in a ball furnace until they were 'dripping hot' – a term used to signify that their slag content was oozing out and melting because of the heat. The still dripping pile was taken over to the hammer and forge

Figure 7.   Interior of Cooke's forge, with a bloom of wrought iron being forged under the steam hammer (left). Note the two-wheel barrow in the right foreground, as used for transferring balled iron from the puddling furnaces to the forge.

welded into a block. Iron made in this manner (effectively by recycling) was called 'Best Scrap Iron' and was in quite high demand because it has a superior structure to ordinary wrought iron on account of its having been worked under the hammer twice – once as the original articles and once on piling.[8] *The name sounds rather strange to someone not familiar with the industry but was meant to imply this aspect of having been doubly worked, and not that the iron was fit only for scrap!*

At one time all the men in our family were employed at Cooke's. In addition to father and myself, I had four brothers there. Horace, Bill and Jack all worked in the Donkey Shop, where horseshoes were made, [Figure 8]. Tom had the job of hammer 'slekking', which consisted of cleaning scale away from around the base of the hammer. The scale, or slack, gradually accumulated as a by-product of the forging operation but wasn't allowed to go to waste – it was mixed with ground 'tap cinder' (slag from the puddling furnace) and the concoction used to line and repair the puddling furnace hearth. Repairing the hearth – fettling – took place between heats to make good any damage caused by the combination of slag and heat corroding the brickwork. A few shovels of hammer slack were also used to dress the puddling furnace hearth at the very start of each working day.

Eventually the Depression caught up with Cooke's and puddling iron was discontinued about 1926, throwing us out of work. The firm closed down altogether shortly after this, and the site, on Attercliffe Common, is now occupied by Tinsley Wire Industries Ltd.[9]

It was fairly obvious that Cooke's works was past its best years when I joined. I have recently learned of the two blast furnaces that once operated on the site, but these had gone by the time I worked there.

After finishing at Cooke's I was fortunate to get a job as a furnace hand at Turton Platts, Meadowhall, then worked briefly on crankshaft drop stamping at Shardlows. In 1937 I moved to Istelco Ltd on Grange Mill Lane where I stayed until 1964, when the firm went into voluntary liquidation. I was then transferred for my last few working years to the Waverley Works of Henry Rossell & Co Ltd on Effingham Road.

I suppose I had quite a varied working life, but of all the jobs I did, puddling at Billy Cooke's made the biggest impression. Perhaps it was due to the primitive, basic nature of the work. It's a rather strange feeling to think that I am probably the area's last ex-puddler[10] *– a final link with a centuries-old bygone industry.*

Figure 8. Cooke's horseshoe manufactory

Appendix

The rise and demise of wrought iron puddling

The following data, complied mainly from official returns, give some indication of the overall size of the UK wrought iron industry, which was based largely in Derbyshire, Lancashire, Shropshire, Staffordshire, Teesside, Yorkshire, Scotland (Lanarkshire) and South Wales. The figures quoted refer only to primary puddled iron output and do not take into account reworked material, i.e., 'Best Scrap Iron'. Although the Bessemer process for making mild steel was generally accepted from about 1860 on, such was the sheer size of the wrought iron industry that its expansion was not checked by its mild steel rival until 1875, a good 15 years later.

In 1861, at the birth of the mild steel industry, there were 213 wrought iron works, puddling iron in 4147 furnaces, and rolling it in 439 mills.

By 1875 this had increased – at a more or less even rate – to 314 works, 7575 furnaces and 909 mills. Output had increased such that the total wrought iron production in the early 1870s was in the region of 4½ million tons per annum, a staggering one thousand times greater than the corresponding figure for Bessemer and Siemens steel. Indeed, the figures for 1875 were an all time high for the industry.

A decade or so later, in 1886, they had decreased to 227 works with some 4500 furnaces (a third of them out of use) and 666 mills. By 1890, wrought iron and mild steel output figures were on a par, both being some 2 million tons.

Wrought iron had become very much second fiddle to steel by the turn of the present century. In 1906 the number of puddling furnaces had dwindled to 1535, with puddled bar output for the year being approximately one million tons. Steel output, on the other hand, was running at $6^{1}/_{2}$ million tons per annum, and expanding steadily.

Output of wrought iron remained at the 1 million tons per annum level until the Great War, but by the 1920s had dwindled to one quarter of this total. By this time the principal production centres were located in South Staffordshire, Teesside, Yorkshire and Scotland (Lanarkshire). In two of the industry's former strongholds, Lancashire and South Wales, wrought iron production had been largely superseded by mild steel production, notably from Siemens openhearth steelmaking facilities installed after the turn of the century. This trend was subsequently mirrored to some extent in the later-surviving wrought iron producing areas, until commercial production of the metal ceased.

Notes

1. A general and historical account of the Tinsley Works of William Cooke & Co Ltd can be found in Pawson & Brailsford's *Guide to Sheffield* – the 1889 and 1899 editions are particularly useful. There is, incidentally, no connection between William Cooke & Co Ltd and the present day foundry business of William Cook plc based on Parkway Avenue, Sheffield.
2. This tool was also known as a rabble in the industry.
3. This phenomenon was widely known as puddlers' candles, though the term was not known to Mr Barraclough. The appearance of the flames signifies loss of carbon from the melt, which eventually results in malleable iron being left in the furnace.
4. The Anglo-Saxon word 'bloma' means lump, hence the origin of bloom – literally a lump of forged iron. The term bloom is still used in modern steel terminology, and nowadays is limited to describing rolled or forged steel over about five inches (13 cm) square section.
5. Mr Barraclough confirmed that in his time at Cooke's three other mills – the 9-inch Mill, the 14-inch Mill and Wire Rod Mill – were all still in use for re-rolling material from the Forge Mill down to a variety of finished sections.
6. Such moves were widely practised, but were of psychological rather than technical benefit, with the 'physic' often consisting of nothing more sinister than salt, or similar harmless chemicals. In the quantities added these had little or no effect on the process.
7. So-called because they were used to ball-up or amalgamate small items of iron into larger ones.
8. It should be noted that making quality B.Y. Iron was not just a matter of raw material selection but also involved suitable pre-rolling treatment. To minimise directional properties – due to weakening slag streaks in the metal – bars from the initial hammer forged blooms were crosspiled, reheated and forged together to produce a fresh bloom with no one favoured direction of the slag streaks.
    Material crosspiled in this manner was referred to as merchant bar or best iron. If bars of this material were sheared into lengths, crosspiled, reheated and forged together again, the product was now best best iron. Finally, if best best (or BB) iron was crosspiled and forged yet again the outcome was best best best iron (BBB or treble best iron) – the highest grade. Needless to say these grades

carried price premiums, and were used for products where high material integrity was vital – for example coupling links for railway vehicles, mine cage hoists, anchor chain and so on.

In the heyday of wrought iron production, even more elaborate reworking was practised. Merchant bar was then known as single crown iron – and often stamped with a crown motif. Crosspiling single crown iron gave best iron, after which the sequence was as elaborated in the preceding paragraph. In other words, a total of four reworkings to get from the original forged and rolled product – often called 'muck bar' – to treble best iron.

9.   These recollections are confirmed by Mr W. Lane, who as a youth of 16 was working behind the shingling hammer at Cooke's when puddling ceased in 1926–27. Mr Lane also recalls the Donkey Shop closing at about the same time.

10.   The rolling of wrought iron was carried out as late as 1973 by the Midland Iron Company Ltd at Rotherham, but by this time all the feedstock was re-piled iron – or Best Scrap Iron to use the industry's own terminology. Widely known as 'Masbro Forge', the Midland did once puddle pig iron but discontinued the practice on a regular basis about 1957, and efforts to locate ex-Midland puddlers have not been successful. Coincidentally, Mr Barraclough's father once worked there.

Acknowledgements

The introductory section draws heavily on my study of wrought iron production at Park Gate Works, Rotherham, which first appeared in *Steel News*, the newspaper of British Steel. See in particular *Steel News* (Rotherham edition) for December 1983 and March 1984, which covered respectively 'Park Gate – Early Partners and Products' and 'The Golden Years of Wrought Iron'.

The major part of this account is based on the oral recollections of the late Frank Barraclough, with whom I spent several most enjoyable evenings in 1988 talking shop. My original intention was to have the account published shortly after these visits but sadly this did not prove possible. Fortunately, Mr Barraclough saw and approved the completed draft.

I am also pleased to place on record the help I received over many years from the late W.K.V. (Keith) Gale, doyen historian of the iron industry of South Staffordshire. His classic work, *The Black Country Iron Industry* (published in 1979 by the Metals Society) should be consulted by any student keen to learn more of the technicalities of the wrought iron trade.

Most of the official government returns on wrought iron production quoted in the appendix have been taken from relevant issues of the periodical *Iron & Coal Trades Review*. Some of the earlier data – up to 1890 – appeared in Griffiths' *Guide to the Iron Trade of Great Britain* by Samuel Griffiths. Originally published in 1873, the book was reprinted in 1967 by David & Charles (publishers) Ltd, Newton Abbot.

10. THE SHEFFIELD WORKHOUSE NEAR KELHAM ISLAND

by T. J. Caulton

Is it the fact that the workhouse is an old cotton mill? – It is really a fact, that it was once a cotton mill.

Is it in a good airy situation with land around it for the purposes of gardening, and the inmates working in it? – Certainly not.

What acreage have you for your garden? – No garden; the smoke of Sheffield would prevent any garden.

Extract from 1862 Select Committee on Poor Relief [1]

Introduction

IN 1984, THE AREA SURROUNDING Kelham Island Industrial Museum was designated an Industrial Conservation Area. Today, the cutlery firm of Richardson occupies the site of the former Globe Steel Works, flanked by lanes with the intriguing names of Cotton Street, Cotton Mill Row and Cotton Mill Walk. In fact, the older

Figure 1. The West Elevation of the Sheffield Workhouse *c. 1947. Kelham Island Museum collection, photographic record of new factory for Woodhead Components Limited, 1950, not catalogued*

buildings on the Richardson site belonged to a steam-powered cotton mill which had been erected on the site of a former water-powered cotton mill destroyed by fire in 1810, which itself replaced a water-powered silk mill on the site which had been destroyed by fire in 1792.[2] The success of the third textile mill on the site was short-lived, for the premises came up for sale in 1815, and despite being offered as 'perhaps the most favourable opportunity for entering extensively and beneficially into the cotton spinning business that ever offered', the cotton mill remained unoccupied between 1815 and 1829.[3] After 1829, the cotton mill buildings (Figure 1) were used as the Sheffield Union Workhouse, until Fir Vale Workhouse opened in 1881.

This article is a history of the workhouse near Kelham Island, which formed the subject of a University of Sheffield Division of Continuing Education local history research project in 1986.[4] The main workhouse buildings suffered severe war-time bomb damage in 1940, and were demolished in 1946–7. In the mid-1980s, several subsidiary buildings survived on the site which the research group was able to investigate, although it is believed that there has been some subsequent demolition. However, map evidence suggests that the row of buildings backing on to Alma Street to the left of the current entrance to the site were not only part of the workhouse, but also date back to the first cotton mill in 1805. Since the official workhouse records were lost when Sheffield Vestry was bombed during the Second World War, the evidence has been pieced together from a number of archive sources, including official reports of the Poor Law Commissioners.

The Poor Laws originated in 1601 when overseers of the poor were empowered to levy a poor rate for the relief of the sick, aged and unemployed. By the early nineteenth century, poor rates nationally had risen markedly, provoking protests from ratepayers. Opposition was particularly strong to the practice of granting outdoor relief to employed labourers (particularly in southern rural districts), thereby subsidising low wages out of poor rates. By the 1830s pressure for reform culminated in the New Poor Law of 1834. The new law, like its predecessor, accepted the principle that every necessitous person had a claim to relief, but this was now only to be given under very strict conditions: relief for those outside the workhouse was to be abolished, and all claimants had to enter within.[5]

This article is a grim reminder of the harsh realities of Victorian life. It encapsulates Victorian morals and changes in attitude to the urban poor in a period of rapid city growth, before and after the New

Poor Law. It details local opposition to the New Poor Law, and the subsequent bitter conflicts between national government and local administration over the continuing practice in Sheffield of giving outdoor relief to the unemployed. It includes arguments from reformers concerned with the suitability of the cotton mill for a workhouse, objections from ratepayers unwilling to fund an alternative building, and provides an insight into the not-infrequent scandals within the workhouse walls.

Early history: the poorhouse and outdoor relief

The previous workhouse in West Bar had been open since 1733.[6] On 4 August, 1828, a public meeting in Sheffield resolved, 'that the present workhouse in West Bar should be abandoned and the materials sold, and that the cotton mill formerly occupied by Messrs. Heathfield should be purchased and fitted up for the reception of the poor.'[7] Detailed elevations and plans of part of the cotton mill complex survive from 1828, apparently after at least part of it had been taken over for use as a workhouse.[8] On 18 June, 1829, 'The paupers having been removed from old workhouse to the new one, formerly the cotton mill, they were treated to 280lb of beef and 320lb of pudding; 317 paupers sat down.'[9] White in his *Directory of Sheffield* for 1833 notes that the cotton mill had been purchased for £7,500 to become a 'gigantic asylum for the destitute and helpless poor', and that 'several additions have been made to the buildings, and the whole enclosed with a strong wall, with a neat lodge for the principal entrance.'[10]

When cholera struck Sheffield in 1831–2, the workhouse buildings were partially converted to enable the upper floors to be used as a hospital. One local paper wrote, 'No town could have such an advantage as Sheffield in employing their workhouse for such a purpose, from its airiness and cleanliness, and also from it being walled around.'[11] In July 1831, the paper had issued a warning:

The cholera is likely to come to Sheffield. It attacks chiefly the dirty, the idle, the drunken and the disorderly. If the cholera rages in Sheffield, all the poor cannot get doctors to attend them at their own homes . . . for these reasons, a place has been provided where there will be plenty of fresh, pure air, clean linen, comfortable beds, proper medicine and the best food; there will also be provided attentive and humane nurses, skilful and kind doctors – ready to attend day and night upon all who require assistance. Conveyances will be provided for carrying the sick as soon as they are taken ill, and in the most comfortable manner, to this House of Recovery . . . It is confidently believed that the poorer inhabitants of Sheffield are too wise to remain at home and die, rather than go to the Cholera House of Recovery.[12]

Perhaps understandably, the Board of Health had great difficulty in obtaining domestic servants, porters, nurses and washer women, and had to pay high wages to overcome the fears of potential employees. However, by November, 1832, the epidemic had almost passed, and the hospital was closed down and reverted to its former workhouse function: in total, between July and December 1832, there had been 403 deaths from cholera in Sheffield.[13]

In its early years, the workhouse near Kelham Island was administered under the old system by four Overseers of the Poor, who were selected from tradespeople in the town. It was considered to be more of a poorhouse than a workhouse, with accommodation for 600 inmates (although it had an average of only 316 inmates throughout the period 1830–36).[14] In comparison, 800 'regular poor' (infirm old people, cripples, idiots, and orphans) received outdoor relief, together with the 'casual poor' who received occasional assistance in times of sickness or other temporary misfortune. About 942lbs of bread were given weekly to the casual poor and to gaol inmates. The average cost of keeping an inmate within the poorhouse was 2s 4d (£0.12) for food, but 3s 6d (£0.18) when coal, candles, soap and clothing were included. Whilst it was much cheaper to offer relief outside the poorhouse, life within the walls was clearly basic:

At the same time, it is necessary to state, that the accommodation afforded is not such as to make it a place to be desired or sought after; and God forbid any of those little indulgences, which at present contribute to the comforts of the aged, should be curtailed or disallowed, so as to make it an asylum still less desirable.[15]

In 1834, the Sheffield workhouse was the subject of a detailed enquiry by the Commissioners on the Poor Laws. This revealed that not only were men and women separated from each other, but children were kept apart from adults, and the 'dissolute are kept apart from the unfortunate, but more respectable, inmates.'[16] Relief was given to able-bodied men outside the workhouse, but in return they had to work for eight hours on repairing roads, or on breaking stone.[17] Able-bodied men within the workhouse were also put to work breaking stone for roads in a stone-yard adjoining the workhouse. Once broken, the stone was sold on to surveyors, and the income provided offset the costs of poor relief.[18] Some men could break two tons of stone a day, although four or five tons a week was more common.[19]

Much of the report concentrated on how funding would be provided for children born outside marriage, and it was revealed that occasionally a woman was bribed 1s (£0.05) to name the father. It also contains the minutes of a meeting in December, 1832, at which it was resolved that the bodies of the unclaimed poor would be made available for anatomical research. Full accounts for the year 1831–2 are provided, providing an intriguing insight into life within the workhouse under the old Poor Law: for example, £8 9s 6d (£8.48) was spent on apprehending run-away husbands, and £34 8s 7d (£34.43) on leeches for bleeding.[20]

The New Poor Law: conflict with central authorities

Two Unions were formed to administer the New Poor Law in the Sheffield area. The Kelham workhouse was in the Sheffield Union, which comprised the townships of Sheffield, Brightside, Attercliffe and Handsworth. The Ecclesall Union comprised the townships of Ecclesall, Upper and Nether Hallam, Norton, Totley, Dore and Beauchief.[21] One of the main aims of the new legislation was to substitute indoor for outdoor relief, and to cut back drastically on the amount of outdoor relief. Many local people were shocked by the prospect of people being herded into huge workhouses, arguing that the cyclical nature of the Sheffield trades meant that large numbers of workers needed occasional outdoor relief, but these periods were often too brief to justify breaking up their homes, which in many cases were also their workshops.[22] The people of Sheffield considered themselves to be in a special position not only because of the cyclical nature of work, but also because of the large number of widows in the town owing to the high death rates amongst dry grinders.

A petition against the application of the New Poor Law gained 16,000 signatures, and in 1838 an Anti-Poor Law Society was formed.[23] One local philanthropist, Samuel Roberts (1763–1848), campaigned vehemently against the New Poor Law. Roberts was the author of an immense number of books, pamphlets and broadsheets on a diverse range of subjects from slavery to Chartism. The self-styled 'Pauper's Advocate', Roberts highlighted many cases of abuse within the workhouse, which he used to support his arguments against the New Poor Law.[24] He was particularly concerned with the excessive cost of the New Poor Law, with the overbearing attitudes and behaviour of the Guardians, and with the adverse effects on the destitute and poor.

The depression in 1838 forced the new Board of Guardians not only to continue, but to extend the system of outdoor relief.

Evidence to the Select Committee on the Poor Law Amendment Act in 1838 suggested that although the workhouse was almost full with 600 inmates, opposition to the New Poor Law had quickly subsided since the Sheffield Guardians had continued to give outdoor relief.[25] In the depressions of 1842 and 1847, over four times as much was spent on outdoor relief as on relief within the workhouse.[26] In 1849, in a different initiative to prevent able-bodied men from entering the workhouse, over 50 acres of land at Hollow Meadows was leased from the Duke of Norfolk to set up a workhouse farm for the able-bodied poor. The scheme was evidently very successful over a long term, for in 1862 the Guardians were negotiating to lease further land.[27]

Despite the local preference for outdoor relief, numbers within the Sheffield Union Workhouse on Kelham Street increased as the New Poor Law was implemented, and as local trade suffered badly in the 1840s. In 1843, £6,000 was spent on enlarging the workhouse.[28] By the time of the publication of the 1853 Ordnance Survey map (Figure 2), a hospital, asylum, boys school and other buildings had been constructed around the old cotton mill, expanding the buildings on the site fourfold. But despite these and later additions, the site was hardly ideal for the poor of the city, and the use of the build-

Figure 2.   The Sheffield Union Workhouse in 1853. *Ordnance Survey*

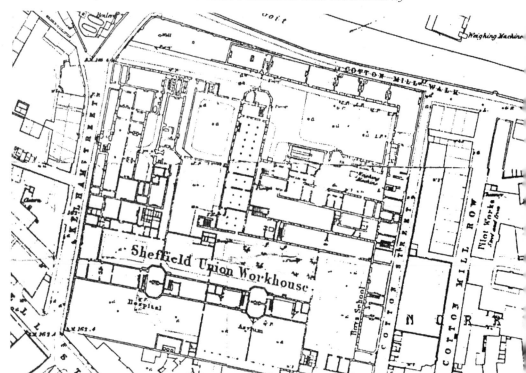

ing remained controversial throughout the period. The Ecclesall Bierlow Union had built a new workhouse in 1842, which later became the Nether Edge Hospital.[29] In 1854, the Poor Law Inspector urged the Sheffield Guardians to erect a new workhouse, but they resolved 'that it is inexpedient to do so at present.'[30]

In 1855, the Poor Law Inspector reported that five per cent of the local population were paupers, compared to three per cent in the remainder of the district. As a result, the Guardians resolved to spend £30,000 to purchase 50–60 acres of land at Darnall to build a new workhouse with accommodation. This was violently opposed by the ratepayers, but supported by the Government Poor Law Board, who gave their authority, and directed a site to be selected. At the elections of Guardians in 1856 and 1857, opponents of the scheme were elected with large majorities, and they refused to complete the purchase of the land at Darnall. The vendors threatened legal proceedings, so the new Guardians had to complete the purchase and asked for permission to resell the land. Meanwhile, the Guardians proposed an alternative scheme whereby the existing workhouse on Kelham Street would be improved at a cost of £4,000, by converting the condemned day and night wards into stores, and the stores into wards. The Poor Law Board refused to agree to these proposals, stating that a new workhouse was the only satisfactory solution to the problems at the Kelham workhouse. A deadlock existed until 1858, when permission was granted to sell the land at Darnall, and to make improvements at a cost of £5,900. By 1862, children had been moved out of the Kelham workhouse into separate premises at Pitsmoor.[31]

On Christmas Day in the workhouse

In 1862, a Select Committee on Poor Relief made a detailed investigation of practices within the Sheffield workhouse.[32] Henry Crawshaw, Chairman of the Sheffield Union, claimed that the local Guardians should have more independence from the Poor Law Board as they had a better knowledge of local problems. He was particularly concerned that the local Guardians should have more discretion to administer relief and to alter their premises as they thought appropriate. For example, the local Guardians preferred to make their own decisions on appropriate diets for inmates of the workhouse, and in some cases, they preferred to offer cash rather than food as outdoor relief.[33] It is clear that a tradition of hostility had arisen between the central authorities trying to impose the New Poor Law, and the local Guardians who felt that the nature of the

Sheffield trades required special consideration. One persistent problem was that the local Guardians refused to appoint a Church of England chaplain as required by law, owing to the large number of non-conformists in the town. This caused hostility from the local Church, who were always quick to expose any malpractices or scandals:

Mr Chester, in his letter, mentions the following circumstance: that on Christmas-day, 'during the absence of the governor, but with the express permission and encouragement of some of the officers of the house, a party of bedizened prostitutes infected with a loathsome disease were let loose to sing amongst the sick and dying in the hospital, and afterwards being joined by some able-bodied paupers, they were permitted to proceed to the insane wards, where they remained until 11 o'clock at night. The officers who took part in these disgusting orgies, to which the dying poor were exposed on the evening of their Saviour's birthday, were reprimanded by the chairman.'[34]

Clearly, the events on Christmas Day in the Kelham workhouse were rather different from those in the traditional poem! The criticisms did not stop there:

The men have been in the habit of leaving the house in large numbers on Wednesdays, on pretence of seeking work, but really, in many instances, to go on the 'spree', as was proved by a large number of them returning under the influence of liquor. The Poor Law inspector having pointed out its illegality, it was determined to discontinue a practice which worked so badly. The whole of the able-bodied inmates, excepting fifteen, in consequence, refused to work yesterday, and when several policemen were called in, they swore great oaths and set upon them with oakum, hitting the officers in the face.[35]

Reverend Chester's criticisms to the Select Committee also concentrated on the physical state of the cotton mill building, and internal arrangements within it. This resulted in the district inspector compiling a report:

In a few instances the day rooms are five or six inches below the level of the ground, but I see nothing objectionable to the rooms being used for the intended purpose on that account. The men generally sleep two in a bed when the workhouse is at full, which is very objectionable; and although the master and the porter state that they have never seen three men in the same bed, they could not deny that they had heard of such being the case from the inmates themselves . . . As regards females, a ward with a separate yard was provided for depraved women, and was used as such until lately, when, from the

large stock of picked oakum on hand, the master has improperly filled
the ward with it until it can be sold, and removed the women into the
general able-bodied women's ward . . . Several men . . . were on the
verandah of the male sick ward, from which place they were able to
see into the sick women's yard, and also to look into the windows of
the lying-in yard . . . In the male venereal yard, seven men were in
four beds, and in the male itch ward, two men were in the same bed
. . . The Board think it necessary that every adult able-bodied pau-
per, particularly when suffering from disease, should have a separate
bed.[36]

The Sheffield Flood, 1864

In 1864, when the Dale Dyke Dam at Loxley burst, Kelham Island
took the full force of the ensuing flood. The workhouse was flooded
to a depth of four feet, with water entering the hospital and lunatic
wards on the ground floor not only by the doors, but also by the sew-
ers.

A score of able-bodied paupers were told off for special duty, and
despatched across the yards to the rooms occupied by the children
having measles and small pox, and also to the women's venereal
wards. The task of these men was one of great peril, as they had to
wade through the water, which was not only exceedingly cold, but also
a considerable depth . . . The men carried the women and children,
who had nothing on but their night dresses, through to the upper
rooms of the female hospital. There were many narrow escapes, but
happily no life was lost. The damage to the property was considerable
. . . In the dead house several bodies were in coffins, which were placed
on high benches. They were reached by the water, but were not moved
from their position. A thick deposit of mud was left over the entire
area of the premises.[37]

After the flood, 124 victims were taken to the workhouse for identi-
fication, where they were laid out on straw. Twenty-three were never
identified, and 56 were interred at the expense of the poor law
authorities.[38]

The bodies presented every possible appearance. Some were serene
and beautiful in death, without a limb torn, or a feature distorted –
clam and peaceful, as though they had passed away dreaming that
they were borne along on the river of life for a better land. There was
the lovely form of an infant, with a smile still playing on its placid
face. There was the fair maiden, cold in death, with the long tresses
dishevelled over her marble brow. But all were not thus pleasing to
behold. Some there were with gaunt and ghastly forms, with clenched

fists, closed teeth, and rugged features, as though they had died in a desperate struggle with the foaming waters and uprooted trees by which they were surrounded. [39]

With the tramps and the rats: a night's experience in the Sheffield workhouse

The Sheffield workhouse continued to have problems throughout the 1870s, with development on the site effectively blighted. In 1874, the Local Government Board had refused to agree to the proposal from the Sheffield Guardians to buy land adjoining the workhouse on Kelham Street for £15,000. Consequently, in September that year the Guardians decided to abandon any long-term commitment to the Kelham site, and agreed to purchase 42 acres of land at Fir Vale for £13,500 for a new workhouse. [40] The foundation stone was laid on 16 September, 1876. [41] Thereafter, the problems at the Kelham workhouse compounded. In July, 1877, attention was drawn to the enormous quantities of ale (35,424 pints), wine (5000 pints) and spirits (400 pints) drunk by inmates in the previous year. [42] In February, 1878, the workhouse schoolmaster was compelled to resign for cruelly beating a boy (presumably at the Pitsmoor site). [43] Within a week, paupers travelling to the workhouse farm at Hollow Meadows on a daily basis went on strike because the food provided was sour, and they refused to undertake their punishment of picking half a pound of oakum. [44]

The Guardians at that time felt there was a spirit of insubordination within the workhouse, and this may have inspired a local journalist to find out for himself. In 1866, a London journalist had gone undercover in the Lambeth workhouse, and his experiences were serialised in the *Pall Mall Gazette* as *A Night in the Workhouse* under the pseudonym 'The Amateur Casual'. [45] In 1878, a local journalist ('our own Amateur Casual') copied the technique, dressing as a tramp and spent a night in the Sheffield workhouse. The article describes how twenty-one tramps, many of whom had skin diseases, had to wash in one bath of filthy water, before sleeping on wooden benches in a room 50–60 feet long, by 18–20 feet wide. The room had a dank odour, and only a jet of gas at one end for light. The journalist was woken at 7 a.m. and had to pick 1lb of oakum ('the customary task of criminals and paupers'): this involved picking hard tar off strips of old rope, and reducing the rope to its constituent fibres. At 11.30 the oakum was weighed, and the tramps were given a 'half pint of milk and water in a filthy can' together with sour bread. [46]

In conclusion, let me say that if any one has doubts as to the picture

*I have drawn, the Sheffield Union Workhouse is within easy reach,
and he can try the hospitality it affords, and prove for himself how
much needs doing, and endorse the words of one who has seen the
casual's ward at its worst, and doubtless at its best.*[47]

The problems identified by the reporter may have been embellished
for the readers of the paper, but the problems must have been real
enough, for in 1880 one pauper, Frederick Jupp, committed suicide
by leaping from a window of the workhouse. Four days later, another
inmate, Samuel Oldfield, killed himself with a knife at the inquest
on Jupp.[48]

The end of an era

The new purpose-built workhouse at Fir Vale opened on 22
September, 1881.[49] Significantly, outdoor relief always exceeded
indoor relief throughout the history of the Kelham workhouse,
although the gap between the two steadily declined in relative terms
after 1853. The absolute amount expended on outdoor relief started
to be reduced after 1882, although it was not until 1891 – well after
the cotton mill ceased to be used as a workhouse – when indoor relief
exceeded outdoor relief for the first time.[50]

The provision of a new workhouse at Fir Vale effectively ended
this era in the life of the cotton mill. The old workhouse was offered
for sale on 26 September, 1882,[51] and eventually purchased by
Messrs. Ibbotson Brothers and Company for £15,000 in 1889.[52]
Ibbotson Brothers owned the Globe Works on Penistone Road, and
renamed the old cotton mill Globe Steel Works. By the time of the
publication of the 1890 Ordnance Survey map, Ibbotsons had
demolished the buildings on the corner of Alma Street (formerly
Cotton Mill Walk), and rebuilt the entrance, gatehouse and office
block, along with the Globe Steel Works sign on Alma Street.[53]
Ibbotsons provided some large infill buildings to the south of the
original cotton mill building, effectively enclosing the space between
the additions made by the workhouse authorities. Furthermore, the
courts and yards to the west of the site were acquired, and the Globe
Steel Works built over Kelham Street, formerly the main thoroughfare into Sheffield from Kelham Island and the workhouse. The tail-
goit from the Britannia Corn Mills (formerly Kelham Wheel) opposite Globe Steel Works was culverted, and Cotton Mill Walk was able
to be widened. Renamed Alma Street, this became the new main
thoroughfare through the district. Kelham Street does not exist
today, although one can still see an enamel sign for Cotton Mill Walk
by the lane running alongside the Fat Cat public house.[54]

Figure 3. The East Elevation of the Sheffield Workhouse c. 1947. *Kelham Island Museum collection, photographic record of new factory for Woodhead Components Limited, 1950, not catalogued*

The development of the cotton mill site was virtually complete by the turn of the century, by which time water-power had long ceased to be used, and there had been little further development by 1941.[55] The mill-race for the site, a secondary goit from the Kelham Wheel mill-race, was canalised and built over, and remained in 1986 (when water was still being drawn from it for cooling purposes by Apollo Steels for their adjacent hand-rolling mill, which closed down soon after). The main cotton mill buildings were demolished in 1946–7 by Woodhead Components, who recorded the building in a series of photographs (see Figures 1 and 3), before building their new factory behind the gatehouse and old buildings fronting Alma Street.[56] The main cotton mill buildings had brick arches, cast iron columns and sections, and one-quarter inch thick lead gutters on the roof. An account of the water-mills in Sheffield in 1934 had drawn attention to two architectural features: the porticoed ventilator and the fine lead spouting which bore fleur-de-lys and were dated 1809.[57] The Council for Conservation of Sheffield Antiquities noted in 1956 that one of these had been preserved,[58] and this now forms part of the collections in store at Kelham Island Museum.

When the local history research group investigated the site in 1986, several former workhouse buildings survived on site, and the former entrance on Cotton Street could be clearly identified by changes in brick pattern. The only complete buildings which survive today are those fronting Alma Street, which are a relic not only of the workhouse era, but are believed to date back to the first cotton mill built in 1805. In 1815, the sale plan of the second cotton mill shows these buildings were being used as a kitchen and four workshops, but plans and elevations of the workhouse in 1828 show them to be a scullery (the former kitchen), with a kitchen and pantry next door, then the matron's room, and a school room. On the first floor was the laundry women's bedroom, the matron's bedroom, and the sick room. On the second floor (which no longer exists) there was a girls' garret, lunatics' room and boys' garret.[59] Other former workhouse buildings existed in part in 1986. Part of the hospital shown on the 1853 Ordnance Survey map was being used as an open store, whilst part of the hospital and asylum wall had been incorporated into more recent buildings. Another building on the eastern side of the site adjacent to the 1853 boys' school (a warehouse in the 1815 cotton mill) also still existed in 1986, although its function within the workhouse is not known. At the time of the research project, the hand rolling mill of Apollo Steels, on the land adjacent to the workhouse site, was still in operation, although the buildings on the workhouse site were empty. Several steelworkers claimed to have witnessed 'Workhouse Mary', a friendly ghost who inhabited the Woodhead Components building erected in 1950 on the site of the former workhouse. A more tangible link with the past was that provided by another worker who had unearthed a copper workhouse token on the site (the kind given out as out-relief to exchange for bread), but he had passed it on to a coin collector.

In conclusion, this history of the Sheffield workhouse near Kelham Island provides a grim reminder of the harsh realities of Victorian life, encapsulating Victorian morals and changes in attitude to the urban poor in a period of rapid city growth, before and after the New Poor Law. The cotton mill near Kelham Island was always a controversial choice for a workhouse, and its deficiencies were exacerbated when the New Poor Law necessitated large numbers of people living within its walls. Local ratepayers were reluctant to spend large sums of money on funding a suitable replacement for this workhouse, and bitter conflicts arose between local and national administrators over the failure of the central authorities to recognise that the economy of Sheffield deserved special consideration. The local Guardians resented the intrusion of national administrators into all aspects of the service, but in particular they felt the continuing practice of giving outdoor relief to the unemployed was a cost-effective way of meeting the problems of local workers undergoing temporary hardship. In total, whilst there is very little evidence surviving on the ground of the workhouse at Kelham Island, its 52 years as a workhouse has left behind a fascinating legacy of Victorian Sheffield.

Notes and References

1. Parliamentary Papers, *Select Committee on Poor Relief*, 1st Report, 1862, (181), vol. X, pp. 154–5.
2. Further information on the water-mills at Kelham Island can be found in D. Crossley *et al.* (eds.), *Water Power on the Sheffield Rivers*, Sheffield Trades Historical Society/University of Sheffield, 1989, pp. 14–6.
3. Sheffield City Archives, Sale Plan, April 13 1815, Lot 1; W. White, *Directory of Sheffield*, 1837, p. 46.
4. The author acknowledges the contributions made by members of the Local History from Kelham Island group in 1986 towards this research.
5. See, for example, J.F.C. Harrison, *The Early Victorians 1832–51*, Panther, 1973, pp. 106–12.
6. R.E. Leader, *Sheffield in the 18th Century*, 1901, pp. 322–3.
7. *Sheffield Local Register*, entry for 4.8.1828.
8. Sheffield City Archives, EBu 99S – Ebu 111S.
9. *Sheffield Local Register*, entry for 18.6.1829.
10. W.White, *Directory of Sheffield, 1833*, p. 112.
11. *Sheffield Courant*, 11.11.1831. For a detailed history of the role of the workhouse in the cholera epidemic, see J. Stokes, *The History of the Cholera Epidemic of 1832 in Sheffield*, 1921.
12. *Sheffield Courant*, 1.7.1831.
13. J.Stokes, op. cit., pp. 41–7.
14. R.E. Leader, *Statistical tables and observations*, Sheffield City Archives, WWM Handbills 173.
15. *Ibid.*
16. Parliamentary Papers, *Administration and Operation of the Poor Laws*, App. B2, Pts I and II, 1834, (44), vol. XXXV.
17. *Ibid.*, App. B2, Pts III, IV and V, 1834, (44), XXXVI.
18. Parliamentary Papers, *Select Committee on the Poor Law Amendment Act*, 3rd Report, Pt I, 1838, (140) vol. XVIII, p. 19.
19. Parliamentary Papers, *Administration and Operation of the Poor Laws*, App. A, Pt I, 1834, (44), vol. XXVIII, pp. 851–60.
20. *Ibid.*
21. M.Walton, *Sheffield: its story and its achievements*, 1948, pp. 172–3.
22. *Ibid.*
23. S. Pollard, *A History of Labour in Sheffield*, 1959, pp. 39–40.
24. S. Roberts, 'The bone-gnawing system', *Local pamphlets*, vol. 13, 6; 'Death of James Andrew', *Local Pamphlets*, vol. 249, 10.
25. Parliamentary Papers, 1838, *op. cit.*, pp. 15–22.
26. S. Pollard, *op. cit.*

27. Pawson and Brailsford, *Illustrated Sheffield Guide*, 1862, p. 33.
28. J. Furness, *Records of the Borough of Sheffield*, 1893, p. 77.
29. P. Speck *et al.*, *The Institutions and Hospital at Fir Vale, Sheffield*, 1978, p. 5; J. Flett, *The Workhouse and the Hospital at Nether Edge*, not dated.
30. J.M. Furness, *op. cit.*, p. 103.
31. *Ibid.*, p. 108; Pawson and Brailsford, op. cit., p. 33.
32. Parliamentary Papers, *Select Committee on Poor Relief*, 1st Report, 1862, (181), vol. X, pp. 148–65; *Ibid.*, 2nd Report, 1862, (321), vol. X, pp. 14–16.
33. *Ibid.*, (181), P. 153.
34. *Ibid.*, p. 158.
35. *Ibid.*, p. 155.
36. *Ibid.*, (321), pp. 14–15.
37. S. Harrison, *A Complete History of the Flood at Sheffield*, 1864, pp. 77–9.
38. *Ibid.*, pp. 79, 89–90.
39. *Ibid.*, p. 89.
40. J.M. Furness, *op. cit.*, p. 196.
41. Pawson and Brailsford, *Illustrated Sheffield Guide*, 1879, pp. 65–7.
42. *Sheffield Local Register*, entry for 25.7.1877.
43. *Ibid.*, entry for 20.2.1878.
44. *Ibid.*, entry for 27.2.1878.
45. J. Greenwood, 'A night in the workhouse', in P. Keating (ed.), *Into Unknown England, 1866–1913*, Fontana, 1976, pp. 33–54.
46. 'With the tramps and rats: a night's experience in the Sheffield Workhouse', *Sheffield and Rotherham Independent*, 28.2.1878.
47. *Ibid.*
48. *Sheffield Local Register*, entry for 10.6.1880.
49. *Ibid.*, p. 260; Pawson and Brailsford, 1879, *op. cit.*, P. Speck *et al*, op. cit., pp. 5–6.
50. J.M. Furness, *op. cit.*, p. 563.
51. Kelham Island Museum collection, Sale Plan of Old Workhouse, not catalogued. Reprinted in a Sheffield City Museums publication, *Kelham Island Round Trail*.
52. J.M. Furness, *op. cit.*, p. 444.
53. Kelham Island Museum collection, Plan of Globe Steel Works, 25.3.1890, not catalogued.
54. The main extensions to the site were completed by the time of the publication of the 1890 Ordnance Survey map. Further extensions were made by the time of the publication of the 1906 Ordnance Survey map.
55. Kelham Island Museum collection, Plans of Globe Steel Works, 25.3.1890 and 10.12.1941, not catalogued.
56. Kelham Island Museum collection, Photographic record of new factory for Woodhead Components Limited, 1950, not catalogued.
57. W.T. Miller, *The Water Mills of Sheffield*, 1934, p. 18.
58. Council for the Conservation of Sheffield Antiquities, *Survey of the Mills and Dams on the Rivers of Sheffield*, 1956.
59. Sheffield Archives, Sale Plan, April 13 1815, Lot 1; Sheffield Archives, EBu 99S – Ebu 111S.

11. A Changing Landscape: Darnall in the Nineteenth Century

by Sue Turton

THE LITTLE KNOWN DISTRICT OF DARNALL lies approximately three miles to the east of Sheffield's city centre. Approaching Darnall by road from the city centre, via Attercliffe Road and Staniforth Road leading in to Main Road, there is little to demarcate Darnall first from Attercliffe and then Handsworth, the neighbouring districts, other than Darnall's suburban shopping centre. Along this route, the predominant domestic building style is the bay-windowed terraced house of the early twentieth century also found in many other Sheffield districts. The side-streets leading off Staniforth Road, which formerly consisted of long rows of flat-fronted terraced houses with their shared backyards, have largely been re-developed within the last twenty years. Some old streets have been demolished and replaced by small estates of modern council houses with gardens, whilst others have been levelled and overlaid with grass. Approaching Darnall by the alternative routes of Greenland Road from Tinsley Viaduct or Prince of Wales Road from the Sheffield Parkway, also creates the impression that much of Darnall has been built in the twentieth century. The Greenland estate, however, is another example of the re-development of older terraced streets, whilst the Greenwood, Littledale and Bowden Wood estates, off Prince of Wales Road, were laid out on Darnall's former green fields as part of post-World War 2 housing expansion.

Addressing the need for more and better housing during the twentieth century made considerable demands on the landscape local to Darnall. Following the routes described above, it may appear that the district has lost all vestiges of its nineteenth century past. However, discovering indications of Darnall's history amongst so many changes is not quite the fruitless search it may seem to be initially. There is yet another approach from Attercliffe leading to Darnall; an older route which from 1761 had formed part of the Attercliffe to Worksop turnpike road and was known until the mid-1860s as Worksop Road, but thereafter the section through Darnall was re-named as Darnall Road and Main Road.[1] This was already an old route before being made into a turnpike road and the village of Darnall is thought to have been consciously laid out along it during the twelfth century.[2] Nineteenth century housing expansion in Darnall shows a similar focus on the road, with development during the first half of the century along it, whilst later houses were accommodated in side-streets leading off it. Thus the road played a significant rôle in the censuses from 1841 to 1891; either as a census enumerator's route between 1841 and 1861, or in the later censuses as a starting point for an enumerator's itinerary. Whilst most of the buildings and side-streets the census enumerators recorded have been demolished, there are a handful of named buildings, such as Holy Trinity Church, Darnall Hall and most of Darnall's public houses, which can still be related to all the censuses. Admittedly, almost all of these are not the original buildings seen and recorded by the enumerators, but they have all retained the same locations in Darnall's landscape and, for the most part, the same names. The only building which has had a change of name is Darnall Hall. Popularly known locally as the 'Libs', it has housed the Darnall Liberal Club for the present century and, due to alterations and additions, largely goes unrecognised as the remnant of an early eighteenth century mansion.

Apart from where Main Road intersects Prince of Wales Road and Greenland Road, the route of the Darnall and Main Roads has not been substantially altered. It is still possible to follow its course in the present day using the 1855 Ordnance Survey map of the Darnall district, reproduced in Figure 1.[3] This route is also a reconstruction of the main route of Darnall's two census enumerators in 1861, when one recorded the north side and the other the south side. Darnall Road may be approached from Attercliffe by leaving Attercliffe Road at Worksop Road and following its course to the Canal Aqueduct. Darnall Road begins at this point and the route takes an uphill course to pass the *Ball Inn*, which stands on the north side of the road as indicated on the map. As the course of the road becomes level and begins to descend, it is re-named as Main Road. At the foot of the descent, Main Road bends to the right at the *Duke of York Inn* and then rises slightly in passing to the right of the *Old Bradley Well* (Figure 2) at the foot of the narrow Fisher Lane, an approach to Darnall Hall (the Liberal Club). Within a short distance, at the present day, Main Road is linked to the right with the limit of Staniforth Road. On the 1855 map, Main Road is seen to pass farm buildings on the end of Turner Lane, a field lane which later provided the foundation for Staniforth Road in Darnall. The continuation of Main Road, both now and in the past, then turns left to pass Holy Trinity Church and the *Wellington Inn* on the right. However, after

Figure 1.
Darnall and
surrounding
area in the
mid-nine-
teenth century,
reproduced
from the 1855
O.S. map.
*Sheffield City
Libraries, Local
Studies Library*

this point, past and present again diverge. Currently, Main Road crosses the intersection of Prince of Wales Road and Greenland Road, before bearing left to begin the ascent towards Handsworth and, at the iron bridge crossing the railway, is now re-named as Handsworth Road. All the nineteenth century census schedules terminated at the point where the road bears left (in modern terms, just beyond the *Rose and Crown*). On the 1855 map, two minor roads branched off Main Road, Catcliffe Road and Owlergreave Road, leading into Darnall's fields. Catcliffe Road still exists, although part of it was destroyed when Greenland Road was built across it, and Owlergreave Road was widened and extended in the building of Prince of Wales Road. The status of Darnall's old principal road has diminished to that of a quiet back route in the modern landscape, which is probably due to the Canal Aqueduct. The solidly stone-built Aqueduct incorporates two pedestrian footpaths on either side of the roadway but, having been constructed in the early nineteenth century with only reference to contemporary ideas of vehicle height and width, it imposes restrictions on modern traffic and is impossible to widen.

Just as the route along Darnall Road and Main Road has been superseded by newer roads, Darnall's ancient boundaries have been obscured by development and revised by administrative changes. In the twentieth century, for example, under the provisions of the Sheffield Corporation Act of 1900, Sheffield's eastern boundary was extended to include land formerly belonging to the parishes of Tinsley and Handsworth.[4] Among the gains to Darnall were Tinsley Park Cemetery (previously only the approach road to it lay in Darnall), Infield (or Hill Field) Lane and High Hazels Park. These landscape features had belonged respectively to Tinsley and

Figure 2.   The nineteenth century *Old Bradley Well* public house, demolished c. 1907. *Collection of Mr H. Clayton*

Handsworth parishes and Infield Lane formed the boundary and an old bridleway between the two parishes. The 1900 boundary change also lengthened Darnall's share of the old road, to include that part which leads to Handsworth and terminates at the iron railway bridge. Officially, this was re-named as part of Main Road, but the older name of Handsworth Hill is still used locally. As this extension of the eastern boundary approaches its hundredth anniversary, enough time has passed for the land to be regarded as an integral part of Darnall. However, parts of the original boundary, Carr Brook, which separated Darnall from Tinsley and Handsworth can still be found. The Carr Brook not only formed the eastern boundary for Darnall, but was also incorporated into Sheffield's older boundary for much of its length. Darnall's ancient boundaries can be seen in Figure 1. The curving southern boundary, separating Darnall from Sheffield Park and extending from Bowden Housteads Wood, intersected both Carr Brook and another small stream, Kirk Bridge Dike. On the map, Kirk Bridge Dike runs north to join the turnpike road at just beyond the point labelled *Darnall T B* (the toll bar) and formed the western boundary, distinguishing Darnall from Attercliffe. However, the remaining boundary further demarcating Darnall and Attercliffe, is not marked on the original 1855 O.S. map but was reconstructed for Figure 1 by referring to a set of maps of Attercliffe and Darnall dating from 1819.[5] The 1841 and 1851 census enumerators followed a route which began with the toll bar and terminated at Carr Brook and in doing so recorded the extent of the manor of Darnall.

With the insertion of the northern boundary, the modest scale of the manor of Darnall is re-introduced into the landscape; or to be more precise, under the complex niceties of the feudal system, the sub-manor of Darnall in the lordship of Hallamshire. The boundaries of Darnall contained about 340 acres but even such a small manor had four areas of common lands. These comprised Owler Green and Darnall Green, both adjacent to the eastern boundary, Darnall Common, chiefly lying alongside the northern boundary and, at the western boundary, Darnall Lesser Green, the wedge-shaped piece of land lying between Kirk Bridge Dike and the turnpike road. The manorial records for Darnall are sparse. Sheffield Archives holds only a few seventeenth and eighteenth century documents relating to Court Baron, whereby transfers of property in Darnall, either by sale or inheritance, were recorded.[6] In time, this function of the manor waned to be gradually replaced by the Registry of Deeds at Wakefield, which was established exclusively for the registering of freehold land in the former West Riding and has records dating from

1704 to 1970. The surviving records for Court Baron refer to the manorial court of the Spencer family, lords of the manor of Darnall from the mid-seventeenth century. Apart from this specific rôle, the Spencer family appear to have maintained few connections with Darnall. They did not live at their Darnall manor house which, with 23 acres of land, is recorded as leased to a tenant in the 1740s and by the early nineteenth century had become the property of the Steer family.[7] The Spencers lived at Attercliffe Hall and, as the Sheffield Archives documents record, by the mid-eighteenth century lived at Bramley Grange in Braithwell, when a steward became their local representative. A system for local government was already in place even before the Spencers had left the district. Darnall, Carbrook and Attercliffe, each a separate manor with their own lords, had been grouped together as the township of Attercliffe cum Darnall. The administration of the township was undertaken by the various over-seers, elected annually from amongst the local ratepayers. Nevertheless, by virtue of title rather than the amount of land held in the township, a Spencer of the early nineteenth century could still claim the right to be part of a process which made a substantial change to the local landscape.

In 1810 a survey was made of Attercliffe cum Darnall by Joseph Bishop and Josiah Fairbank, land surveyors, who observed:

> . . . *we have enquired into the Boundaries of the said two Townships of Attercliffe and Darnal and that we have found the same suffi-ciently ascertained and distinguished except where the same Townships adjoin each other between the Worksop and Attercliffe Turnpike Road and the Township of Tinsley. And we have ascer-tained set and determined and fixed the Boundary . . . which Boundaries we have caused to be marked by stakes . . .*[8]

This boundary followed the same line as the reconstructed northern boundary on Figure 1, using the 1855 O.S. map. However, the field outlines which can be seen skirting the upper north-eastern part of Darnall's boundary on Figure 1 did not exist in 1810. At the time, the area was still Darnall Common and the boundary reconstructed by the land surveyors was to distinguish between it and Attercliffe Common. This was a preliminary move towards the specific task of enclosing the 238 acres of common and waste lands and 50 acres of open fields within Attercliffe cum Darnall township. To carry out this procedure had required an Act of Parliament, which was passed in 1810 and appointed Messrs Bishop and Fairbank as the enclosure Commissioners. The preamble to the Act stated

> *And whereas the most noble Charles Duke of Norfolk is Lord of the*

> *Manor of Attercliffe and Frances Spencer is Lady of the Manor of*
> *Darnal and the said Duke of Norfolk Gamalial Milner John Shaw*
> *John Deakin William Deakin Joseph Read George Bustard Greaves*
> *Samuel Staniforth George Steer John Beldon and others are propri-*
> *etors of the said Commons wastes and open fields it would be of*
> *advantage to them if the same were divided and specific parts there-*
> *of allotted to them and the other persons interested . . .* [9]

The advantage to the above people did not lie with the enclosure of
Darnall's four previously described common lands, which in total
measured slightly less than 40 acres. The real attraction was the vast
expanse of Attercliffe Common. In comparison to the gains made by
the Duke of Norfolk, Frances Spencer's award of one eighteenth part
of Darnall's commons was very slight. However, the Act maintained
the right of both within their respective manors to:

> *. . . any Mines, Ores, Minerals or Coal in or under the aforesaid*
> *Commons or waste lands respectively but that they and their respec-*
> *tive Lessees Agents Servants and Workmen shall have full and free*
> *liberty at all times hereafter to search for, work, dig, win, raise and*
> *carry away all such mines, minerals and coal as fully and effectual-*
> *ly as if this act had not been passed.* [10]

At the time, perhaps, this was not of real value to the Spencer family but may have had more significance later, when the deep mining
of coal became possible. Documents held at Sheffield Archives show
that coal had been mined in Darnall from at least the mid-eighteenth
century.[11] A map of 1763 reveals that all the land north of the turnpike road, including Darnall Common and some Spencer landhold-
ings in Tinsley, had either already been worked or was in the process
of being worked for coal. In addition, the area had been considered
worth the investment of a pumping engine, or fire engine as it is
called on the map, to remove water from the coal face.[12] In 1897, the
Nunnery Colliery leased '. . . about 101 acres of Freehold and
Common Silkstone Coal situate in Attercliffe and Darnall' from
Messrs Spencer's devisees for a term of 44 years.[13] Judging by the
accounts from the early years, however, the seam was initially difficult to work and not particularly profitable. It may be that a hundred
years elapsed between the award of the mineral rights in Darnall and
some gain being made from it by the Spencer heirs.

Enclosure was undoubtedly a lengthy process which could take
several years. For example, the enclosure of the area comprising
Upper Hallam, Nether Hallam, Fulwood, Morewood, Stannington,
Storrs and part of Dungworth took fourteen years, but it was an area

of 6,000 acres.[14] In the case of Attercliffe and Darnall, from the passing of the Act by Parliament to the enactment of the award, took ten years. This does seem a little excessive although the delay may have been due to any number of reasons. For example, the cost of the enclosure was to be offset by the sale of small parcels of common land, but the potential purchasers may have needed time to raise the money. Among the directions to the Commissioners contained within the Act were the provision of public watering places and public stone quarries to provide materials for repairing roads, excluding the turnpike road, and the setting out of new roads. However, some of the 'new' roads mentioned for Darnall may already have been in place but the Act gave them 'official' status. The Owlergreave Roads, for example, are mentioned as 'new roads' but as they seem an obvious route into the fields south of the village, it would seem likely that they existed before enclosure as footpaths or cart tracks. Above all else, the Commissioners had to make a scrupulously fair division of the common lands amongst the many freeholders who were entitled to claim a share, albeit their holdings were of widely disproportionate amounts. Samuel Staniforth, for example, Darnall's largest landholder with over a 100 acres, including the Darnall Hall set in nearly two acres of grounds as shown on Figure 1, was awarded eleven plots of land scattered over the four Darnall common lands amounting to nine and a half acres. At the other end of the scale, John Innocent qualified for the share of one perch of the former Darnall Green as he had land measuring 18 perches, which appears to have included a garden of 400 square yards held on a 199-year lease at the yearly rent of one pound and one shilling (£1.05).[15] However, one of the Commissioners, Josiah Fairbank, was connected with another project which may have brought the enactment of the award to a standstill. That was the construction of the Sheffield to Tinsley Canal begun in 1815, and for which Mr Fairbank had surveyed the land and drawn the plan in 1814.[16]

The canal had been a long-standing proposal, intended as the final link between Sheffield and the navigable River Don at Tinsley. However, the canal was disapproved of by successive Dukes of Norfolk, lords of the manor for much of Sheffield as well as Attercliffe, who saw the canal as a threat to their income. On the one hand, the canal would break the monopoly the Dukes had in supplying the Sheffield market with coal from their various mines and, on the other, to make alterations to the River Don would affect the water-powered industries on sites rented from the Norfolk estate. The latter objection was overcome when the canal's designer and engineer, William Chapman, proposed that water extracted from nearby coal mines, supplemented by Kirk Bridge Dike and Carr Brook, was a viable alternative. Also, by ensuring that a branch-line, the Greenland Arm, was made from the canal to the Norfolk estate coal mines on Attercliffe Common, the best advantage could be made of both the mineral rights awarded under the enclosure and of supplying coal to the Sheffield market.[17] As can be seen on Figure 1, the L-shaped Greenland Arm lay mainly in Attercliffe, but the foot just crossed the boundary into Darnall. Perhaps less evident is the reservoir constructed on the Carr Brook, half in Darnall and half in Tinsley, which lay off Main Road and just north of the *Duke of York* public house. The reservoir was also the property of the Sheffield Canal Company and appears to have been part of the Greenland Arm's supply.

The many changes to the Attercliffe and Darnall landscape, because of both the Enclosure and the canal, meant that the local administrators found new maps of the township were a necessity, especially as local taxes were property-based. In the handsome volume which was produced in 1819, the Darnall area was drawn up as five maps, two of which were comprised exclusively of fields.[18] Each field was given an identifying number as were the numerous carefully drawn properties and small plots of land within the village. The numbers can be traced in the schedule accompanying the maps and gives the names of owners, tenants, the names of fields or a description but not names, of the properties and the area of the field or property measured in acres, roods and perches. The initial information that can be extracted from the 1819 schedule is that at the time Darnall village consisted of 158 houses, seven homesteads, two schools, two public houses (not named, but from their locations these were the *Ball Inn* and the *Old Bradley Well*), a butcher's shop, a blacksmith's shop, a wheelwright's shop, a cutler's shop, eight other workshops, seven shops, two steel furnaces, besides an assortment of stables, barns, cowhouses and some piggeries. Apart from seven owner-occupied houses, all these premises were rented or leased to a named tenant, or named the principal tenant but referred to sub-tenants as '& others'. The majority of the houses occupied only a small area and are illustrated on the maps as short terraces. Very few groups of houses had only a yard, usually there were garden plots attached and other gardens of various sizes were available to rent separately. However, all these premises and gardens comprised only a small part of Darnall's landscape and it is when the principal feature of the district, the fields, are examined that some of the complexities for local farming are revealed. The outlines of Darnall's fields show little change between the 1819 maps and the 1855 O.S. map, at which time, particularly south of the village, some fields still retained the form of medieval strips. The pattern of the fields perhaps reflected the piecemeal acquisition and ownership of the land. Samuel Staniforth, for example, may have been the largest landowner locally with over a 100 acres, but the Staniforths had gradually built up their holdings over a period of nearly 200 years and the fields were unevenly distributed in the Darnall landscape. The current popular concept of a farm may be of a farmhouse, with outbuildings and adjoining fields, which may be leased by a tenant as a consolidated holding, but Darnall in 1819 had only one example to offer. This was the property of George Steer, formerly the Spencer estate, lying between the north-eastern end of the turnpike road and the reservoir and comprising 25 acres. If a farmer wished to work a similar sized area of fields as a convenient group in another part of Darnall, he may have had to lease land from as many as four different owners. On the other hand, if a farmer leased land exclusively from one owner, then the fields were most likely to be in quite different parts of the manor.

Viewed in isolation, the 1819 maps and schedule may appear to be only a 'snapshot' of the landscape and property ownership at a known date, but the information contained within them is unique. The 1819 documents provide the foundation for studies of the changes and developments within Darnall's nineteenth century landscape and may be used in conjunction with a wide range of other documents. They can be related to the decennial censuses currently available for examination from between 1841 and 1891, for example, in studies of Darnall's domestic buildings; their continuity, increase and, in some instances, deterioration. In addition, the detailed drawings of the properties on the 1819 maps makes them almost the counterpart to the 10 feet to the mile O.S. maps of 1893.[19] As might be expected with a gap of 70 years between the maps, the expansion of Darnall is the predominant feature, but closer scrutiny can reveal where certain earlier buildings had been lost or altered in the intervening period. Such a comparison also highlights that the 1855 map contains inaccuracies and distortions in its rendering of some of the properties, although it remains a convenient and useful reference map for a study of Darnall's fields. The 1819 maps and schedule are also the basis for using the Registry of Deeds at Wakefield which has an extensive source of documentary evidence relating to property. Records are found by using an uncomplicated name-based index and may contain many details, for example, the names of the people involved, their status or occupation, a description of the land or property changing hands and references to adjoining properties or landscape features. There are two other sources of information which offer an alternative perspective of Darnall's lost buildings; photographs and the memories of local people can give an appreciation of the elevation and proportion of buildings which maps and written documents lack. Many of the photographs of Darnall which have come to hand are reproduced from picture-postcards which date from an era when postcards were more widely used as a form of cheap and rapid communication, that is, from about the mid-1890s and into the early twentieth century. The subject matter was intended to appeal to a broad market and, judging by the number of such cards still extant, local scenes, including streets, appear to have been popular. Occasionally, photographic evidence has to be treated with caution as the surprising longevity of some of Darnall's domestic buildings means a greater probability that they had been substantially altered.

One group of cottages which usually had a full complement of tenants in all the censuses, suggesting that it was affordable accommodation for miners, cutlers and labourers, was **Dunkirk Square**, which stood on Main Road facing the *Old Bradley Well*. The illustration of Dunkirk Square, reproduced as Figure 3, probably dates from about 1900 to 1910, based on the clothing of the children in the foreground. This property not only survived until the 1940s, within living memory for older Darnall people who were able to confirm its identity, but it was considered very old in the mid-1840s. Judged by its appearance in the photograph, however, there is little evidence to suggest that it was other than a group of workmen's cottages, possibly of early nineteenth century origin. Its location can be found on

Figure 3. Dunkirk Square in the early twentieth century, demolished *c.* 1947. *Collection of Mr H. Clayton*

Figure 4, reproduced in simplified form from the 10 feet to the mile map of 1893, where the property is indicated as **Court 7**. Comparing the map and the photograph reveals that the full range of buildings making up Dunkirk Square is not shown in the photograph, which comprised eight cottages on the right, four facing the viewer and four cottages on the left. The map also shows that there were other buildings to the rear and a long garden extending down to the Carr Brook. Unfortunately, only the general arrangement of the property was shown on the 1855 map, although the garden was drawn in some detail. All properties on the 1855 map were reduced to simple shapes, so that the row of eight cottages of Dunkirk Square and an adjoining row, which formed part of Jones Square according to the 1851 census, were rendered as a rectangle, whilst the four cottages in Dunkirk Square facing the road were drawn as L-shaped.

A reconstruction of the same site taken from the 1819 maps and schedule (Figure 5) not only reveals that this set of buildings was not L-shaped, but that extensive alterations must have been made to Dunkirk Square before 1855. In the 1819 schedule, the property was

Figure 4. Location of Dunkirk Square, labelled as Court 7, on Main Road, simplified from the 1893 10ft/mile O.S. map. *Sheffield City Libraries, Local Studies Library*

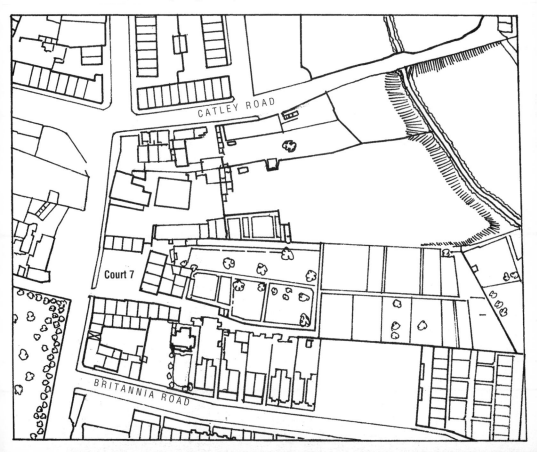

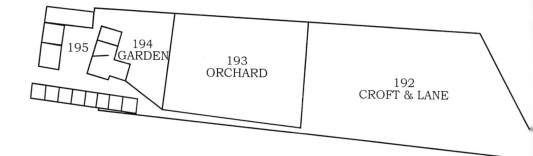

Figure 5. Reconstruction of the buildings comprising Dunkirk Square and associated land in 1819. *M.A. Turton*

described as twelve houses and a barn owned by Samuel Younge and tenanted by William Taylor and others. The whole, inclusive of the yard to the houses, the garden, orchard and the croft with its lane, measured one acre, one rood and thirty-two perches. In 1827 this property was purchased by William Hardcastle, licensee of the *Wellington Inn* at Darnall, from Samuel Younge, who was described in the deed registered at Wakefield as 'Mercer and Draper Dealer and Chapman a Bankrupt'.[20] So that there was no doubt of which property at Darnall was changing hands, the deed gave an elaborate description which both complements the 1819 schedule and maps and provides additional details:

> . . . *All that Capital Messuage Dwellinghouse or Tenement with the Outbuildings Garden and Croft adjoining and lying near and belonging thereto situate standing and being in Darnall in the Parish of Sheffield in the County of York heretofore in the possession of Elen Chaloner afterwards of Samuel Wheeler and now of William Taylor or his Undertenants also all those eleven several Dwellinghouses or Tenements adjoining and lying near to the said Capital Messuage now or late in the several tenancies or Occupations of Thomas Wilkinson Joseph Grayson Joseph Shaw Samuel Wheeler Charlotte Mirfin Hannah Fisher George Leversidge Isaac Wheeler George Staniforth and John Cheetham and three in a State of Delapidation and unoccupied all which said hereditaments including the said Buildings contain together by Survey one Acre one Rood and thirty two perches or thereabouts the same more or less and are Extended on or towards the North by land and Buildings now or late belonging to Joshua Jepson Oddy and towards the South by land and Buildings*

belonging to William Jones and towards the West by the Turnpike road leading from Worksop to Sheffield and towards the North East by Land lately sold to the Sheffield Canal Company on which a Reservoir is or was intended to be made And also three Sittings in a Pew in Attercliffe Chapel occupied with and belonging to the said Capital Messuage . . .

It would appear that some of the buildings already had the status of workmen's cottages at this period. Where the named tenants can be traced in local parish registers, their occupations are shown as pocket knife cutlers, coal miners or labourers.[21] William Taylor, the principal tenant, also appears in the 1819 schedule as the tenant of a butcher's shop which adjoined the *Old Bradley Well.* On the other hand, this unassuming group of cottages acquires a different status when described as a 'Capital Messuage', meaning a large house. With its area of attached land and 'three Sittings in a Pew in Attercliffe Chapel', this tends to suggest that it was once a property of a very different stamp. Tracing the changes of ownership through detailed examination of deeds, wills and inventories at the Wakefield Archives may reveal that this was once quite an important property in Darnall. However, the records at Wakefield, which commence in 1704, may not go back quite far enough. A small volume published in 1844 and entitled *Walks in the Neighbourhood of Sheffield,* suggested that Dunkirk Square was built before 1700.[22] At about this date, it was said to have become the home of William Walker, a detail that was still remembered in the nineteenth century, because Darnall legend would have it that he had been the executioner of Charles I. The evidence for this was probably more speculative than truthful, as the author pointed out, but he gathered his information on Dunkirk Square from William Hardcastle, who gave some interesting details of the property he had bought:

Passing through the outer door, which was strongly studded and barred with iron, an ordinary earthen floor presented itself. Upon removing this dirt, the purchaser was agreeably surprised to discover a substantial oaken boarding, resting on solid joists of the same material. Behind this building, now converted into four tenements, may be observed the orchard originally attached to the place. The old trees here, reveal a date even anterior to the time referred to. The wanderer will find the whole worth gazing at – the old and still retained name of the place, is Dunkirk, and it will be found midway in the village fronting north-east.

Whilst in Darnall Mr Hardcastle was the licensee of the *Wellington*

Inn and a small-scale farmer; in his native Handsworth he had been a mason and so the alterations to Dunkirk Square may be attributed to him.[23] The full extent of the changes can only be guessed at and there may have been considerable re-building, but perhaps there are a few hints of the original building to be found in the photograph (Figure 3). For example, the cottage at the far left of the four facing the road had a different roof-line, and such a steep pitch was usually meant to take heavy stone roof tiles, not slates. All four cottages had heavy stone lintels to their entrance doors, unlike the other two rows of cottages forming the left and right hand sides of Dunkirk Square, where brick was used. However, deciding where the outer door 'strongly studded and barred with iron' had been, is slightly problematical, as the two cottages at the left both appear to have had doorways with a substantial stone surround.

The buildings of nineteenth century Darnall spanned many periods and styles, from the seventeenth century farmhouse and the eighteenth century mansion to the contemporary cottage accommodation. Nor was the Staniforth family's Darnall Hall the only example of an early eighteenth century house, there was also the modest **Darnall Cottage**, near the *Ball Inn*, and the spacious **Darnall House**, which had become **Darnall Vicarage** by the time of the 1871 census. However, the few large houses in Darnall remained beyond the means of the majority of the local population throughout the nineteenth century, whose needs more usually were met by the affordable accommodation of the small terraced houses. The working men living in Darnall ranged from foremen, 'little mesters', skilled and semi-skilled men and labourers, and their accommodation often reflected their income. Single men appeared in all the censuses as lodgers and some Darnall households took in two or even three men as lodgers. On the other hand, it was rare to find two separate families sharing a house and, on the whole, families in Darnall seem to have preferred a house to themselves. This becomes more explicable with the 1891 census, which recorded how many houses consisted of four rooms or less, and revealed that the majority of Darnall's houses were of four rooms, with some of three and a few of two rooms. Up to and including the 1871 census, the largest single group of Darnall's workers were coal miners, whilst men employed in the cutlery and allied trades, chiefly pocket knife makers, formed a smaller but still important group. By the time of the 1871 census, there was evidence of an alternative form of employment in Darnall, at John and Alfred Craven's wagon works and timber yard. By the 1881 census, the workforce at Craven Brothers' wagon works formed a significant and recognisable group, but the employees were rarely local to Darnall, the vast majority being incomers. Another noticeably large group at this period were the iron and steel workers, who hitherto had scarcely been represented in Darnall.[24]

From comparisons of the 1819 schedule with the consecutive censuses, it becomes apparent that the need for affordable accommodation was addressed in two distinct periods. In 1819 there appears to have been a total of 167 possible homes (the 158 houses, seven homesteads and two public houses). The totals for the census years 1841–1891 are:

Census year	Occupied	Uninhabited	Building	Total of houses
1841	215	10	1	226
1851	213	7		220
1861	221	20	2	243
1871	384	79	29	492
1881	638	121	1	760
1891	858	5	7	870

Evidently, there had been an increase to the local housing stock between 1819 and 1841, but this was not necessarily the result of new building, the conversion of existing buildings to make homes also made some contribution. Mr Hardcastle, for example, not only altered part of Dunkirk Square into four tenements, by 1822 he had also made three houses adjoining the *Wellington Inn* into five houses.[25] Unfortunately, the 1819 schedule and the 1841 census for Darnall are not readily comparable, as the earliest census contains not only minimal details of the community, but the barest details of addresses. Whilst the enumerator for the south side of the turnpike road recorded a few indicators which could be used, the enumerator for the north side referred only to 'Worksop Road'. However, close examination of the 1841 and 1851 censuses revealed that it was possible to 'interpret' the 1841 records using the 1851 information. Both the 1851 and 1861 censuses contained a wealth of local detail, including the information that certain properties had specific names, Darnall Cottage and Darnall House, for example. References were also included to the small property owners or builders. Four houses near the *Wellington Inn* were specifically labelled as 'Hardcastle property' for example, and there were several instances of personal names attached to other small developments of between five and seven houses. There was, for example, **Cawthorne Row** on Main Road and **Wright's Row** and **Cheetham's Row**, both on Catcliffe Road. Cheetham's Row (Figure 6) was the property of George Cheetham, whose principal occupation was as a coal miner, but the 1819 schedule included his name as the owner of a small plot of land on Owlergreave, which may have led to his designation as a 'farmer' in the White's Directory of 1841.[26] Mr Cheetham does not appear to have been the builder of the houses but may have sold his land to pay for them, perhaps viewing the houses as a better investment and a potential source of funds in retirement. The original owner of the land and possibly the builder of the houses which stood on it, was George Handley, who had bought the plot when parts of the former Darnall Green were offered for sale to fund the Enclosure Award. All the Rows were later made anonymous by house numbers, but some may be identified in the 1891 census and on the 1893 O.S. map amongst the groups of houses labelled as 'Courts'.

A number of means may have been adopted to begin the next major phase of house building in Darnall, including the small, speculative builder, freehold land societies or building societies. The indexes at Wakefield Registry of Deeds contain references to many such societies in Sheffield, particularly for the period 1849 to 1863 when the items indexed for Sheffield occupy nearly two volumes. Darnall, too, appears to have had its share of new developments through building societies, including the Norfolk Benefit Building Society and the third and fifth Borough Benefit Building Societies. The freehold land society was a group venture, whereby funds to buy a piece of land were raised by mortgage which was transferred to elected Trustees who administered the funds on behalf of members

Figure 6. Catcliffe Road showing at far right the houses recorded as Cheetham's Row in the 1851 census, demolished *c.* 1968. *Collection of Mr H. Clayton*

of the society.[27] The earliest clue to a land society in Darnall was found in the 1861 census where six houses, which stood on Darnall Road between the Ball Inn and Darnall Cottage (Figure 7), were referred to as *Freedom Hill*. The 1871 census confirmed that these houses were part of the *Freedom Hill Land Society*, but the name was also used in the 1881 census for further houses built on a narrow strip of land behind the original six. Examination of a deed relating to the 'Attercliffe Freedom Hill Benefit Building Society', dated 1853, revealed that the six houses were already built before the society was formed.[28] In the 1819 schedule and maps the site was occupied by two houses and a barn, although the deed referred to the six houses as '. . . heretofore part of and constructed out of an ancient Barn or Laith . . .'. The bulk of the deed was concerned with setting out the main parcel of land which had consisted of a close and a small part of the former Darnall Common. The land was divided into 22 plots and included a carriage road, fifteen feet in width, and a well for use by the occupants. Under the rules of the Society, the owners of the individual plots were not to build:

> . . . *any House or other Permanent Building of Brick or Stone except according to such Elevation and in such a position on the Land and at such a height above the level of the said New Carriage Road as should be approved by the major part in number of the Trustees . . .*

The original aspirations of the *Freedom Hill Society* members may have been towards the ownership of land and a well-built house. Very few members may have achieved this as the later censuses reveal not only changes in occupancy more suggestive of rented accommodation, but the building rules had been relaxed to permit the erection of a two-roomed wooden house. By the 1891 census all the houses illustrated in Figure 7 were numbered as part of Darnall Road and the remainder of Freedom Hill had been re-designated as Basford Street.

As can be seen from the census figures, accommodation in Darnall nearly quadrupled between 1861 and 1891 and Figure 8, reproduced from the 1893 O.S. map, reveals the extent of the side-streets. The pattern of the side-streets did not entirely hide the older Darnall, however, careful comparison with the 1855 map showing that many followed the original field lines. York, Surrey and Helen Roads, for example, may be seen to have followed the curves of the old Reservoir for the Greenland Arm, but including Cravens Road, they also fill the expanse of the former Hunt Meadow. (Darnall Burial Board had few problems in buying up land from a series of

Figure 7. The terrace of six houses which originally comprised Freedom Hill with Darnall Cottage on the far right, Darnall Road, demolished *c.* 1968. *Collection of Mr H. Clayton*

owners for the cemetery – they bought Great Meadow.) Although the 1871 census revealed that many of the side-streets off Darnall Road and Main Road had been already laid out and named, some of the longer streets, such as Industry and Station Roads, took nearly two decades to reach completion. Included in the number of 'uninhabited' houses in the 1871 census were a large number of properties that had been only recently completed. The census enumerator recorded five occupied houses on Poole Road but indicated that fifteen houses were 'recently built' and a further twelve houses were 'unfinished'. In contrast, the large number of 'uninhabited' houses in the 1881 census on the whole referred to untenanted houses. The census appears to have coincided with one of the periodic trade 'slumps' that Sheffield was susceptible to throughout the nineteenth century. Albert White, one of the census enumerators, recorded his occupation as 'Clerk, out of employ'. However, what is most apparent from the 1893 map is how much room there still was within the narrow

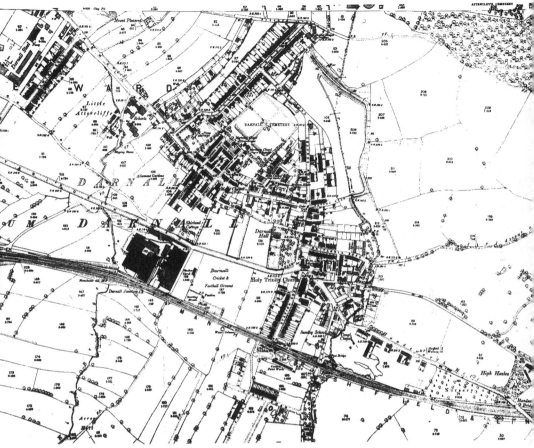

Figure 8. The extent of the side-streets and developments along Darnall Road and Main Road shown by the 1893 O.S. map. *Sheffield City Libraries, Local Studies Library*

confines of Darnall's boundaries for further housing expansion. The latter part of the twentieth century may be seen as a time of sweeping changes to Darnall's old buildings, but in the nineteenth century Darnall experienced radical changes to its ancient landscape. As the end of the millennium approaches, there is the certainty that Darnall will change again in the future.

Notes and References

1.   C.A. 15/3 (*Attercliffe cum Darnall Vestry Records*, 1819 to 1884), Sheffield Archives.

2.   D. Hey, *The Fiery Blades of Hallamshire: Sheffield and its neighbourhood, 1660–1740*, Leicester University Press, 1991.

3.   Ordnance Survey, Yorkshire 295 full sheet, County Series, 1855.

4.   *White's Sheffield District Directory*, Kelly's Directories Ltd., London, 1902.

5.   C.A. 13/1 (*A book of maps of the Township of Attercliffe cum Darnall with Numbers referring to a Survey thereof by W & J Fairbank, 1819*), Sheffield Archives.

6.   Catalogue of Sheffield Deeds, volume 3, Sheffield Archives; D. Hey (ed.), *The Oxford Companion to Local and Family History*, BCA, 1996.

7.   T.C. 293, Sheffield Archives; M. Walton, 'The Three Darnall Halls', *Transactions of the Hunter Archaeological Society*, Vol. V, Part III, March 1940, pp. 126–130. Mary Walton's article identified the site of the Spencer manor house as near Darnall Cemetery. Two maps subsequently deposited with Sheffield Archives show that in the late eighteenth century this site contained two substantial houses, but only one remained by 1819. There is also some slight confusion within the article between the two properties, Dunkirk (which is illustrated in the present article) and the house allegedly called Old Darnall Hall. The 1893 O.S. map and the 1871 census enumerator may have given credence to the name, but no other supporting evidence has been found and local memory recalls the house as Stackyard Farm.

8.   C.A. 364, Sheffield Archives – the document quoted from is a loose leaf inserted into the front of the volume.

9.   C.A. 364, Sheffield Archives; C. Paulus, *Some Forgotten Facts in the History of Sheffield and District*, Independent Press, 1907, contains a copy of the Act and an indignant interpretation of its consequences.

10.   C. Paulus, *Some Forgotten Facts . . .*

11.   T.C. 804, 805, 819, Sheffield Archives.

12.   NBC 440, Sheffield Archives.

13.   NBC 543, Sheffield Archives.

14.   C. Paulus, *Some Forgotten Facts . . .*

15.   John Innocent's lease is mentioned in Book FO, page 148, number 192, Registry of Deeds Office, Wakefield.

16.   NBC 383(10), Act of Parliament relating to Sheffield to Tinsley Canal, 1815, Sheffield Archives.

17.   *Sheffield East End History Trails, Lower Don Valley, No 1 The Sheffield & Tinsley Canal*, Sheffield City Libraries, 1987.

18.   C.A. 13/1, Sheffield Archives.

19.   Ordnance Survey, Yorkshire (West Riding) Shefield, Sheet CCXCV 5.9, 1893.

20.   Book IY, page 750, no 731, Registry of Deeds Office, Wakefield.

21.   P.R. 28/13, Attercliffe Christ Church Baptisms, 1813–1838, Sheffield Archives.

22.   John Thomas, *Walks in the Neighbourhood of Sheffield* (Second Series), Robert Leader, Sheffield, 1844.

23.   337/X2/4, Bishop's Transcripts for St Mary's Church, Handsworth, Sheffield Archives.

24.   S.E. Turton, 'Change and Continuity in Darnall between 1841 and 1881', unpublished MA thesis, University of Sheffield, 1993.

25.   Book HO, page 120, no 119, Registry of Deeds Office, Wakefield.

26.   W. White, *General and Commercial Directory of Sheffield*, Sheffield, 1841; Book PI, page 103, no 106, Registry of Deeds Office, Wakefield.

27.   V.S. Doe, 'Some Developments in Middle Class Housing in Sheffield 1830–1875' in S. Pollard and C. Holmes (eds) *Essays in the Social and Economic History of South Yorkshire*, South Yorkshire County Council, Sheffield, 1976.

28.   Book SO, page 558, no 319, Registry of Deeds Office, Wakefield.

Acknowledgements

My sincere thanks are offered to the many people who have taken a friendly interest in my Darnall studies for their help, advice and encouragement in both the research and writing of this article. I would also like to take this opportunity to acknowledge the unfailing kindness and courtesy of the staff, past and present, of Sheffield Archives and Sheffield Local Studies Library.

Advice and help has come from many sources for both the research and writing of this article and my sincere thanks is owed to many individuals.

12. PARADISE LOST? SHEFFIELD'S HISTORIC PARKS AND GARDENS

by Joan Sewell

Introduction

ONE OF THE MOST ENDURING IMAGES of Sheffield has to be its greenness and open spaces. Parks, gardens, allotments, cemeteries and green spaces weave through the fabric of the city creating an environment that is inspiring and intriguing. How did one of the most notoriously dirty towns of the last century come to be so well endowed with open space and greenery?

The diversity and variety of historic parks and gardens in Sheffield is staggering. Four sites in the city are listed on the National Register of Parks and Gardens of Special Historic Interest, compiled by English Heritage. Three are historic urban parks: Sheffield Botanical Gardens; Norfolk Park; and Weston Park. They represent some of the earliest recreational spaces in Britain. Sheffield Botanical Gardens, for instance, was open to subscribers and shareholders in 1836. Norfolk Park, was laid out by the Duke of Norfolk in the early 1840s and opened to the public in 1848.

Features, settings and styles combine to give each park and garden a unique character. The quality of Norfolk Park, with echoes of an early nineteenth century Landscape style, contrasts with the Gardenesque style of Sheffield Botanical Gardens with it broad lawns and intriguing miniature landscapes. Similarly, the historic gardens of Ranmoor, ' the finest residences in the neighbourhood – the homes of the merchant princes of Hallamshire'[1], grand in scale and elaborate in features, contrast with the small vernacular cottage gardens behind the estate cottages in Norfolk Park. All, in their way, a reflection of the city's past.[2]

A number of nationally acclaimed designers have been involved in commissions for both public and private space in Sheffield. Robert Marnock (1800–1889) was the designer and first curator of Sheffield Botanical Gardens. He was an exponent of the Gardenesque and was influential in the design of villa gardens and indeed whole neighbourhoods within the town. George Wostenholme involved Marnock in the laying out of the Kenwood district and many private commissions followed from this.[3] William Goldring (1854–1919), who towards the end of the nineteenth century was a leading figure in landscaping, was commissioned to adapt Endcliffe Woods for public use in 1885 (Figure 1). Clarence Elliott (1881–1969), nationally acclaimed horticulturalist, plant hunter and nurseryman, was involved in the creation of 'Little Quarry' at Whinfell Quarry Gardens.[4]

The association of parks and gardens with significant events and local dignitaries provides a fascinating insight into the lives and tastes of past generations of Sheffield people. The Royal opening of Firth Park on the 16 August, 1875, well documented in local newspapers, was a memorable event in the history of the town. It caught the imagination of local people and boosted civic pride.[5] During the two day visit, the Prince and Princess of Wales opened Firth Park and came in contact with three of the most prominent gardens of the time, Oakbrook, Endcliffe Hall[6] and The Farm, the latter two of which have largely disappeared.

This article arises from research done over the last three years into the historic parks and gardens of Sheffield. The original brief for Sheffield City Council was to identify the most important historic parks and gardens in the city for recording on a Local Schedule.[7] It soon became apparent, however, that the research was as much about what has already been lost as about what remained. Lurking behind this apparently green facade is a story of neglect and vandalism, one that should both disturb and motivate all concerned with the future

Figure 1. Endcliffe Woods in the early 1900s. *Ian Mitchell's postcard collection*

of the city's heritage.

The development of the City's historic parks and gardens

Three main factors have influenced the development, pattern and rate of growth of the city's historic parks and gardens. They are: geographical factors; the economic and cultural progress of the city; and the effect of Government legislation through time. Sheffield lies at the meeting point of the northern and western uplands and the eastern lowlands. This creates dramatic topographical contrasts which have influenced the character and growth of the city. Huge waves of landscape present a contrast of elevated heights, important in the siting of the elegant Victorian villa gardens, and sheltered valleys suitable for industry.

The free availability of rich geological resources in close proximity was guaranteed to produce industrial growth. In medieval times, for instance, charcoal was used to exploit the exposed coal measures containing iron ores. The availability of fine quality clays for refractory linings assisted the development of Benjamin Huntsman's crucible steel manufacture during the 1740s. Various grades of sandstone outcrops were available to add an edge to the finished blade in the cutlery industry. Streams such as the Porter, Rivelin, Loxley, Sheaf and Don presented the potential for water power and the impetus for early industrial development.

The types of goods produced were strongly influenced by the geographical isolation of the town. These had to be easily transportable and of high quality. The manufacturing centre of Sheffield was becoming distinct from the agricultural hinterland by the mid-eighteenth century and with the creation of the first turnpike in 1756 – the Sheffield-Chesterfield-Derby turnpike – a more reliable means of transporting goods was available. Improvements brought about by the use of coke instead of charcoal for reheating blister steel in crucibles, resulted in higher quality steel than had previously been possible. The installation of the first steam engines by 1782 provided a powerful impetus to the growing steel industry. The development of the town gained momentum.

Towards the end of the eighteenth century, the town was still compact extending from Park Hill in the south-east to Netherthorpe in the north-west. The rest of the parish was a patchwork of fields and woodland. At the meeting of roads small clusters of buildings formed the early nuclei of villages such as Nether Green, Ranmoor and Grimesthorpe. Within that matrix were larger houses or halls such as Whiteley Wood Hall and Fulwood Hall.[8]

By the beginning of the nineteenth century, the industrial scene in the town was expanding rapidly. In 1819, the building of the Sheffield and Tinsley Canal, completing the canal system into the town, and the opening of the Sheffield to Rotherham railway in 1838, both had a major influence on the siting of heavy industry. The lower Don valley became the new centre of gravity for the steel industry. Huge steel works were created concentrating all the processes involved on one site, where both owners and workers lived. Names such as Cyclops and Globe Works give an impression of the sheer scale of such ventures.

By this time living conditions for both employer and employee were becoming unbearable. Back-to-back houses, with their high density and poor amenities, provided unhealthy living conditions. The urgent need for open spaces was becoming a national and local issue. This was highlighted in the Report of the Select Committee on Public Walks, produced in 1833. It stressed the need for open space for recreation and the lack of appropriate recreation for the working classes in the major towns in England. Access to open spaces was worst in the largest and most rapidly expanding centres of population. By the 1830s there was a middle class perception that contact between the classes in parks would promote pride and competition, where cleanliness, neatness and appearance would be important, and would improve the lower classes. Rational recreation, as it was called, would provide a more suitable alternative to the other forms of recreation associated with public houses! John Silk Buckingham, for example, then MP for Sheffield, was particularly proactive for three years in succession in pushing through bills to establish walks and playgrounds. The Select Committee on Public Walks recommended changing the law concerning the bequest of land. This had a far-reaching impact at a local and national level.[9]

Sheffield Botanical and Horticultural Society was formed in June 1833 with the intention of creating a botanical garden to promote healthy recreation and self education. Robert Marnock won a competition for the design of the gardens which were laid out in Gardenesque style. This involved the creation of small scale landscapes to promote beauty, animation, variety and mystery. Expanses of grass, curvilinear paths with seating and shelters and the careful planting of trees to simulate parkland typified the style. Sheffield Botanical Gardens was opened in 1836, with admission limited to shareholders and annual subscribers except on four Gala days when the general public could gain admission.[10]

Between 1841 and 1848, the 12th Duke of Norfolk laid out

Norfolk Park on the last vestige of Sheffield Deer Park. The Earls of Arundel, now the Dukes of Norfolk, inherited Sheffield Manor and Park through marriage. By the early eighteenth century, much of the woodland had been cut down and the land divided into farms. It was on that template that Norfolk Park was developed. It was simple in design with open spaces for cricket and football and a wide peripheral walk with regularly placed seats (Figure 2). This philanthropic gesture provided much needed relief from the pressure of urban life and work, and made the surrounding land more desirable for development. Norfolk Park is significant as one of the first parks to be opened to the public in Britain by a public benefactor, six years before Birkenhead Park.[11]

At this time, many of the steel magnates, the foundry owners and other employers, decided to move to the west of the town, to fresh air and spectacular views. On the crests of hills and on south facing slopes, a pattern of villas in often elaborate gardens was superimposed onto the existing template of small villages. These villa gardens were influenced by the style of the newly completed Sheffield Botanical Gardens. They also incorporated features using materials, such as crucible pots, recycled from industry. Local nurseries, such as Fisher Son and Sibray at Handsworth, supplied plants locally and regionally to furnish such gardens.

In 1860 the Public Improvements Act gave local authorities the power to levy rates to pay for maintenance of open spaces. This was

Figure 2. An early view of Norfolk Park. *Sheffield Local Studies Library*

in contrast to what had previously happened when local authorities struggled to maintain their affairs with the help of aristocratic public benefactors and private charity. The Public Health Act of 1875 gave local authorities further powers to acquire and maintain land for recreation with the possibility of government loans. This break-through had an impact at national level with an unprecedented increase in the number of parks and a great upsurge in civic pride. At a local level, 1875 marked a second phase in the development of the network of parks in the city.

The Victorian municipal parks including Firth (opened 1875), Weston (opened 1875), Endcliffe Woods (opened 1885), High Hazels (opened 1895), Meersbrook (opened 1890) and Hillsborough (opened 1892) formed a 'green necklace' around the town and provided much needed breathing space in the sometimes appalling living conditions at that time.

The problem of access to recreational space remained a problem in the densest parts of towns. At a national level, the creation of small recreation grounds and the transformation of disused burial grounds was intended to solve this situation. The Town Planning Act of 1909 meant that local authorities could make effective plans for the future. In Sheffield this marked the beginning of a further expansion of the network of open spaces. The completion of the electric tram system in 1903, with its low fares, promoted a greater degree of mobility than had hitherto been possible.

From the end of the nineteenth into the early twentieth century, the city continued to expand rapidly. The new parks both attracted development and halted the loss of open space. Parks such as Abbeyfield and High Hazels provided valuable breathing space in the densest housing areas. Also in the early twentieth century, elaborate gardens were created to house collections of unusual plants such as at Whirlow Brook and Whinfell Quarry Gardens.

The Beautiful Sheffield League was formed in 1910, composed of architects, artists, amateur gardeners, ministers, professors, teachers and 'others interested in cultivating the love of the beautiful'. The League wanted to transform the city. Its objectives were:

1. to cultivate among the young and old a spirit of pride in their city and a desire to make it beautiful;

2. to preserve natural beauty in and around the city;

3. to encourage the planting and preservation of trees, shrubs, etc;

4. to promote the acquisition of parks, open spaces, and playgrounds;

5. to advocate artistic town planning;

6. to encourage the erection of beautiful buildings, and secure the preservation of buildings of artistic or historic value;

7. to support all efforts for preventing the pollution of the air of Sheffield, and the streams and rivers of the neighbourhood.[12]

The annual report of 1914, refers to the League's connections with schools and to the many advances made towards 'beautifying' the city. In particular, it noted houses being built with more generous gardens and the continuing demand for allotments.

In the early 1920s, Patrick Abercrombie prepared a plan for Sheffield encompassing all aspects of the city's future needs including housing, transport and open space. In his proposals Abercrombie promoted the Council's commitment to a substantial open space network. The fruits of this can be enjoyed today by following the Porter Valley Parks, a green corridor of naturalistic parks that mingle loosely in and out of the urban fabric, drawing nature into the city in one direction and inviting exploration of the wilds beyond the city in the other.

Throughout the first half of the century, parks were often acquired with the help of public benefactors. For example, Millhouses Park was laid out and designed by Sheffield City Council in 1909, with part given as a gift by Earl Fitzwilliam and the Marquis of Zetland. Graves Park was presented as a gift to the city by Alderman J.G.

Figure 3. Views of Graves Park. *Ian Mitchell's postcard collection*

Graves in phases between 1925 and 1935 (Figure 3). More recently the gardens of Whinfell were presented to the city in 1968 by James Neill Holdings Ltd., in memory of Sir Frederick Neill, the first High Sheriff of Hallamshire, who had lived at Whinfell since 1933.

The decline of the steel industry, the destruction caused by the Second World War and a major cultural shift in outlook prompted the demise of much of the city's heritage. In looking to the future, the city swept the past away, leaving behind Victorian values and fabric. That change in attitude is well documented in the loss of historic features and the gradual erosion of garden layouts and boundaries. In particular, the often extensive grounds of Victorian villas and public parks presented a difficult maintenance burden for both the private and public sector.

In the vignettes of various historic parks and gardens that follow, reference will be made to this loss of character. In the city's parks, this has involved the removal and degradation of features, facilities, entertainments and activities. This in turn has produced a shift in public perception. The demise of entire historic gardens, features and settings has been taking place on an unprecedented scale. Such large houses in extensive and elaborate grounds have presented prime locations for offices with car parks and low maintenance levels or for inappropriate housing developments.

The demise of Sheffield's historic parks

The degradation of Sheffield's historic parks has become a cause for concern in recent years. All the parks have suffered. Changes in mobility and the use of leisure time mean many people will drive into the Peak District rather than support the local park. In the past the presence of a park warden often prevented anti-social behaviour and vandalism. It is now no longer financially viable to provide such supervision. The changing financial fortunes of the local authority is reflected in reduced maintenance levels in all parks and the decay and vandalism of features. Primarily, many of the historic parks were created and intended for another generation and a different outlook, as reflected in this description of **Firth Park** early this century:

> *A rough calculation gave the number of visitors on Good Friday as 30,000 and somewhat on a par were the assemblies of Easter and Whit Mondays. On fine afternoons that are not general holidays Brightside, Attercliffe, and Pitsmoor folk flock to it by hundreds; Ecclesfield, Shiregreen, and Thorpe send occasional contingents; and sometimes wagonettes ply thither from Chapeltown.*[13]

The following brief studies highlight three aspects of loss in historic parks: the loss of features; the fading out of music in the parks; and the decline of horticultural excellence, once one of Sheffield's proud boasts.

Loss of features

Weston Park, the 'jewel in the crown' of the city's Victorian parks, epitomises the demise of the city's historic parks. Sheffield Corporation purchased Weston Hall and its grounds from the Harrison Trust in 1873 to create the first municipal park in the town (Figure 4). Robert Marnock advised on the layout. He converted an existing lake into a focal feature giving it a sinuous edge, perimeter path, two bridges and occasional seats. The main tree lined walk led through the park to the southern end of the lake and used to continue along the southern bank to the original entrance on Winter Street. The lake proved popular:

> *A favourite place is the People's Garden, where, in the bright summer days, the children most do congregate to watch the swans disport themselves in the cool water – . . . very grateful to the eye of the town toiler who has just left the dusty highway or the stony street . . . There is no part of Weston Park more appreciated than the Lake . . .* [14]

In the 1950s the Corporation agreed to the demolition of the Winter Street entrance (which had gates similar to those recently stolen), together with its lodge and outbuilding, to allow for the construction

Figure 4. Bridge over Weston Park Lake, *c.* 1904. *Ian Mitchell's postcard collection*

of the University library. The lake is now a shadow of its former self, having lost its perimeter walk and original bridges, and is often in need of maintenance.

When William Goldring modified **Endcliffe Woods** for public use, a well loved amenity was conceived, popular with all ages. Along a short stretch of the Porter a magical landscape was created with bandstand, stepping stones, winding paths and a small bathing pool fed from the stream (Figure 5). The OS map of 1920 shows the location of the pool. An entry in the Annual Surveyor's report of 1905 comments on the poor condition of the pool, a regular source of complaint. The water was often emptied during the winter and mud cleared out. This pool has now gone completely.

It was not just water features that were to disappear, but also miniature landscapes. In **Meersbrook Park** one of the early features was a broad promenade walk called 'The Avenue', typical of Victorian parks where people could stroll in their Sunday best (Figure 6). This was situated above the Hall, then the Ruskin Museum, and afforded good views across the town. 'The Rosary' was a small ornamental rose garden that could be viewed from the elevated position of the Avenue drawing the eye to distant views and landmarks such as Sharrow Church.[15] A path led from here down into an intimate rockery and cascade walk, known as 'The Glen'. The Avenue remains but the other features have virtually disappeared.

Figure 5.   Endcliffe Woods Bathing Pool. *Ian Mitchell's postcard collection*

Figure 6. The Avenue, Meersbrook Park, *c.* 1906. *Ian Mitchell's postcard collection*

There are many other examples too numerous to detail, for example: the disappearance of **Weston Park** gates; the loss of the lake at **Firth Park**; the degradation of the Westran fountain at **Meersbrook Park**; the infilling of **High Hazels Park** lake; the decline of water facilities at **Millhouses Park**; the demise of the 'Paxton' pavilions in **Sheffield Botanical Gardens**; the dereliction of **Whinfell Quarry Gardens**.

Music in the Parks

The last remaining Victorian bandstand in the city stands in **Weston Park**. Decaying and boarded up against vandalism, it symbolises the way the soul has gone from many of the historic parks. By 1901 permanent bandstands had been constructed in **Weston, Firth, Hillsborough** and **Meersbrook Parks**, and **Endcliffe Woods** and these supported seasons of 'Special Band Performances'.[16] Evening concerts were popular and arrangements were made to illuminate the bandstands for such events, as in 1913:

A special feature in connection with Music in the Parks has been the illumination of the exterior of the Bandstands at Weston Park and Endcliffe Woods.

About 700 8-candle power lamps are fixed to the roof, eaves, and sides of each of the Bandstands and also 9 50-candle power lamps in the interiors of Endcliffe, Firth, Hillsborough, Meersbrook and High Hazels Park bandstands.[17]

The money for this, a sum of £400, was given to the Bands Sub-Committee by the Tramways Committee, confirming the relationship between the expansion of the tram network and the success of the parks. To complete the magical scene, in **Endcliffe** and **Weston Parks**, the Tramways Committee voted that a further £300 be given to install Fairy Illuminations in the trees!

Music had established itself as a popular pastime by the turn of the century and the Music in the Parks seasons (Figure 7) supported a wider interest in the town in all things musical and ensured good attendances to the parks generally. The well established and popular programmes of brass and military band concerts became a tradition in the parks. Thus, in 1940, when the Government urged local authorities to provide entertainment and recreation for workers, encouraging them to take holidays at home, Sheffield was more than prepared. Already the 1941 programme was well advanced with plans for some 80 events. Bands were central to the programme but other events included cricket weeks, galas, fairs, open air dancing and variety shows (Figure 8). Sheffield was outstanding nationally in the scale and popularity of its programme and there is no doubt that during the 'Holiday at Home' seasons the relationship between the city's parks and local people was at its height.[18]

Another sphere of town life 'sang the soul' into many of the parks. Whit Sings were popular events in the town calendar. In **Meersbrook Park** long processions from all the local chapels made their way along roads lined with large numbers of people, to reach special enclosures roped off in the lower part of the park. At **Hillsborough Park** on Whit Monday, all the local churches and choirs would join together to form a mass choir.

1957 marked the last season of band engagements at **Hillsborough Park**, with only the Sheffield Transport Band and Hallamshire Battalion York and Lancaster Regiment giving performances that year. In March 1958, the City Council approved the parks committee's resolution to demolish the bandstands in **Meersbrook, Hillsborough** and **Endcliffe Parks**. It was the end of an era.

(SHEFFIELD DISTRICT CENTRE.)

HYMNS & TUNES

For WHITSUNTIDE.

CONDUCTORS :

Endcliffe Park - Mr. H. CHISHOLM JACKSON, F.T.S.C.

Bole Hills - - - Mr. H. P. BRUFTON.

Figure 7. Programmes for 'Music in the Parks' and Whit Sings. *Sheffield Local Studies Library*

PRICE ONE PENNY.

Programme ...of... Music in the Parks

SEASON 1908.

ESTON PARK, WEDNESDAY, JULY 26, BAND OF H.M. SCOTS GUARDS, 3 to 5 and 7-15 to 9-15 STWICK,

CITY OF SHEFFIELD.

Music in the Parks & Open Spaces,

SEASON 1911.

GRAND SPECIAL BAND PERFORMANCE

BY KIND PERMISSION OF LT.-COLONEL ENDERBY AND OFFICERS, BY THE BAND OF THE

2nd Battalion Northumberland (the Fifth) Fusiliers,

Bandmaster, Mr. W. F. COOPER.

MEERSBROOK PARK, THURSDAY, July 20th, 7-15 to 9-15 p.m.

Figure 8. Theatrical production at Graves Open Air Theatre, Holidays at Home Season, 1944. *Sheffield Local Studies Library*

Horticultural decline

What has happened to the Festival of Britain Conservatory in **Weston Park** in recent years, symbolises the decline in horticultural stewardship. When first built, displays of seasonal plants were presented in the conservatory, with house plants and educational exhibits. Individual specialist societies were encouraged to display. There was also an elegant ornamental pond with goldfish. Now the beautiful timber and glass conservatory set in its formal garden, once so popular as a lunchtime venue, is sadly neglected. A Eucalyptus is growing through its roof.

Vivid annual displays of bedding plants, ever popular with the public, continue to enhance the Victorian character of many parks. The tradition for this started in the mid-1860s when the use of bedding plants were considered ideal for polluted conditions. Plants could be placed out for one season securing horticultural interest and providing a visual display for the poor. Today, concern must focus on the mature banks of trees and shrubs inherited from Victorian times. In many parks these need attention not just for aesthetics but to improve a sense of personal security, currently a big issue with many park users.

However, the manpower needed for this is currently beyond the scope of the Council's spending power. Again, taking Weston Park as an example, before 1910 there were nine gardeners working in the park (Figure 9). By the 1960s this number had dropped to six and by the mid-1990s the equivalent of one and a half gardeners carry out occasional maintenance. The vicious spiral of lack of maintenance and absence of security is at the core of many of the historic parks' problems.

Historic Gardens under Threat

A full study of the city's historic gardens, their development and details is beyond the scope of this article. The following examples illustrate some typical features and highlight the main threats: changing ownership; lack of resources; lack of awareness of value; and

Figure 9.   The gardeners at Weston Park, 1910. *Sheffield Local Studies Library*

pressure for development.

An early pleasure ground

Pleasure grounds were one of the earliest forms of recreational space. Patrons came from a wide cross-section of the community and paid an entry fee. This was in contrast to, for example, botanical gardens, often open to subscribers only. Often communal ventures, they would be open at night and offered elaborate entertainment to their clientele. There were a few of such places in Sheffield before 1850.

Although written documentary evidence is scant, the 1850 OS map of Sheffield (Figure 10) shows that there was a pleasure ground to the west of the junction between Sandygate Road and Coldwell Lane, in the Sandygate district of town. This was surrounded by a patchwork of fields with the occasional small hamlet such as Hallam Head or individual properties such as Carsick Hall. The Sandygate pleasure ground was elaborate in layout with two levels of castellated terraces, known as 'The Roundabout'.[19] These acted as viewing plat-

Figure 10.   1850 OS map showing Sandygate Pleasure Grounds.

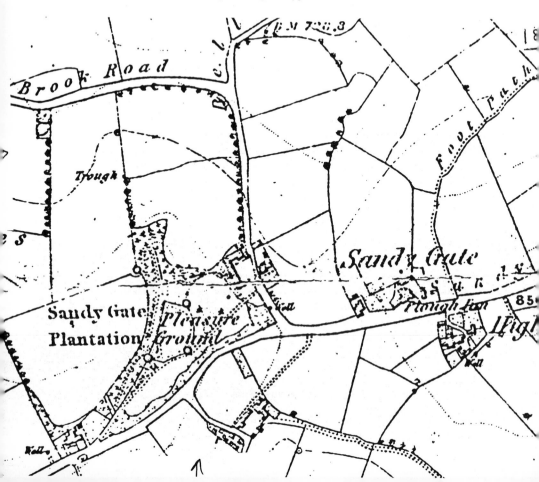

forms over the distant landscape. Sandygate Plantation formed the western boundary of the grounds and offered natural glens and woodland walks. A small natural cavern or grotto, dated 1812, may also have formed part of the attractions. It is said that one George Woollen laid out the grounds in the early part of the last century. A George Woollen is referred to in White's Directory as a miller and dealer in flour with connections to Rivelin Mill, which is easily accessible from the pleasure grounds.

In 1896 'The Towers' was built, a residence in the Scottish Baronial style designed by Flockton and Gibbs for Christopher David Leng, editor of the *Weekly Telegraph*. The house was built on the northern part of the grounds on the edge of the castellated walls of the 'Roundabout' (Figure 11), very much echoing the style of the grounds. The pleasure ground became the garden for the house, with, henceforth, no public access. In 1905 the house was enlarged westwards, a U shaped stable block was added to the north of the house and a lodge was built at the Sandygate Road entrance. The driveway was modified allowing unimpeded views towards the house and its unique setting.

Leng influenced many buildings in the area including the establishment of a model dairy next to Sandygate Farm and the transformation of a derelict quarry into a huge rock garden and pool on the opposite side of Sandygate Road.

In 1921 Christopher Leng died and the estate was sold off. Unfortunately, four houses were built on parts of the original pleasure grounds, on the lower terrace of the Roundabout. After a succession of owners, the property was empty by 1990. The present owners, in occupation since 1993, are committed to restoring the gardens. Although half of the original pleasure grounds has been lost to development, many original features remain including castellated walls, stone turrets, grotto and mature vegetation.

Queen's Tower

Samuel Roberts (1763–1848) built Queen's Tower, in the Norfolk Park district, between 1834 and 1837 in a commanding position with magnificent views over Sheffield and beyond. The intention was to create a romantic setting for the house, situated as it was in beautiful countryside

Figure 11. Sandygate Towers. *British Architect, 19 July, 1895*

surrounded by fields and woodland. Inspired by the Manor Lodge, he commissioned the firm of architects, Woodhead and Hirst of Doncaster, to design a house in romantic (florid) Gothic style, and named it after Mary Queen of Scots. He was a great admirer of Mary and wanted very much to create a house that would reflect her life and times. Castellated turrets, a gateway and portcullis were duly added to the building.

The grounds of Queen's Tower, 'which are extensive and beautiful'[20] were designed by Robert Marnock. The 1851 OS map (Figure 12) gives an impression of the grounds with terraces and lawns, a small lake and sinuous pathways. At the bottom of the garden was a portion of the Manor ruins, rescued as the Manor fell into dereliction. A portion of the old wall and mullioned window through which Mary was supposed to have looked were moved from the Manor and incorporated into the garden. The following tribute was carved on a small marble stone:

> *Alone, here oft may Scotia's beautious Queen*
> *Through tears, have gazed upon the lovely scene;*
> *Victim of villany, of woman's hate,*
> *Of fiery zeal, of wiles and storms of state;*
> *Torn from her throne, her country and her child,*
> *And cast an exiled monarch on this wild,*
> *She here was taught, what youthful beauty ne'er,*
> *While seated on a throne had deigned to hear;*

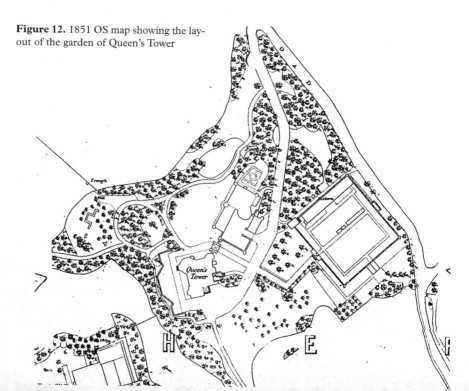

Figure 12. 1851 OS map showing the layout of the garden of Queen's Tower

> *To say, submissive at the closing scene,*
> *''Tis well that I have thus afflicted been;'*
> *Then calmly on the block, in faith, resign*
> *Three heart-corrupting crowns for one divine-*
> *Reader, the ways of God are not like thine.*[21]

To the east of the house was also a large walled garden which originally incorporated glasshouses. The grounds of Queen's Tower were extensive and impressive for its time (Figure 13).

By 1958 concern was expressed that the Manor ruins were overgrown. The house was offered by the Duke of Norfolk for Basque Refugees in 1939 but it was subsequently used by the Army during the Second World War after which it fell into disrepair. In the 1950s the property was purchased by a Sport and Leisure Group who promptly roofed over the entire area of the walled garden to form a squash court. In recent years plans to develop a hotel, casino, disco and restaurant on the site have met with opposition. Although the extent of the garden is unchanged, virtually all the features are overgrown or lost. The Manor ruins appear to have been buried and there are few signs of other original features.

Lynwood

Two gardens have been in the news recently in connection with pub developments. Both caused public outcry – Lynwood House (formerly Broom Bank) on Clarkehouse Road and Ecclesall Library or Weetwood House on Ecclesall Road. Both have been taken over either in part or whole by Tom Cobleigh PLC, of 'Unspoilt pubs for Nice People' fame. Weetwood formerly 'The Knowle', had beautiful grounds, evidence of which can still be seen in the elegant layout of the front garden. The kitchen garden, however, has been the main casualty. It proved an ideal location for the pub car park. (Kitchen gardens, and walled gardens in particular, are nationally under much pressure for development.) In the case of Weetwood the grounds remain largely intact. Lynwood was not so lucky.

Early maps indicate that Broom Bank was one of the largest and earliest gardens of its type to be established in the town. This is confirmed by its appearance on a map of 1832. The house was almost

Figure 13. Queen's Tower *c.* 1850. *Sheffield Local Studies Library*

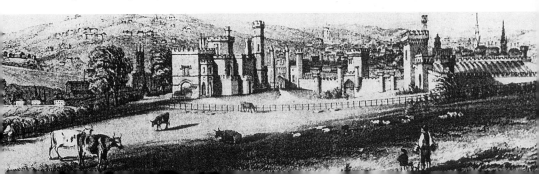

certainly built for a *nouveau riche* industrialist. From White's Directory of 1841–1865 a 'John Webster Esquire, Gentleman', occupied the house. Broom Bank and the neighbouring garden at number 5 were created following the original field boundaries of 1795, with the addition of high walls.

By 1851, roads had been laid out in the Broomhall Park area and a number of large residences built. This is detailed on the 1851 OS map which shows spacious gardens around early houses in Broomhall Park and those off Glossop Road. Many of the gardens were built with walkways, ponds and tree planting, particularly around the boundaries. Land was cheap during this period and there was the labour to maintain it.

The accent at Broom Bank appears to have been informality and spaciousness with a large sweeping lawn below the house. There was a woodland along the southern boundary of the garden (see Figure 14). This woodland contained a small stream following Broom Spring Vale.

Between 1851 and 1905 about one third of Broom Bank garden was sold for new houses along Clarkehouse Road and Antrim Avenue. The owner by this time was a brewer, Mr H. Simpson of T. Rawson & Co. By this time a new feature had appeared at the bottom of garden, a crozzle wall and grotto, in the existing wooded ravine, probably to screen off the new houses on Park Crescent.

Figure 14.   1889 OS map showing the layout of the garden of Broom Bank.

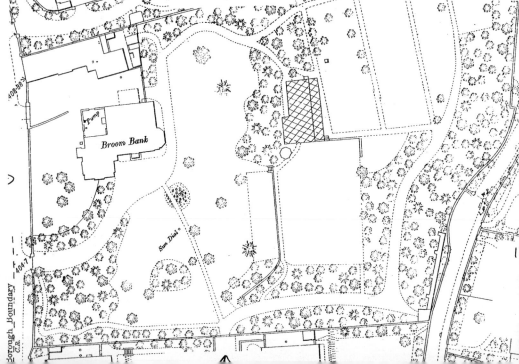

Crozzle is an indestructible material made at high temperature by baking the grit and oil from grinding wheels. Also added to the garden by this time were grassed terraces connecting to the wooded ravine, extensive kitchen gardens and a large glass house.

In 1905, Broom Bank was taken over by Sheffield City Education Committee as a boarding house for King Edward VII Grammar School and renamed Lynwood. Tom Cobleigh have recently developed the house as a pub and taken over a large part of the grounds for unsympathetic parking and childrens' play areas. The property frontage to Clarkehouse Road has been much altered. Lynwood has been renamed Aunt Sally's! This example of loss of character is deplorable and could have been avoided by city planners.

Despite attempts by Council workmen after winter gales in 1993 to demolish it, the crozzle wall with its grotto remains, though in a derelict state. They stand as a monument to the need to conserve all things historic in Sheffield in general, and its gardens in particular.

The nursery of Fisher Son & Sibray

By the beginning of the nineteenth century, the firm of Fisher Son & Sibray had established a large nursery on 150 acres at the west end of Handsworth village, growing fruit, shrubs and forest trees, with extensive glass houses. By October, 1886, this had expanded to over 200 acres. Parts of the nursery were used to display various plants. For example, hollies were a speciality and 70 varieties were planted in an avenue of single specimens. *Ilex aquifolium* 'Handsworthensis' was one of many varieties to be developed by the nursery. A Rhododendron avenue and a golden yew avenue planted in the 1830s were equally impressive. By all accounts, the nursery was quite something and could supply both the indoor and outdoor requirements of their clientele, often the *nouveaux riches* of the town.

The nursery, no longer in existence, obviously served a wide hinterland with records of deliveries appearing in the accounts of Thornbridge Hall, Derbyshire. Plants from the nursery found their way into most of the villa gardens in Sheffield in the form of holly, yew, Aucuba, laurels and ivies, all of which adapted well to the polluted conditions, and it is interesting to see this collection as a living chronicle of the tastes of the times.

Paradise Regained

If this article raises awareness of the significance of the city's historic parks and gardens and their current demise then it will have served its purpose. It is always the case that things taken for granted are missed once they have gone. In many of the examples described above, features have been lost which can never be regained. Despite the losses, much remains to be conserved.

In recent years the City Council has shown a commitment to recognising and protecting the city's historic parks. Policy BE21 in the Unitary Development Plan (Deposit Copy) states:

> *The character, setting and appearance of Historic Park and Gardens will be protected.*

The research already done will inform planning decisions and provide guidelines for conservation. Sheffield Leisure Services have also commissioned a series of studies into park regeneration and heritage strategies. With various new sources of funding becoming available, there may be hope for the future of the inheritance.

There has historically been a strong tradition of caring for all things green in Sheffield. Combine this with an outlook that is both resourceful and determined and it is no surprise to discover that for some time various volunteer groups throughout the city have been acting as stewards of the city's parks and gardens. Every credit must be given for this. Such groups have in many cases halted the process of decay. Public awareness of the importance of historic landscapes has also improved and many individuals now have commitment to conserve valuable historic features.

Traditionally, Garden History Societies have been volunteer 'watchdogs' for historic sites. They pioneer research and establish links with community groups, local businesses and local authorities. A Yorkshire Gardens Trust has been formed and this association of experts, interested parties and laypeople will contribute much to the debate regarding the future of such landscapes. Education will be one of the key issues tackled. The next generation must be able to make informed decisions about the future of the city's past.[22]

Notes and References

Abbreviation: SLSL – Sheffield Local Studies Library.
1.   *Visit of Their Highnesses The Prince and Princess of Wales to Sheffield, August 16th and August 17th, 1875,* a large leather bound volume with descriptions of some of the prominent gardens of the time, SLSL.
2.   For a full description of 20 heritage sites in Sheffield see Joan Sewell, *A Strategy for the Heritage Parks & Green Spaces in Sheffield,* September 1996, SLSL.
3.   See Nether Edge Neighbourhood Group, *They Lived in Sharrow and Nether Edge,* SLSL.
4.   See Saskia Holtkott, Whinfell Quarry Garden & Limb Valley Management Plan,

unpublished thesis, Department of Landscape, University of Sheffield.

5. A full description of the opening of Firth Park is in *Visit of Their Highnesses The Prince and Princess of Wales to Sheffield, August 16th and August 17th, 1875*, SLSL.

6. See D. Hindmarch & A. Podmore, *Endlciffe Hall*, for a description of the formal Italian gardens that were once there, SLSL.

7. Consult Sheffield City Council, *UDP Policy Background Paper No. 4, Historic Parks & Gardens in Sheffield*, March 1993, SLSL.

8. 'A Map of the Parish of Sheffield in the County of York', Wm Fairbank & Son, published 1796, SLSL.

9. Hazel Conway, *People's Parks*, 1991, Cambridge University Press.

10. Jon Carder, *The Sheffield Botanical Gardens*, 1986, Sheffield City Council.

11. Report by Michael Ellison to the Duke of Norfolk, 22 October, 1855, Sheffield Archives.

12. Leaflet regarding the Beautiful Sheffield League, 1910, SLSL.

13. *Newspaper Cuttings relating to Sheffield, Volume 48*, p. 130, article on Firth Park, one of series by Antaeus, 'Round the Sheffield Parks', SLSL.

14. *Sheffield Illustrated, 1885*, Volume 2, p. 50, SLSL.

15. See *Sheffield & Rotherham Independent*, 13 August , 1887, article and sketch of the 'Rosary', SLSL.

16. *City of Sheffield Annual Report of the City Engineer and Surveyor for the year ended 1901*, SLSL.

17. *City of Sheffield Annual Report of the City Engineer and Surveyor for the year ended 1913*, p. 9, SLSL.

18. *Holidays at Home*, leaflet produced by Sheffield Libraries and Information Services, SLSL.

19. J. H. Stainton, *The Making of Sheffield, 1865–1914*, 1924, SLSL.

20. *Sheffield Illustrated*, Volume 2, SLSL.

21. *Transactions of the Hunter Archaeological Society*, Volume 6, pp. 81–82.

22. For a general bibliography consulted for this research see Joan Sewell, *A Strategy for the Heritage Parks & Green Spaces of Sheffield*, pp. 195–202.

Acknowledgements

I would like to thank all the research assistants who have made this work possible, particularly Janet Hannary; the staff at Sheffield Local Studies Library for their attention and patience; John Stead for information regarding Lynwood; and Ian Mitchell, Sheffield Leisure Services, for the use of his postcard collection.

13. ENDCLIFFE HALL: THE RESIDENCE OF A GENTLEMAN INDUSTRIALIST

by *Julie Goddard*

BY USING THE FURNISHING OF ENDCLIFFE HALL as an example, this article will attempt to describe the nature of Sheffield taste and its origins in respect of domestic furniture during the mid-nineteenth century.

The building of Endcliffe Hall (Figure 1) between 1863–1865 for the industrialist Sir John Brown provided a rare opportunity for the Sheffield furniture industry to both exercise and advertise its skills. It was claimed £100,000 was spent on the building and a further £60,000 on the furnishings. Such was the rarity of public, private or corporate building on this scale in Sheffield that upon completion Sir John opened the Hall to the public for three days, attracting huge crowds and lengthy eulogies in the local press.

Born in 1816, the son of a Fargate slater, John Brown was educated at Mr Robert Thompson's school in Portobello where he met Mary Schofield, daughter of a local auctioneer, whom he later married. After finishing his education at Mr Wilkinson's school in Broomhall Park and rejecting his father's wishes to become a linen

Figure 1. Endcliffe Hall and Conservatory from the Italianate Gardens. *Sheffield City Libraries, Local Studies Department*

draper, Brown became apprenticed to Earl, Horton & Co. where he accepted a partnership with the aid of a £500 loan. In 1844, he started his own steel manufacturing business in Orchard Street gaining considerable success with his invention of conical steel spring buffers for railway carriages. In 1856 he entered the arms race, manufacturing armour plate from Bessemer steel at his new Atlas Works. Wealth and recognition followed. In 1862 he entertained the Prime Minister, Lord Palmerston, at his home, Shirle Hill, and in 1863 held a reception there for the Lords of the Admiralty and 'all the neighbouring nobility' after an inspection of the rolling of armour plate at his works.[1] In local affairs, he held numerous posts including Mayor, Master Cutler, Deputy Lieutenant of the West Riding of Yorkshire, J. P., Council Member of the Sheffield School of Art, Chairman of the Sheffield School Board and Town Trustee.

Shirle Hill was a spacious home, 'fitted up with every convenience, and decorated at great cost for the owner's occupation and comfort'. It had seven bedrooms, a conservatory, 'pleasure grounds tastefully laid out and containing the choicest Shrubs and Evergreens', stabling, a vinery, peach house, pine pits, potting houses and large amount of land.[2] In the turbulence of the mid-nineteenth century, *nouveaux riches* industrialists had begun to oust the aristocracy from their positions of power and emulate their way of life. Neighbouring businessmen, such as Crossley, Salt and Lister were building new homes incorporating the latest fashions and technology[3] and as one of the nation's leading industrialists Sir John undertook the building of Endcliffe:

> ...*specially adapted for dispensing hospitalities on a scale worthy of such distinguished visitors.*[4]

Endcliffe was, and still is, the largest private residence to have been built in Sheffield and easily achieved its function as an impressive aid to Sir John's career. He was one of many Sheffield industrialists whose entrepreneurship enabled him to acquire a home far beyond the means or dreams of his forbears who, hitherto, had left the town few buildings of note. Prestigious civic or corporate building activity was virtually unknown whilst domestic building had been constrained by the custom of successful businessmen leaving the area once their wealth had been made rather than fostering the cultural development of their own town.[5] During the nineteenth century this trend was slowly reversed with substantial middle class suburbs appearing to the west of the town centre providing well built and spacious accommodation for Sheffield's growing middle classes. Despite their custom of being architect-designed, these homes emphasised comfort and convenience. Of Birchlands, the home of John Newton Mappin, the *Sheffield Weekly Telegraph* reported:

> *It is a roomy and comfortable house, with no ostentatious architectural features to arrest attention or excite remark. Birchlands was built for the comfort and convenience of its owner, more than as a show house for the multitude.*

Even local nobility appeared content with the comfortable, providing little opportunity for designers to be innovative or cabinet makers to test their skills.[6] The author of the article *A Visit to Wortley Hall* wrote:

> *The residence of Lord Wharncliffe was in no way a 'show place', after the fashion of Chatsworth House and Welbeck Abbey . . . Wortley Hall possessed no State Rooms and was essentially the home of its resident . . ., the absence of ostentation and the air of homeliness (in the best sense) pervaded the place.*[7]

Sir John was determined Endcliffe should be the showhouse he clearly believed Sheffield lacked, and further determined to employ Sheffield craftsmen whenever possible. The latest developments in fashion and technology were used to confirm Endcliffe as the home of a wealthy and sophisticated technocrat, at ease with industrialists, politicians and the aristocracy.[8] Designed by the Sheffield architects Flockton and Abbot in the French Italian style, the 36 room mansion (see Figure 2) was built upon the site of a much earlier hall bought and demolished by Brown to create a 40 acre parkland base in the town's increasingly affluent western suburbs. The Hall's public rooms included a 60 foot long Saloon, containing his art collection and a water powered 32 stop organ, a conservatory, billiard room, dining room, drawing room and large open court, whilst the library and morning room were for the private use of Sir John and Lady Brown. Upstairs, nine bedrooms, including the 22 feet x 19 feet State Bedroom with a walnut and gilt four poster bed, had their own bath and dressing rooms together with views over the Italianate gardens and parkland.

The house was virtually fireproof, iron joists and concrete floors being supplemented by a large cistern in the tower providing water for domestic use and firefighting as well as powering the organ. The ground floor windows could be protected against burglary and sunlight by retractable Belgian-made louvred iron shutters. At night, large mirrors, stored in the wall cavities, masked their appearance and threw light back into the rooms. The cooking ranges could use gas or coal whilst all rooms were linked by an electric bell system to

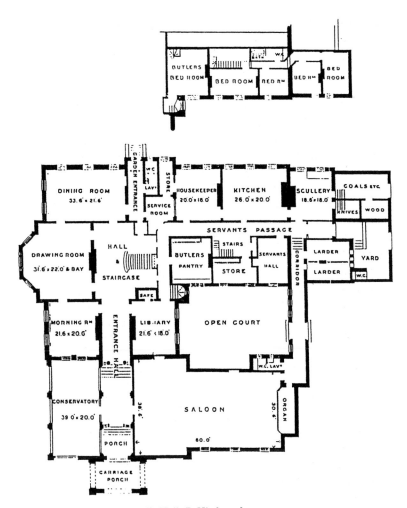

Figure 2.   Plan of Endcliffe Hall. *D Hindmarch*

the kitchen. Ornamental gaslights lit the driveway which led to a covered porch protected from the weather by large plates of glass. The
two large conservatories exemplified the use of modern plate glass
and iron as construction materials.[9] Glass houses had been popular
on the estates of the nobility and gentry throughout the eighteenth
century where early conservatories had had walls of masonry with
just the interstices being glazed. It was not until the 1860s that cast
iron ribs extending from a masonry base had become common, the
method used at Endcliffe.[10]

'The public advantages of personal munificence', a highly enthusiastic article describing Endcliffe Hall, appeared in the *Sheffield
Daily Telegraph* of 24 May, 1865, and took up the theme of technical
innovation and skill, especially as most of the work was carried out
by Sheffield companies. The paper acknowledged the rarity of giving
such work to local companies and rightly praised the building of
Endcliffe as a showcase for Sheffield craftsmanship. The firms
employed included:

Flockton & Abbot	Architects.
John Jebson Smith	Cast iron balustrades for the Grand Staircase. The best stove and chimney pieces.
Messrs. Longden & Co	Coal and gas kitchenstoves.
Messrs. Robertson & Carr	Stoves and chimney pieces.
Mr Ellis, George Street	'Warming up apparatus'. Iron work in the Saloon and vineries, etc.
Joseph Hadfield, Norfolk Lane,	Chimney pieces made to designs supplied by George Eadon's and John Manuel's.
E. W. Wyon	Carvings of The Four Seasons.
Messrs. Craven	Carved and moulded plasterwork-ceiling designs by Charles Green. Masonry and joinery.
Mr William Gibson, Oxford Road, Ecclesall	Carpentry.
Mr Bissett	External plumbing.
Mr Pitt	Internal plumbing and glazing.
John & Joseph Rodgers	Decorating.
John Manuel & Son	Furniture, furnishings.
George Eadon	Furniture, furnishings
William Johnson	Furniture and furnishings.

Much was made of Endcliffe's style of architecture – French in the
Italian style – as it set the tone for furnishing and was a means of
assessing Sir John's social status. Classical architecture had a strong
tradition in England having begun with the designs of Inigo Jones in
the early seventeenth century. Being popular with the aristocracy,
classicism was associated with men of wealth and taste. It underwent
several transformations from its inception until the nineteenth cen-

tury through Palladian, Grecian, Neo-Classical and Italianate. Changes in furniture design went hand in hand with the evolution of domestic and palatial architecture with each variation being refined and honed under the scrutiny of a sophisticated clientele and experienced craftsmen. Gentlemen furnished their homes to a prescribed style and format regardless of the source of their wealth or their outlook upon life. The turbulence of the nineteenth century together with the rise of a competitive, volatile and industrialised *nouveau riche* society terminated the linear development of classicism and there evolved the social minefield which became known as 'The Battle of the Styles'. Self-expression, ostentation, novelty, quantity, embellishment, comfort, informality, cleanliness, polish, clutter: all contrasted sharply with the restraint, elegance and formality of eighteenth century design yet became watchwords for the Victorian household. Two main branches of furniture design, described as the classical and the picturesque, began to form as cabinet makers followed the precedents set down by architects. Each, initially, had distinct characteristics:

> *The Classical character . . . is that of stately, symmetrical, refined balance and repose with simple, elaborate elegance in the ornament: the Picturesque character that of unsymmetrical, vigorous, sparkling piquancy with the ornament not so much refined as animated.*[11]

The Battle of the Styles became one largely fought between the variations of style available under the Classical and Gothic (or Picturesque) banners. The classical style, preferred by the gentry and aristocracy, continued to be popular during the reign of William IV and in the early Victorian period. It was also favoured by the furniture trades as being easier to manufacture than the more elaborate and asymmetrical Gothic. Loudon summarised the major styles present in 1833:

> *The principal styles of design as at present executed in Britain may be reduced to four, viz., the Grecian or modern style which is by far the most prevalent; the Gothic or Perpendicular style which imitates the lines and angles of the Tudor Gothic architecture; the Elizabethan style, which combines the Gothic with the Roman or Italian manner; and the style of the age of Louis XIV, or the florid Italian, which is characterised by curved lines and excess of curvilinear ornaments.*[12]

By 1871, Robert Kerr could list ten different styles of domestic architecture from which clients could choose – Elizabethan, Palladian, Revived Elizabethan, Rural Italian, Palatial Italian, French Italian, English Renaissance, Mediaeval or Gothic, Cottage Style (inferior Rural Italian) and Scottish Baronial. This variety of design, available to those who could afford to employ an architect, was a source of great debate:

> . . . the client . . . is expected to make a choice from amongst half a dozen prevailing 'styles', all more or less antagonistic to each other, all having their respective adherents and opponents, and all very likely to prove more and more mysterious the more they are examined.[13]

With such variety and debate upon the subject of style, the furnishing of nineteenth century middle class homes became the focus of numerous journals and books targeting the *nouveaux riches* who, it was feared, might possess the wealth akin to gentry but may well lack their taste and sophistication. It was possible to gain assurance and advice, albeit often conflicting, upon every aspect of home management and furnishing. To demonstrate the extent to which Sir John chose to follow or disregard convention at Endcliffe, the form and furnishing of the dining room and drawing room in particular will be examined alongside advice from some of the most popular publications of the day.

The reliable Mrs Beeton, familiar with the young housewife's 'great ordeal' of entertaining her husband's clients and colleagues, strongly advised 'the introduction of any particular new book, curiosity of art, or article of vertu' into the drawing room to ease conversation amongst guests as they waited the call to dinner. Others concentrated upon the character and layout of particular rooms. A writer in an article in the *Art Journal Illustrated Catalogue of the Paris Exhibition of 1867* claimed:

> The dining room furniture of England, as distinguished from the furniture suited to a drawing room, should be substantial, massive, handsome, and in colour somewhat sombre rather than gay. The sideboard is the piece de resistance, in which these characteristics usually reach a climax: this is the article in which dinner-giving Englishmen take a pride, and, as usual, our cabinet-makers here put out their utmost strength.

The dining room should be square or rectangular with windows facing south and west so that the sideboard, ideally in a recess along the north wall, should bask in reflected light. The dining table should be the same shape as the room. A servants' entrance to one side of the sideboard would facilitate the flow of courses with minimum disruption to guests. The room should look good in artificial light, being most frequently used at night, and generally its whole appearance should be that of 'masculine importance'.[14] Loudon recommended that '. . . the characteristic colouring of a dining room should be warm, rich and substantial'.[15] Popular colour schemes included extensive use of gold and crimson. The ideal floor covering should be a Turkish carpet in similar colours, the same shape as the room although an Axminster or a Brussels square could suffice.[16]

Next to, but distinct from, the dining room should be the drawing room, the most important day room in the house. In middle class homes this was the room upon which most money was lavished and in which most time was spent. Used for socialising, guests would gather here before and after dinner to be impressed by the variety and fashion of furnishings, ideally a variation of the curvaceous and opulent looking Louis style. The drawing room was considered a female domain and was expected to have a lighter, more cheerful appearance than the sombre, masculine dining room.

Pastels, white and gilding, combined with satinwood, walnut or rose-wood furniture, were recommended as the basis for a feminine colour scheme.[17]

The use of the latest classical style – French in the Italian manner – at Endcliffe was calculated to show Sir John both as a modern technocrat and a gentleman. It hinted at his modernity yet aligned him with a tradition embraced by the English aristocracy for over two hundred years.

As prescribed, the principal rooms at Endcliffe faced south and west to take full advantage of the sun and views across the estate. The domestic quarters and service rooms were on the north side and arranged so that the public rooms could be accessed with the minimum disruption. The rectangular dining room (Figure 3), 33 feet 6 inches by 21 feet 6 inches, was located at the rear of the Hall on the south-west corner with five windows to take full advantage of the light and view. A servants' passage linked it to the kitchen and housekeeper's room via a small service room separated from it directly by the garden entrance to minimise the noise of courses being cleared from intruding upon conversation. The furniture and doors were made from oak with the room being dominated by a large, mirror back, carved and panelled sideboard 9 feet 6 inches wide (Figure 4) and a five foot telescopic dining table which could extend to 22 feet with the addition of ten extra leaves. Although the room lacked a recess in which to place the sideboard, it was on the north wall to help reflect light and the impression of an alcove was given by it being flanked by a servants' door and a false door to provide balance. The colour scheme consisted of crimson cloth curtains, green

Figure 3. The Dining Room taken from the Sale Catalogue prepared by Maple & Co. Ltd., London, 1896. *Sheffield City Libraries, Local Studies Department*

moroccan leather uphol-stery, a rectangular, multi-coloured geometric Turkish carpet bordered by a Brussels carpet, a blue and crimson wool table cover together with fifteen green wool and figured silk d'oy-leys and four crimson table mats. The curtains were

Figure 4. Oak sideboard designed and manufactured by Eadon's. *Sheffield City Libraries, Local Studies Department*

worked with silk rep borders and bullion fringe valances. They were held back by heavy gold tassels and were supported on large, ornate gilt poles which allowed them to sweep along the floor, a practice roundly condemned in 1864 by Eastlake[18] but which remained popular in Sheffield for some considerable time.[19] The room was further decorated by an elaborately moulded and painted ceiling, a carved marble and bronze overmantel with a polished steel stove and tiled hearth over which was a large carved and gilt oval top mirror surmounted by urns and a cartouche. Two other mirrors, one 40 inches x 19 inches and another forming part of an 11 feet 6 inches marble top, wood and gilt pier table reflected light from a pair of 36 inch French bronze and cut glass gilt candelabra and three companion pairs for the sideboard, console table and walls. Seating was provided by a 34 piece suite which consisted of fourteen gentlemen's dining chairs, a carver chair and fifteen ladies' chairs all with Sir John's coat of arms stamped in gilt upon the back. More informal seating was provided by a pair of open arm elbow easy chairs, a lady's reclining chair and a 7 feet 6 inches sofa all of which were deep buttoned.

The drawing room at Endcliffe (Figure 5) , some 31 feet 6 inches x 22 feet, was located between the dining and morning rooms opposite the grand staircase. Having a large bay window which overlooked

Figure 5.   The Drawing Room, 1896. *Sheffield City Libraries, Local Studies Department*

the gardens, its shape was more rounded requiring furniture of a more feminine appearance, made from walnut, as befitted the character of the room. Photographs from the sale catalogue show a room filled with deep buttoned and fringed upholstered chairs, sofas, footstools and ottoman, together with stands, firescreens, games-, writing-, centre- and occasional tables, and an elaborate inlaid walnut china cabinet. The colour scheme was somewhat darker than might have been expected with brown ribbed silk upholstery, amber curtains and a crimson floral design Axminster carpet. The furniture in this room was made by John Manuel & Son who also designed and made the curtains, fixtures and fittings (Figures 6a – 6e).

In all, three firms were approached to provide furniture for Endcliffe and all had to submit designs for approval prior to manufacture. From a total of 68 surviving drawings[20] some 30 are signed by Eadon although only three are countersigned by Sir John, implying approval of the designs, whilst 31 of the 34 presented by another Sheffield firm, John Manuel & Son, appear to have been accepted on this basis. To ensure his requirements were met Sir John took as active a role in the planning of his home and its contents as he did the running of his business:

> *Mr Brown was not only the architect of his own fortunes, but he was the architect of his own works. He not only planned the buildings as they were needed, but most of the machinery used in the production of plates, forgings, railway bars, steel springs, and railway material generally was either wholly designed or improved by himself.*[21]

The drawings made by Eadon's and Manuel's[22] covered a wide range of furniture including beds, davenports, dining chairs, occasional and dining tables, candelabras, mirrors, overmantels, fire surrounds,

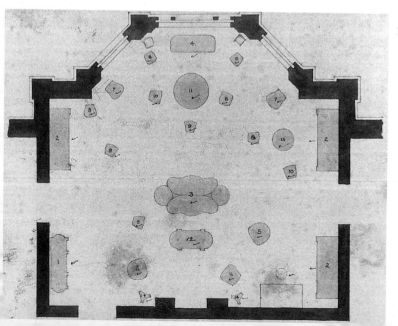

Figure 6a. Proposed floor pl[an] of the Drawing Room by John Manuel & Son. *Sheffield City Libraries, Local Studies Departmen[t]*

Figure 6b. Proposed furniture for the Drawing Room by John Manuel & Co. From left to right: credenza, door curtains, sofa. *Sheffield City Libraries, Local Studies Department*

Figure 6c. Proposed Drawing Room furnishings by John Manuel & Son. Clockwise from top: sofa, spoonback nursing chair, conversation sofa, spoonback armchair. *Sheffield City Libraries, Local Studies Department*

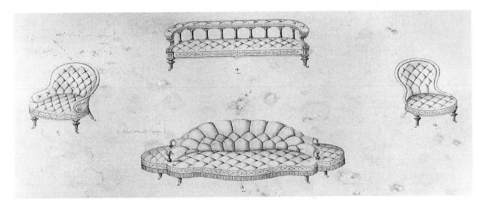

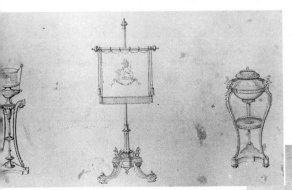

Figure 6d. Proposed Drawing Room furnishings by John Manuel & Son. Left to right: torchiere oil lamp stand, firescreen, torchiere oil lamp stand. *Sheffield City Libraries, Local Studies Department*

Figure 6e. Proposed Drawing Room furnishings by John Manuel & Son. Clockwise from top: mirror, nursing chair, centre table, games table. *Sheffield City Libraries, Local Studies Department*

sofas, firescreens, a billiard table and organ. Drawings were also made of windows with suggested curtains and pelmets (Figure 7), many of the latter being embellished with Sir John's coat of arms. For some rooms designs for doors and wall panelling were also provided as well as plans for siting individual items of furniture.

All the furniture in the dining room was made by George Eadon & Son of New Church St. and Fargate, Sheffield. George Eadon of Ecclesfield, served his apprenticeship under John Hill, a carver and gilder, 'who had himself been a fellow apprentice with [Francis] Chantrey at [Robert] Ramsay's . . .'[23] Eadon began his own business around 1818 as a carver, gilder and looking glass manufacturer. For some time he also supplied artists' materials before expanding into cabinet making and upholstery. He provided the designs for the tables made for the third Cutlers' Hall in 1832 and was commissioned to make the Master Cutler's chair.[24] The 1851 Census listed him as the resident of 170, Clarkehouse Road, aged 55, a carver, gilder & cabinet maker, employing 31 men and head of a household comprising of himself, his wife, five daughters, two sons and one female servant. To live away from his work premises and in one of the town's western suburbs showed him to be a successful businessman and throughout the mid-nineteenth century Eadon's was one of Sheffield's leading cabinet makers and house furnishers. By 1861, he was classed as a Master carver and gilder, now living at Tapton House, Glossop Road, with his wife, a daughter, nephew and two servants. After his death in 1862, his son, Edward, continued the business but soon diversified into auctioneering.

The furnishing of the drawing room was given over to John Manuel & Son, a firm established

Figure 7.   Curtains and pelmets designed
John Manuel & Son. *Sheffield C*
Libraries, Local Studies Departmen

c.1845 as Allott & Manuel[25] but thereafter listed by trade directories as John Manuel trading alone. The Census of 1851 listed John Manuel, born in Knapthorpe, near Newark, aged 36, cabinet maker, living at 87, Devonshire St. with his wife, son, two daughters and brother-in-law Samuel Bland, an apprentice cabinet maker. He was then an employer of 22 men. By 1871, like Eadon, he had moved to a house in the western suburbs and employed 45 men, five boys and ten women. His highly successful business expanded to include cabinet making, upholstery, all forms of house furnishings, removal and storage facilities.

Throughout Endcliffe the furniture reflected a variety of styles including Italian, Louis XIV, Empire, Louis XVI, and Arabian (arabesque) prevalent throughout the mid-Victorian era and frequently used together.[26] It is probable that Sir John visited the Great Exhibition in 1851 and saw the great diversity of furniture on show there. He attended the 1862 Exhibition as an industrialist at the height of his powers and conducted Queen Victoria around the Sheffield Court where his own company had won a Gold Medal for armour plate manufacture.[27] Probably on the spur of the moment he purchased a mantle and stove for the drawing room at Endcliffe despite Manuel's having provided designs (AP 38. 27, 29). Several items of Sir John's furniture bear many similarities with items displayed at various international exhibitions held in the 1850s and early 1860s. The half tester bed designed by John Manuel & Son for Sir John's bedroom bears many similarities to that shown by Rogers and Dear of London at the Great Exhibition (Figure 8). The winged wardrobe in the State Bedroom, also designed by Manuel's, bears a close resemblance to one made by Messrs.

Figure 8.   Half tester bed designed by John Manuel & Son in green, gold and crimson. Registered design showing similarities with that designed by Rogers & Dear, London, for the Great Exhibition (Yapp, Plate LXIII). *Sheffield City Libraries, Local Studies Department*

Trollope, again shown in 1851, 'composed of the choicest woods and inlaid, and the whole work executed in the most finished manner'. The cartouche on top of this wardrobe cornice, supported by two cherubs and flanked by finials appears to have been closely inspected, for some fourteen years later a copy appears on top of Sir John's bed, which nevertheless had its design registered.[28] The 1862 Exhibition had a bedroom suite manufactured by the Manchester firm of Bird and Hull made from sycamore and alder[29] which closely resembled that made by Manuel's for Lady Brown's bedroom suite, also in sycamore.

Industry used these exhibitions to demonstrate their latest designs and advancements whilst furniture firms attended to show their skills and gain publicity. This necessitated their exhibits to be flamboyant and eye catching; it was rarely their intention that display goods should pass into everyday production.[30]

This differentiation may not have been detected by Sir John. Whilst some of the ideas shown at these exhibitions would have passed into mainstream use, their incorporation into furniture for Endcliffe suggests that Sir John specifically requested such goods or that the Sheffield firms had the measure of their man. However, despite the odd touch of flamboyance, which mainly occurred in the bedroom furnishings, most of Endcliffe's furniture conformed to a pattern expected of a wealthy and established merchant. The standard of workmanship was high. Most processes were carried out by hand as the items made were one-offs, leading to high unit costs. The materials used were also of the best quality. Brown appears to have had a fondness for mahogany and the sale catalogue frequently cites the use of the high quality Spanish variety. Oak, walnut and Hungarian ash were employed according to the protocol of the day: oak in the masculine dining room, walnut in the feminine drawing room, mahogany for a man's bedroom, ash for a lady's boudoir. The common Victorian trap of novelty for its own sake appears to have been avoided. There is little mention of items made from exotic or novelty materials such as papier maché, iron, carton pierre or leather.

Conformity to the protocol of the day appears to have been closely followed at Endcliffe. The greatest tokens to individuality were the inclusion of Sir John's coat of arms either as a whole or its various elements of a lion, bee, star and a coil on many items throughout the Hall.[31] As well as appearing over some doorways, elements of Brown's coat of arms, sometimes with the motto, *nec sorte nec fato* (neither by chance nor destiny) were incorporated into the designs of many pieces of furniture. They could be seen on designs for the firescreens and inlaid pedestal table of the drawing room, the bed, wardrobe, linen press mantle and curtain pelmet of the state bedroom and bedroom No. 2, and in the dining chairs and chiffonier. Using heraldic devices in this way implied longevity, continuity and stability as well as a degree of pride and desire to be acknowledged as part of the establishment. It is interesting to note the designs for the furniture at Endcliffe were made largely between 1863 and 1865 although Sir John was not knighted until 1867.

Sir John was prepared to use 'new men . . . as artists, draughtsmen and statuaries'[32] from the local School of Art, and new ideas in the form of technology but he was reluctant to break away from the expectations and protocol inherent in furnishing a Victorian home. He was essentially the same as most of his fellow industrialists whose '. . . personal taste [was] associated with their well-earned wealth'[33] – and their wealth had risen predominantly from the shop floor. Often the first generation who could look to furnish homes as they wished, and not be governed by income or necessity, their tastes remained essentially cautious and conservative. Many were technological leaders and industrialists of national importance but few had had the time, education or means to gain sufficient confidence or experience in the fields of art and design to furnish independently from the dictates of current fashion. The cultural and intellectual background of the town was a key factor in developing these tastes and this was an area, when compared with other cities, in which Sheffield was lacking.[34] Although the town was equipped with numerous educational facilities all but the School of Art tended to stress business related subjects which clearly held a wide appeal:

> . . . there are advantages in abundant leisure and in the absence of the cares of business, but along with such advantages there are disadvantages . . . our self-made merchant princes will be leaders in the cause of progress – leaders more effective than any England has hitherto followed. They are no theorists, nor dreamers of dreams.[35]

The new middle classes which formed Sheffield society consisted of:

> . . . doctors, lawyers and clergy, the larger merchants, those who having retired from trade qualified as gentlemen and the few remaining representatives of the older gentry. Manners and habits were not polished when judged by London standards, nor was the intellectual level very brilliant. . .[36]

The south-western suburbs, home to the élite of Sheffield society, did not encourage or inspire dreamers. It has been claimed, perhaps unfairly, that: 'Ranmoor was a centre of local fashion, but not of taste'[37], although it has to be acknowledged that the town did lag behind other industrialised communities such as Liverpool, Leeds, and Manchester in the quality of its architectural heritage and facilities for the arts. Poor communications and lack of economic diversity contributed to Sheffield's relative isolation and inexperience in these fields which was compounded by the absence of influential neighbouring communities and the reluctance of the local population to travel.[38]

During the nineteenth century Sheffield became one of the fastest growing towns in the country but because expansion was so sudden and based solely on industrial output rather than a mixture of commercial activities, the result was a new society eager to express their arrival in material forms but lacking the necessary sophistication and cultural awareness, common to cities with more cosmopolitan cultures. The absence of a locally based and active aristorcracy plus the divisions and inadequacies within local authorities[39] meant commissions for fine furnishings to complement private or public buildings were almost unknown. Such an environment served to deprive local manufacturers of the chance to develop and expand their skills whilst it limited the available source material available to create a lively vocabulary of style from which the *nouveaux riches* could benefit.

The Sheffield physician, G. C. Holland, writing in 1843, noted, amongst his fellow townsmen, that wealth when rapidly created:

is almost invariably associated with a disposition to external display, which manifests itself in every possible form, and is supposed to be necessary to maintain a certain position in life.[40]

John Marshall, the Leeds textile magnate wrote:

The first effects of newly acquired wealth are always seen in the buildings of a town . . . Refinement of taste and manners are of slower growth. It is the next generation which must spend what their fathers have learnt to accumulate.[41]

To its credit, and perhaps due to the lack of visual stimulus, Sheffield appears to have avoided the worst ostentations of Victorian novelty. Most of the furniture destined for the middle class suburbs appears to have been well-made from good materials, practical, durable and comfortable. In these terms, the building and furnishing of Endcliffe Hall must be seen as a triumph not only for Sir John Brown but for Sheffield craftsmen, pragmatism and pride.

Notes and References

1. *Sheffield Daily Telegraph*, 11 August, 1862; *Illustrated London News* 21 November 1863.
2. *Sheffield Daily Telegraph*, Saturday 6 May, 1865.
3. George Sheeran, *Brass Castles. West Yorkshire New Rich and their Houses, 1800 – 1914*, Ryburn, 1993, p.81.
4. *Sheffield Illustrated*, 'Views and Portraits which have appeared in the Sheffield Weekly Telegraph' Vol. II, 1885, p.6.
5. During the period 1680–1740 the practice of Sheffield's few successful manufacturers and professionals retiring from the area was so widespread that the town's social and intellectual development lagged far behind its industrial progress. See Mary Walton, *Sheffield Its Story and Achievements*, 1948, p.103.
6. Probably the most prestigious undertaking by Sheffield cabinet makers in the mid-nineteenth century was the furnishing of the 14th Duke of Norfolk's local residence, The Farm, by George Eadon, 1856–59. See: *Sheffield Independent*, 6 August, 1859; 'The Ducal Residence', *Sheffield & Rotherham Independent*, Saturday, 1 December, 1860; 'Death of the Duke of Norfolk', *Supplement to the Sheffield & Rotherham Independent*, 30 July, 1859; completion of "The Farm", *Sheffield Illustrated*, Vol. 1, 1884.
7. *South Yorkshire Notes and Queries*, Vol. 1, 1899–1901, pp.28–29.
8. Vanessa S. Doe, 'Some Developments in Middle Class Housing in Sheffield 1830–1875' in *Essays in the Economic and Social History of South Yorkshire*, Ed. S Pollard and C. Holmes, SYCC, p.181.
9. The inspiration for large conservatories was Paxton's Crystal Palace, although Brown may have seen Paxton's original construction at Chatsworth where Paxton was architect and landscape gardener to the sixth Duke of Devonshire.
10. Sheeran, *Brass Castles*, p.101.
11 T. W. Symonds & B. B. Whineray, *Victorian Furniture*, 1987, p.19.
12. J. C. Loudon, *Encyclopaedia of Cottage, Farm and Villa Architecture and Furniture*, 1833.
13. Robert Kerr, *The Gentleman's House or How to Plan English Residences from the Parsonage to the Palace*, 3rd edition, revised 1871, p.55.
14. Kerr, *The Gentleman's House*.
15. Loudon, *Encyclopaedia*.
16. James Arrowsmith, *The Paper Hanger's and Upholsterer's Guide*, 1854.
17. Joanna Banham, Sally MacDonald, Julia Porter, *Victorian Interior Design*, 1991, p.38.
18. C. L. Eastlake, *Hints on Household Taste in Furniture, Upholstery and Other Details*, 1868.
19. Examples were still advertised in the *Manual Galleries of High Class Furniture Catalogue*, Sheffield, published c.1900–05. Sheffield City Libraries, Local Studies Department.
20. Sheffield Archives, AP38. 1–68.
21. *Sheffield and Rotherham Independent*, 28 December, 1896, 'Death of Sir John Brown'.
22. A third firm, William Johnson of 82–84 Fargate, whilst one of Sheffield's leading manufacturers, appears only to have presented a few rough sketches and thus received few, if any, commissions, Sheffield Archives AP 38. 42, 59.
23. R. E. Leader, Ed. *Reminiscences of Old Sheffield*, 1875, p.69. Regarding Eadon's apprenticeship, Leader initially claims he was trained by Robert Henderson who in turn was also trained by Ramsay. In the subsequent edition published in 1876, this is changed to his being apprenticed to John Hill who in turn was also trained by Ramsay, a carver, gilder and picture framer of High St.
24. 'Liber Minut Socieat Cutler In Hallamshire In Com: Ebor'. 27 Feb – 11 March 1833. C9/4.
25. See Janet Ball, *John Manuel & Son of Sheffield*, Furniture History Society, 1978, pp. 62–65.
26. *Endcliffe Hall, Sheffield, Yorkshire*. Sale Catalogue, Maple & Co. Ltd. London, April, 1893. Brotherton Library, Leeds. In April 1893, Sir John ordered Endcliffe Hall and its contents to be sold by auction. Having retired some years earlier to Kent in poor health and having suffered several financial difficulties,

Sir John instructed the skeleton staff who maintained the Hall to prepare it for sale. The auction, held on the premises, lasted five days, attracting purchasers from all over the country and considerable local interest. Much of the furniture was bought by local dealers and individuals with John Manuel & Son buying back much which they had manufactured. *Sheffield & Rotherham Independent*, 'The Sale at Endcliffe Hall', 18–22 April, 1893.

27. D. Hindmarch & A. J. Podmore, *Endcliffe Hall in the Manor of Hallamshire*, Sheffield City Libraries, p.29.

28. G. W. Yapp, Ed. *Art Industry, Furniture, Upholstery and House-Decoration*, 1870. Plates XXII and LXIII. Manuel drawing for a half tester bed in green, gold and crimson. AP 38. 62, Sheffield Archives.

29. *Illustrated Catalogue of the International Exhibition 1862*, p.243.

30. '. . . it is important to remember that it [exhibition furniture] was not entirely typical of the furniture trade as a whole. The manufacturers were well aware that novelty and technical skill intrigued the Victorian public above almost everything else and they were at pains that their own exhibits should display those qualities to a greater extent than their competitors . . . the result was that firms tended to display their most costly, most elaborate, most vulgar but least typical pieces.' Symonds & Whineray, *Victorian Furniture*, p.59.

31. Hindmarch & Podmore, *Endcliffe Hall*.

32. 'The Public Advantages of Personal Munificence', *The Sheffield Daily Telegraph*, 22 May, 1865.

33. *Sheffield & Rotherham Independent*, 'The Death of Sir John Brown', 28 December, 1896.

34. It was 1875 before Sheffield's first public museum was opened and 1887 before it gained an art gallery.

35. 'The Public Advantages of Personal Munificence'.

36. 'The Public Advantages of Personal Munificence'.

37. Walton, *Sheffield*, p.225.

38. 'The population of Sheffield is, for so large a town, unique in its character, in fact it more closely resembles that of a village than a town, for over wide areas each person appears acquainted with every other, and to be interested with that other's concern.' Local Government Board, Report on the Small-Pox Epidemic of 1887–8, 1889, quoted in Asa Briggs, *Victorian Cities*, 1990, p.72.

39. Walton, *Sheffield*, pp. 184, 202.

40. G. Calvert Holland, MD, *The Vital Statistics of Sheffield*, 1843, p.240.

41. Asa Briggs, *Victorian Cities*, 1990, pp.43–44 quoting W. G. Rimmer, *Marshall's of Leeds*, 1960, p.103.

14. THE GUITES OF SAMEHILL FARM, RIVELIN, UPPER HALLAM

By Valerie Answer

WHEN WILLIAM FAIRBANK and his son Josiah surveyed the parish of Sheffield, in 1795,[1] the north-west boundary was marked by the River Rivelin, and across the river was the township of Stannington, in the chapelry of Bradfield in the parish of Ecclesfield. On the river the Fairbanks' only named two water mills, Rivelin Mill and Mousehole Forge, three miles apart, and halfway between them, bordering the river, were Upper Hag and Lower Hag. Also marked was the ancient footpath of Hagg Lane, linking Rivelin Corn Mill with the then village of Walkley and the town of Sheffield. By 1850 the same area had been surveyed for the Ordnance Survey by Lieut. Barlow of the Royal Engineers.[2] By that date Upper and Lower Hag had been renamed Samel Plantation and a huddle of buildings went by the name of Samel Yard. The area was also criss-crossed with foot-

Figure 1. 'Soon we came to a cart track which snaked to our right, and there nestling in a hollow was Samehill Farm.' *Bryan Answer*

paths linking the nineteen water mills now working on this small river. Samel Yard is the present-day Samehill Farm.

I first visited Samehill Farm (Figure 1) in late September, 1978. I was taken by a friend who had been visiting the Guites of Samehill Farm* for many years. We walked the same paths the 'little mesters', self employed craftsmen, would have walked from Stannington, dropping down Roscoe Wood, passing Roscoe Wheel, walking alongside the river, passing Iron (Hind) Wheel, now a complete ruin, and climbing the narrow footpath and joining the old Hagg Lane, now renamed Long Lane. Walking on Hagg Lane very little had changed over the centuries; apart from a few hikers the lane was hardly used. Soon we came to a cart track which snaked down to our right, and there nestling in a hollow was Samehill Farm, its chimney puffing smoke and the hens squawking and running all over the place. As we approached, the door opened and a few hens dashed in before us, a sleepy black and white sheepdog gently welcomed us with a slow wag of his tail and we entered the house. The room was small and crowded with possessions of people long dead. I was introduced to Mr

Figure 2. William and Louisa Guite of Samehill Farm, 1978. *Dennis Smith*

William and Miss Louisa Guite and we were invited to sit down. I was offered an old Windsor chair piled high with dusty handmade rag rugs, and Miss Louisa brought out some of her home made wine, which we drank out of dusty glasses. The fire roared, the clock ticked loudly from a corner and the hens ran about. I felt I was intruding on these unworldly people.

My friend decided to take a couple of photographs of them (Figure 2). They didn't object, but sat in silence. I broke the stillness by asking Mr Guite if I could record our conversation on tape. I had just finished my request when Mr Guite began to speak: it was as if he had rehearsed the speech for a play. I had to stop him and quickly

* Key places in the Sheffield area mentioned in the text are shown in Figure 5.

get out my tape recorder which I placed on the table and, in the best tradition of story telling, William Guite, prompted occasionally by Miss Louisa, and with an audience of three, told his tale, and a remarkable tale it is, spanning as it does two centuries, half the globe, and the families of Birks, Seniors and Guites of Samehill Farm.

Out of it will be gleaned no information on William and Louisa or their brothers Thomas or George. Louisa, George and William never married; they lived on the farm together until they died. A distant cousin Mr Vincent Guite, who visited the farm all his life, told me Miss Louisa was beautiful, with long black hair (see Figure 3), and very talented, who would play the piano to almost concert standard, playing Chopin and Liszt, her favourite composers. He remembered as a boy (he was born in 1919) going to the farm and sitting and listening to poetry readings, and choral singing. George and William were both handsome, William being the tallest, and physically very strong. He hardly left the farm all his life, only to deliver milk locally. Did any suitors call at the farm, and were they turned away, and by whom? Why did William Guite beg me to promise not to tell his tale until after he died? I kept the promise. William Guite died on the 29 December, 1992, and Miss Louisa on the 3 May, 1983. They were buried at Crookes Cemetery in a family grave containing the remains of Henry Guite (d. 24.1.34), Clara Guite (d.19.2.52) and George Henry Guite (d.10.6.66).[3]

Figure 3. 'Miss Louisa Guite was beautiful with long black hair.' *Vincent Guite*

William Guite began his tale with John Senior's, his grandfather's regiment, the 18th Royal Irish, which sailed in 1860 to New Zealand via the Atlantic and Cape Horn (see Figure 4) to fight the Maoris.[4] He was stationed in Napier, New Zealand where a son was born in 1862. From there the Regiment moved to Tasmania:

> *My mother was born at the Regimental Headquarters, Hobart, Tasmania, 30 December, 1867. Her father was stationed there for about two years. While my grandfather was there he saw the skull of*

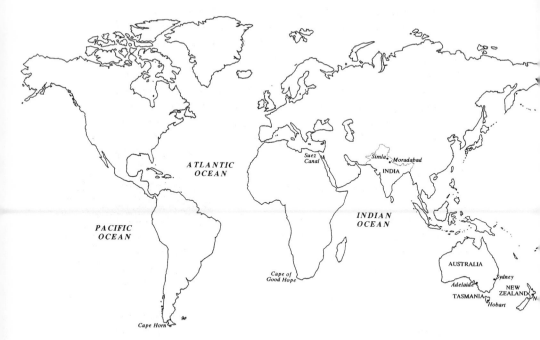

Figure 4.   John Senior's army postings.

the last native of Tasmania, because the doctor had it in his room for a keepsake.[5]

After they left Tasmania, they were transferred to Australia, to Adelaide. They were there a while. I do believe they lost a daughter there. From there they were transferred to Sydney. My grandfather knew the Chief who the land was bought off (Sydney) and they paid him in blankets and hatchets.[6] *When they had been there about two years the regiment had been away from England about five years; they were ordered home. Well, grandfather didn't come he got transferred into a new regiment, Yorkshire Light Infantry. You see he was doing so well out there, he was a sergeant and grandmother was a nurse, in fact grandmother became matron. Grandfather's name was John Senior, but he changed it to join the new regiment, because if he had stopped in that name he would have had to come back, so he altered it to John Simmonite. He had been with that regiment a couple of years when the Australian Government decided to have their own soldiers, so all the English troops were ordered out of Australia. On the voyage coming back to England, when they arrived at the*

Cape of Good Hope, South Africa, the seas were so rough the Captain ordered the ship to go before the wind. They couldn't control it, this threw the ship off course and when the ship docked in Southampton they had been at sea ninety days.

Then the regiment was ordered out to India. Well, when embarking, my mother was a little bit of a stray sort of girl and she got away from them and got lost and they had to hold the ship up to find her. The family then consisted of her, a sister and two brothers and when they were going through the Suez Canal, and going down the Red Sea, my mother's sister couldn't stand the voyage and she died and she was buried at sea; she was just wrapped up in a blanket, a quick service read over her, down the plank and into the sea. They got to India and went up to Simla and Moradabad. After being there a while cholera broke out, and they had to keep shifting about, they called it cholera dodging. Well, in the end mother caught it. The doctor didn't want my grandmother to nurse her because she was needed to nurse the other cases. But she said, 'Who is more likely to look after her child than a mother?' Well, my mother got better but my grandmother caught it and she died. When the doctor saw my grandfather he said, 'I've some bad news for you, you're wife is dead'. Well, my grandfather thought he was going to say you're daughter is dead. You see he didn't know his wife was ill, cramp had set in and she was dead in three hours. She was buried at Simla and grandfather planted a rose tree over her grave.

Well, the eldest boy had just left school, he was thirteen and a half. He had been to school in India. The Band Master asked grandfather if the boy could join the band, he was tall for his age. This left my mother and younger brother nearly like orphans. So the chaplain of the regiment said he would take them in and look after them. The chaplain was a gentleman, he would ride about in a carriage. He was ranked as colonel. He tried to get them in the Lawrence Schools; these schools had been founded and built on donations by the Indian Raj. They were for delicate children of service men, they were built up in the hills. On the plains it was very, very hot in summer, and the children couldn't stand it. Anyhow, they tried to get these two children in but it took two years and that was through influence. There was a general who went from England to inspect the regiment and while he was there the chaplain asked the general about these two children, and do you know they were in the school in a fortnight. Mother was in that school for two years, these were top schools, they nearly turned them out with a university degree.

However, as time went on this younger brother had an accident.

There was a draw well and the top cover had been left off, and it appears he was looking down at his shadow, when he over-balanced and fell down and got drowned. When it got to 1879 my grandfather had done his 21 years and so he was entitled to a pension. He arrived back in Southampton and was transferred to Gosport and he was in that port in that winter of 1879/80, one of the coldest winters they had ever had in this country. They were skating on the ramparts.

At this stage in William Guite's oral history we see John Senior and his daughter moving back to Sheffield. He moved in with his oldest brother, who had built a house on Bramall Lane, on one of the town's numerous garden plots. His daughter, Clara, went to live with her Aunt Mary Barnes[7] who had a shop and house at 84 Wellington Street. Clara was thirteen years old and her birthplace is listed as Hobart, Australia. John Senior's oldest brother was a tailor by trade but his eyesight was very poor. So John Senior went to live with his sister in Portobello Street.

There was only her and her husband and they lived in this little cottage, one up, one down, and he lodged there for some time. Now grandfather was a sick man by then, he had contracted the ague and asthma, and his sickness used to come on him and he would shake like a leaf. Well the doctor got him into a cottage hospital at Glossop, run by the Duke of Norfolk. He was there a while and he eventually married a lady from Ashton under Lyne and that's where he died.

We move now from the Seniors, William Guite's mother's family, to the Guites of Sheffield. The first family member to move into Sheffield was 'Samuel Gyte son of Samuel, Milnhouse Dale, Tideswell, slater, dec, apprenticed to Thomas Palfreyman, Stannington, 1752'.[8] In February, 1787, a Samuel, son of John Guite, was baptised at Ecclesfield. Probably the family lived at Owlerton at that time, because we find in 1793, Samuel son of Samuel, apprenticed to his father, a filegrinder, there.[9] Part of the family then seems to have moved into the White Croft area of Sheffield. We find a dozen or so baptisms from 1798 to 1812 at Sheffield parish church (the present cathedral) of children of Samuel, George and William Guite, all filegrinders.

Married at Sheffield parish church on 14 February, 1833, were Joseph Guite and Susannah Hall. They are listed in the 1841 Census as living at Pearl Town, near Rivelin Bridge, with their growing family of six children, Henry, the eldest, being seven years old. Joseph Guite is listed as a filegrinder.[10] By 1851, Susannah, with her children, Susannah, aged twelve years, and John, aged six years, were living in George Street, both mother and daughter listed as laundress-es.[11] Henry, now aged seventeen was living in Snow Lane, and listed as a filegrinder.[12] Ten years later in 1861, Henry was married and living at Myers Grove, Stannington, with his wife Elizabeth, and children, Sarah aged three years and Joseph aged one year.[13] Two more children, Henry, who would have been three years old, and Elizabeth, a few months old, were baptised at St Philip's Church on 21 September, 1864.

William Guite continued his story with his account of the Sheffield Flood of 1864 in which 240 people lost their lives.

On March 12, 1864, the Great Sheffield Flood happened. My grandfather [Henry Guite] lived on Holme Lane, in a row of houses, near the old tramsheds, Brick Row. Theirs was the corner house and when the flood came it sheared the gable end straight off. It was a wonder the house didn't fall down. Well, it happened at midnight, the dam burst. [Dale Dyke, at Bradfield]. It came down the valley of Loxley crushing everything. The family were all in the bedroom and grandmother kept going to see how high the water was rising. It had got to the window sill. Now my grandfather was troubled with his heart, he had had several stones breaking, he had been knocked about in the wheel.

Henry Guite was a file grinder. He worked at Limberick Wheel [Limbrick Wheel on the Loxley River was always known by the locals as Limberick]. He would sit over his trough or trow, with the grinding wheel sitting on a bed of water. Through the wheel centre would be the turning axle; the axle would go into a smaller wheel, and this was driven by a band or belt which in turn was driven by the water wheel. The grinder would sit astride his horse, or saddle, usually made from a block of oak. Iron bands were placed front and back and attached to these were iron chains to hold it down. The stone would only have to have a slight flaw and the constant use would strain it and it would explode crushing the grinder.

In a while, grandfather said to grandmother, 'Go and look if it's any higher'. Well, grandmother wanted to go up into the garret, but grandfather said, 'Nay lass, we'll stop down here and all get round the crib'. There was my grandfather, grandmother, my father's eldest sister and his older brother, my father [Henry] was the baby in the crib. So they all got round the crib preparing to die together. Grandmother went to have a last look through the window, 'Oh', she said, 'I think it's gone down a bit'. He said, 'Thank God for that, we'll have a chance now'. When it got light they went to go downstairs, and they

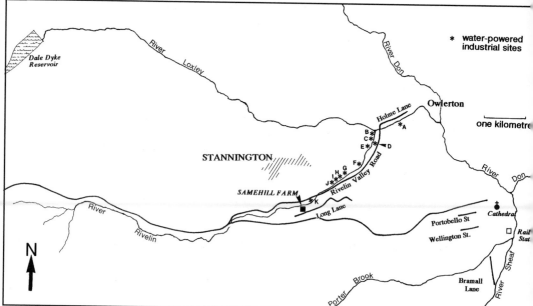

Figure 5.   Key places in Sheffield mentioned in the text. The water-powered sites are: on the Loxley: A – Limb
Wheel; on the Rivelin: B – Grogram Wheel; C – Mousehole Forge; D – Walkley Bank Tilt; E – Riv
Bridge Wheel; F – Spooner Wheel; G – Roscoe Wheel; H – Holme Head Wheel; I – Little London Wh
J – Nether Cut Wheel; K – Hind Wheel

*saw the stairs had gone. They had left all their clothes downstairs, in
them days they used to undress downstairs. Well, they wondered how
they were going to get down. Between them and the people next door
was the dividing wall, so grandfather decided to knock a hole through
the wall, because their house was virtually intact. The flood had taken
everything, they could only find a kettle lid.* [14]

*There was a fund raised and Queen Victoria was the patron. It came
to £200,000, and the Mayor of Sheffield was the chairman of the
fund. The doctor told my grandmother that by no means had grandfather to go and face that committee because he might drop dead. So
she went three times and they said, 'No, you must bring your husband'. They never got halfpenny. They went to live at the top of
Walkley Lane, Hampton View. They didn't stay long because grandfather couldn't climb the hill.*

*A trough came to [became available at] Upper Cut Wheel [Rivelin]
and also a cottage at Glen View, so grandfather came to work in that
wheel as a file grinder. He worked there for some years and eventually found a cottage at Roscoe, and from Roscoe he went to work at*

Spooner Wheel. My grandfather died there, and my great grandfather, they were both forty-nine years old [when they died]*, and both were buried at Loxley Chapel. While they were living at Glen Cottage, they started to get their milk from Samehill Farm. The farm was owned by a man called Samuel Birks. His father had built the farm; it was built in 1815 by Thomas Birks.* [15]

The same year the battle of Waterloo was fought and Thomas Birks volunteered to go and fight against Napoleon and they were practising in a field, twenty to twenty-five of 'em when a soldier came round yon far bend, no roads here then, on a white horse and they all threw their arms up and started cheering. They thought he had come to fetch them, they so wanted to go and fight Napoleon. When he reached them he said, 'Gentlemen, the battle has been fought and we have captured Napoleon, the Duke of Wellington has taken him prisoner'. Then he said, 'For your great patriotism and honour for the country'. He then put his hand in his pocket and gave them half a crown each.

Thomas Birks was born at Stannington in 1789 to Thomas and Mary Birks.[16] A William, son of Thomas Birks, was apprenticed to Enock Drabble, of Storrs, in 1724, in all probability a razor maker.[17] Perhaps the William and John Birks of Norfolk Street, Razor Manufacturers, listed in *A Directory of Sheffield*,1787, were distant relatives?

William Guite continued his story.

Thomas Birks bought this land off the Duke of Norfolk, and started building a house. He engaged a professional builder, and all the beams are made of oak, all the surrounds are made from one big rock, which stood down that hollow and they cut it out before breakfast one morning. They kept adding rooms. At one time there used to be steps outside, where you had to go up to get into the bedroom, but in time they built a kitchen to it and a cellar. In the cellar are three big holes in the wall for keeping the barrels of beer – they used to brew their own beer. There is a place at the top of the cellar steps for putting the barrel they were using. The barrels were a year to two years old before they started on them. They would take the bung out and put a tap in. Then Thomas Birks died in 1865; he left two sons, one married, one single.

In 1851 Thomas Birks was 62 years old, and his wife Ruth was 53 years old. He farmed seven acres. His sons Samuel and John were 23 years and 16 years, both listed as cutlers.[18] In the 1837 Election Poll Book for the West Riding of Yorkshire, Thomas Birks, Rivelin, Upper

Hallam voted for the Hon. John S. Wortley (Wortley received 11,489 votes, Lord Morpeth 12,576 and Sir Geo. Stricken 11,892).[19]

When my father was five or six years old he started fetching milk from here, and instead of going home he used to help Mr Birks [Samuel] *around the farm, building walls and carrying stone. Well, Mr Birks took to him and he wanted him to come and live with him and his mother – his mother was born in 1795.*

Mrs Birks was born Ruth Taylor, baptised at Underbank Chapel, 3 September, 1795. Her father, William Taylor, was a shopkeeper and cutler, and her mother was Hannah, and they lived at Upper Gate, Stannington.[20]

She [Mrs Birks] *lived until she was 90 years old. My grandfather was very poor and there was six of them, so they let him go to live with Mr Birks. My father didn't want to go in the grinding wheel, he was frightened to go in, he had heard so much about stones breaking. So Mr Birks and his mother brought my father up. When he was thirteen he went to school for six months. He went to Stannington School, and Mr Lomas, the owner of J & J Dyson, he was the schoolmaster.*[21]

When he was in his teens he started going to Sunday School. In 1879 the Vicar of Stannington died, and Mr Parkes came [Samuel Parkes, Vicar of Stannington 1880–1907]. *He took an interest in father, and father had a very good singing voice, a tenor, and he sang in the choir for forty years. In 1886 mester* [Samuel Birks] *died and he left my father this place and a life tenancy, that meant when he died the land would go to William Gosling, at Holdworth and his heirs, forever.*[22]

William Guite then recounted how his mother met his father. Samuel Birks had a good butcher and egg round and he produced milk for a man who sold the milk in Sheffield, and one of his customers was a Mrs Barnes in Wellington Street. Mrs Barnes was very friendly with Mrs Ruth Birks and she sometimes visited her, and once she went to convalesce after an illness at the farm and Clara Senior went to visit her and met Henry Guite.

I asked Mr Guite if he could remember the old wheels in Rivelin. On comparing his recollections with the documentary evidence assembled in David Crossley's *Water Power on the Sheffield Rivers*, the unerring accuracy of William's memory was confirmed. Only one point of difference can be found. William said the water wheel at Roscoe Wheel was undershot and Crossley says it was a breast-shot wheel.[23] So starting at Malin Bridge:

Grogram Wheel

Just a small wheel at the beginning. The eldest brother of my father, Joseph, and his youngest brother, George, they were the last to work that wheel. It used to flood in bad weather, they ground files. [Joseph was the grandfather of Vincent Guite, and he lived on Oncha Road.] *George was christened George Snape, after George Snape, a table blade grinder, who died with his wife in the Sheffield Flood. Their house stood below the Limerick Wheel.*[24]

Mousehole Forge

Then came Mousehole Forge and they forged anvils, owned by the Armitages. In due time the Grogham Wheel was abandoned and Mousehole got permission to put some bellows in; they had a pipe fixed up to the wheel and the furnace for extra blowing power. This method was used right up to the end of Mousehole making anvils. Of course, anvils went out of use when the motor car came into being.

Walkley Bank Tilt

The next wheel above was a wire mill, Walkley Bank Tilt, they were wire drawers.

Rivelin Bridge Wheel

The next one above was a little place, it was a grinding wheel, but mostly it was used for corn because the wheel wasn't big enough to drive the grinding stone. The water wheel was very small there wasn't much fall for the water, it hadn't a deal of depth. There was some people called German Wilson, who were corn dealers at Malin Bridge, and they used to bring beans and corn and grind them and they used it as a warehouse for storing the corn.

Spooner Wheel

The next wheel was Spooner Wheel. It was owned by a family called Spooner and they lived at Crookes, a very noted Crookes family. They owned a lot of land at Crookes and they owned that wheel until the Sheffield Corporation bought all the other wheels off the old Sheffield Water Company, between 1895 and 1900. It was when Sheffield was made into a City. Spooner Wheel, my great, great, great grandfather worked there and I understand he ground pocket knives. They used to say that he could carry almost a week's work in his pocket. You know, they used to carry a big satchel over their shoulders, but it was heavy stuff. At one time there was fifty donkeys kept up this valley, they used them for carrying working material to the wheels. The Spooner Wheel turned into a forge for forging blades. Drop hammers. You could hear the forge hammering away, you would think it was going to shake the place down. Well before they turned it into that, when it was a grinding wheel, they used to run short of

*water, there wasn't enough space in the dam to hold enough water to
last them a full day, so they built another dam higher up and they
called it New Dam.*

Listed at Spooner Wheel in the 1881 Census were Henry Guite aged
48 years, file grinder, Henry Guite aged 19 years carter, and John
Guite aged 37 years file grinder.[25]

Roscoe Wheel

*Above that was Roscoe Wheel and that was a very big wheel, about
twenty grinders worked there, and they had upstairs and downstairs.
That wheel was an undershot wheel, that means the water instead of
going over the top of the wheel, the wheel would catch it underneath.
I suppose they built it that way because there wasn't enough fall to
drive the wheel, so you can get twenty to twenty five horse power. I
remember a cutler working there, John Edward Dyson, he just used
one end of it and he must have used the dam because he had some
shuttles put in.*

In 1881 at Roscoe Wheel were recorded Samuel Shaw aged 40 years,
sheep shear grinder, Percy Shaw, son, aged 19 years, sheep shear
grinder, William Banks aged 46 years, moulder. At Roscoe Wood
were James Crooks aged 45 years, razor presser, Henry Crooks, son,
aged 17 years, razor scale presser, Thomas Holland aged 38 years,
table knife hafter, John Gillot, aged 37 years, pocket knife cutler,
James Gilman aged 63 years, pocket blade forger, and Joseph Dale,
razor grinder.

Holme Head Wheel

*The next wheel above that is called Holme Head wheel. I remember
that working, they used to grind razors and table blades. Table grinding wasn't a heavy job, file grinding was the heaviest. Some of the
files were ground for the railways, they were long thins. My grandfather used to have to lift the wheel to grind these files. Well, this Holme
Head got took over by a Sheffield firm and I don't know what they
ground.*

Little London Wheel

*The wheel over that was called Little London. Now that more or less
was a white elephant, because there wasn't enough fall of water to go
into the river, it was a slow fall and when the river was swollen, what
we call a big dyke, instead of the water from the wheel running into
the river, the river used to come and stop the water wheel from working and for years it wasn't worked until a man called Samuel
Dawson took it. He used to work at Wolf Wheel and he was an old
man then, so he took a lease for ten years and when the lease was up*

it was never worked again, and that's fifty years ago [1920s?].

Nether Cut Wheel

The next wheel above was the Nether Cut Wheel. They ground scythes. A family called Kay, father and three sons and they had a closed shop. This one at fourteen, he took him in and couldn't take another of his sons until he was 21 and they worked for Tyzacks.

In the 1881 census William Kay, scythe grinder, Joseph Kay, scythe grinder, Thomas aged 9 years, Joseph aged 7 years, Edward, aged 5 years and Arthur aged 2 years were recorded at Nether Cut Wheel.

The Kay brothers were full of devilment. There was one called Joe, and he was always teasing my father's eldest sister, Sally. They lived at Roscoe then. Well, one day Sally had got all dressed up and Joe got hold of her and pushed her up the chimney. She went up white and came down black. They were all good friends. Another time there was a man in one of the cottages who was a heavy drinker and many a time he would be off work, two or three days. One time he was so drunk, they got a wheelbarrow and they had some tar and they rolled him in some feathers, put him in the wheelbarrow and wheeled him up and dumped him on his doorstep. And his wife was one of these fancy sorts, very clean. Well they left him there, how he went on I don't know. They used to keep a goat and my mother was down there to visit my uncles, (she was nursing the baby Louisa, 1891) so she went and asked the Kays if they would hold billy goat until she passed, so they put the goat down the goyt, so billy would have to go down the tunnel and into the dam till it found dry land.

William Guite finished with his old schoolmaster Reuben Gray, at Stannington Church School, and how he looked after the poor children, sometimes bringing dripping pots from home. Reuben Gray was a local man, his father being a farmer, Benjamin Gray of Greenfold, Dungworth.[26] In 1895 he became schoolmaster at the National School, Stannington.

Postscript

It is nearly twenty years since I visited Samehill Farm. I have tried, where possible, to authenticate events, dates, and people. I cannot fault William: he had a photographic memory. To me it was another time and another place. May I take this opportunity to thank Louisa and William Guite who so graciously let me into their home and told me their family history.

Notes and References

1. A map of the Parish of Sheffield in the County of York by Wm Fairbank and Son, 1795.
2. Ordnance Survey, Six Inch Sheet, No 294, surveyed 1850, published 1855.
3. Sheffield Cemeteries, for Crookes, City Road, Sheffield.
4. Mr Guite interchanged the Regiments 18th Royal Irish and The Yorkshire Light Infantry. A. Swinsen (Ed.) *A Register of the Regiments & Corps of the British Army*, gives the following information:
    – 1751–1881 the 18th (the Royal Irish) Regiment of Foot. Principal Campaigns, Battles – 1863–6 New Zealand.
    – The King's Own Yorkshire Light Infantry formed 1881. 105th (Madras Light Infantry) Regiment – 1861–81. The Regiment was in the pay of the East India Company. 105th, 51st (2nd Yorkshire West Riding) Regiment became Yorkshire Light Infantry.
5. The last surviving male aborigine, Williame Lanne, had died in 1869 and the last female, Truganini, in 1876.
6. It was the custom to hand out hatchets when meeting parties of aboriginals according to Captain Watkin Tench of the Marines, author of *Sydney's First Four Years – Being a Report of a Narrative of an Expedition to Botany Bay, and a Complete Account of the Settlement of Port Jackson, 1789–93*, reprinted by Angus & Roberston, 1961, pp. 176–79.
    Watkin Tench also described how land was allotted to non-commissioned officers and private soldiers in the vicinity of Sydney in the first phase of settlement: ' to every non-commissioned Officer, an allotment of one hundred and thirty acres of land, if single, and of one hundred and fifty acres if married. To every private soldier an allotment of eighty acres, if single, and one hundred acres if married; also an allotment of ten acres for every child, whether of a non-commissioned officer, or of a private soldier.', p. 171.
7. Census, 1881 – on microfilm in Sheffield Local Studies Library, 4630 92, f5.
8. R. E. Leader, *History of the Company of Cutlers in Hallamshire.*
9. Leader, *History of the Company of Cutlers.*
10. Census 1841 – on microfilm in Sheffield Local Studies Library, 1327 p12, Bradfield Parish (Pearl Town).
11. Census, 1851 – on microfilm in Sheffield Local Studies Library, 2336 98F (George Street).
12. Census 1851 – on microfilm in Sheffield Local Studies Library, 2339 481B (Snow Lane).
13. Census 1861 – on microfilm in Sheffield Local Studies Library, 361 p. 18 (Myers Grove).
14. According to Samuel Harrison, in his *A Complete History of the Great Flood at Sheffield,* 1864, p. 47, the flood water rose eighteen feet above the road in Brick Lane, Holme Lane, Hillsborough.
15. The Duke of Norfolk offered plots of land for sale at Hag, Rivelin, Upper Hallam. Sheffield Archives, Fairbank Collection, Field Books. F.B.129 p. 59, F.B. 135 p. 74.
16. Sheffield Archives, records of Underbank Chapel, Stannington.
17. Leader, *History of the Company of Cutlers.*
18. Census 1851, on microfilm in Sheffield Local Studies Library, 2336 301B.
19. West Riding of Yorkshire, Election Poll Book, 1835, Sheffield Local Studies Library.
20. Sheffield Archives, records of Underbank Chapel, Stannington.
21. William Lomas, of the Griffs, Stannington, died on 31 October, 1942, aged 99 years and 11 months. Register of Burials, Christ Church, Stannington.
22. A John Gosling farmed at Parkside, Rivelin. William was his son. *White's Directory of Sheffield*,1879.
23. D. Crossley (Ed), *Water Power on the Sheffield Rivers*, University of Sheffield, 1989.
24. George, Mary and Richard Snape all drowned in the flood of 1864. The body of Richard, aged 17 years, was found in Sheffield on the 12 April, one month after the flood. Harrison, *Great Sheffield Flood*, pp. 94 and 97.
25. Census 1881 – on microfilm in Sheffield Local Studies Library, 4620 31, pp. 28–30 (Roscoe Wood and Spooner Wheel).
26. *White's Directory of Sheffield,* 1888, Sheffield Local Studies, Sheffield City Library.

Other sources consulted:

Ronald B. Dyson, (Compiler & Editor.), *A Glossary of Old Sheffield Trade Words and Dialect*, 1936, reprinted 1979.
R. E. Leader, *Sheffield in the Eighteenth Century*, 1901.
T. W. Miller, *The Water Mills of Sheffield*, 1936.
Samuel Roberts, *Tom and Charles or The Two Grinders*, 7th Ed, 1868.
Stannington, Stannington Local History Group, 1974.
A Directory of Sheffield, Including the Manufacturers of the Adjacent Villages, 1787, Da Capo Press, New York, 1969.

Acknowledgements

The photographs were taken by Mr Bryan Answer, Mr Dennis J. Smith and Vincent Guite. My thanks are also due to Irene and Vincent Guite, who gave me much valued information, the Rev. Philip West, Christ Church, Stannington, for permission to look through the parish burials, and to the staff of Sheffield Archives and Sheffield Local Studies Library.

CONTRIBUTORS

1. THE EARL OF SHREWSBURY AND THE TITHES OF MEADOWHALL

Stephen Cooper was born in 1948 and was educated at the Holt Grammar School, Liverpool and Balliol College, Oxford, where he read Modern History. He qualified as a solicitor in 1972. He was in private practice in Sheffield for a number of years, but joined the Government Legal Service in 1989. He married his wife Gaye in 1970 and they have two daughters, Elizabeth and Rosemary. The family has lived in Thorpe Hesley since 1979. Stephen's interest in local history was awakened in 1985 by the chance discovery of a document relating to a disputed will. This led to the publication of *A House Divided* in 1987, a story of madness and litigation in the late eighteenth century. Stephen's other major publication is *Burglars and Sheepstealers* (1992), which concerns crime and transportation in the early nineteenth century. He is a regular contributor to the *Aspects of Rotherham* series. Apart from history and law Stephen's other hobbies include walking and running.

2. REFORMATION TO RESTORATION: EMERGING NON-CONFORMITY IN SHEFFIELD 1540–1660

Born and bred in Sheffield, **Malcolm Mercer** left school at fourteen in 1939. After seven years in the retail trade disrupted by three years in the Royal Navy (1943–46), he trained as a teacher at Sheffield Training College (1950–52) and taught in several Sheffield schools before being appointed Head of Parson Cross School (1968–83). He gained a Diploma in Education Management (Sheffield Polytechnic, 1971) and MA in Education (Sheffield University, 1979). He has contributed to *The Transactions of the Hunter Archaeological Society*, *The History of the City of Sheffield* (1993) and is the author of *The School at Parson Crosse* (1980) and a history of elementary education in Sheffield 1560–1902 – *Schooling the Poorer Child* (1996). For 28 years he has been a member of the Sheffield Teachers' Choir, a lifelong member of St. Swithun's Church and churchwarden of the parish of Sheffield Manor. Happily married with two children and two grandchildren, he is a long-suffering Sheffield United supporter.

3. MAHLON STACY: AN EARLY SHEFFIELD EMIGRANT

David Hey is Professor of Local and Family History at the University of Sheffield, where he teaches in the Division of Adult Continuing Education. He was born at Jessop's Hospital, 300 yards from his place of work. Educated at Penistone Grammar School and Keele University, he later obtained part-time MA and PhD degrees at the Department of English Local History at Leicester University. His books include *The Making of South Yorkshire* (1979), *Packmen, Carriers and Packhorse Roads* (1980), *Yorkshire from AD 1000* (1986), *Family History and Local History in England* (1987), *The Oxford Guide to Family History* (1993) and *The Oxford Companion to Local and Family History* (1996). His writings on Sheffield include *The Fiery Blades of Hallamshire: Sheffield and its Neighbourhood, 1660–1740* (1991), *Forging the Valley* (with M. Olive and M. Liddament, 1997), the joint editorship of *Mesters to Masters: The History of the Company of Cutlers in Hallamshire* (1997) and the forthcoming *A History of Sheffield* (1997).

4. WOODLAND MANAGEMENT ON THE DUKE OF NOR-FOLK'S SHEFFIELD ESTATE IN THE EARLY EIGH-TEENTH CENTURY

Melvyn Jones was born in Barnsley and educated at the Holgate Grammar School and the universities of Nottingham and Leeds. He taught for seven years at Myers Grove, Sheffield's first comprehensive school, and then for nine years at Sheffield City College of Education before its amalgamation into Sheffield City Polytechnic in 1976. He has recently retired from the post of Head of Academic Resources in the School of Leisure and Food Management at Sheffield Hallam University. Late in life, he has embarked on a career as an independent author. He has written extensively on the economic and social history of South Yorkshire. Recent publications include *A Most Enterprising Thing* (an illustrated history of Newton Chambers at Thorncliffe) and a revised edition of the widely acclaimed *Sheffield's Woodland Heritage*. *Rotherham's Woodland Heritage* was published by Rotherwood Press in 1995. He is co-editor of *Chapeltown and High Green* (1996), a new title in Chalford Publishing's Archive Photographs series. He is the editor of *Aspects of Rotherham* and *Aspects of Rotherham 2*.

5. SHEFFIELD'S TURNPIKE ROADS

Howard Smith was born and bred in Sheffield, and had all his professional career as a schoolmaster and further education lecturer in the city, teaching mainly History and English for 33 years. Immediately following early retirement he studied for an MA in Local History under the tutelage of David Hey, whose teaching and books have inspired much of his own work. His thesis was converted into his first book *A History of Rotherham's Roads and Transport* (1992), but earlier he had produced three 'Turnpike Trails', designed to make certain aspects of local history accessible to the layman. Three more have followed. His specific research area of roads was triggered by his being invited to write a script on the history of local roads for Radio Sheffield in its early days, an interest which has gradually deepened and widened ever since, particularly since retirement. Guide stoops caught his eye whilst researching old packhorse ways, and discovering that there was a gap in the literature on them produced *The Guide Stoops of Derbyshire* in 1996. Howard enjoys the countryside, especially whilst undertaking fieldwork for his research, photography (much of it for archival purposes) and giving illustrated lectures to a wide variety of groups and societies. He is an active member of his Probus club and several local historical societies.

6. THE BUTTONMAKING INDUSTRY OF SHEFFIELD

Dennis Smith was born in Sheffield in 1947, spending much of his life in the Walkley area. Educated at Morley Street County and Myers Grove Comprehensive Schools, he worked variously as cutlery worker, food mixer and cemetery worker. A childhood spent exploring the ruined watermills of the Rivelin Valley was partially responsible for his interest in industrial history. Other influences were his father's reminiscences of Sheffield trades and working conditions. He is possibly remembered by local librarians as the schoolboy who left grubby fingermarks on *The Oxford History of Technology*! Dennis has published booklets on aspects of life in the Bradfield and Cawthorne areas of South Yorkshire. His articles have also appeared in the *Transactions of the Hunter Archaeological Society*, and Sheffield University's *Lore and Language* journal. His other interests include English art, walking and early music. He has also enjoyed wide travel in the British Isles and part of Greece. He retains fond memories of meetings with local people who had worked in the older local industries and spends considerable time attempting to recover details of life from documentary sources.

7. A FORGOTTEN INDUSTRY: THE STOVE GRATE AND LIGHT CASTINGS INDUSTRY OF SHEFFIELD

Chris Morley was born in Manchester but served his apprenticeship as a design draughtsman with the Light Castings division of Newton, Chambers & Co. Ltd. (Redfyre). Until his early retirement he worked as a designer for several domestic appliance manufacturers, designing everything from solid fuel cookers and fires, hairdryers and irons, gas fires, cookers, electric cookers and washing machines, and, for the latter 15 years of his employment, large scale catering equipment. He qualified as a mechanical engineer, and went on to study industrial design, and the utilisation of gas. He is a Chartered Engineer, and has also studied, as an extramural student, Social and Economic History, specialising in the history of the stove grate and domestic appliance industries. This has led him, by 'red herring' routes, to an interest in local history following research into the Walker operations in his own village of Grenoside, and at Masbrough. He and his long-suffering wife have travelled widely in the UK and on the Continent, following leads into early iron making and casting, especially to Coalbrookdale, Falkirk, the Bohemian areas of the Czech Republic and Austria, and to Hungary. When they have not been spending 'Casting' holidays, they have been 'Gattying', researching the biography of the family of the Rev. Alfred Gatty, erstwhile vicar of Ecclesfield, a project that he is hoping to complete when he 'has more time'!

8. THE ELECTRO-PLATE CONTROVERSY

Geoffrey Tweedale has been studying industrial history for nearly twenty years, first at the London School of Economics, then later at Manchester and Sheffield universities. He has published several major studies of the Sheffield steel and cutlery trades, including most recently *Steel City: Entrepreneurship, Strategy and Technology*

in Sheffield, 1743–1993 (Oxford University Press, 1995), and *The Sheffield Knife Book* (Hallamshire Press, 1996). He is currently Senior Wellcome Fellow at Manchester Metropolitan University, where he is writing a book on the history of occupational health in the asbestos industry.

9. THE WROUGHT IRON ERA WITH RECOLLECTIONS OF SHEFFIELD'S LAST PUDDLER

Sheffield born and bred, **Trevor Lodge** was educated at Abbeydale Grammar School, and Manchester and Sheffield universities. An industrial chemist by training, he had an early career which comprised spells of teaching interspersed by a memorable (but all too brief!) period as research chemist with Newton, Chambers & Co. Ltd at Chapeltown. He eventually 'found his feet' in South Yorkshire's special steels industry, retraining as a metallurgist in the early 1970s, largely through development work carried out at British Steel's Templeborough Steelworks. Possessing considerable working knowledge of many of South Yorkshire's other iron and steelworks, both past and present, he currently works as an Information Officer in the region's special steels industry. A growing interest in all matters mechanical and industrial has led him to carry out research since the mid-1960s into the UK's heavy industries (coal, steel and engineering) and the railways that served them. His most notable published works – the histories of the Park Gate Iron & Steel Co. Ltd, Steel Peech & Tozer Ltd., and Samuel Fox & Co. Ltd. – appeared in serialised form in British Steel's *Steel News* and United Engineering Steels' Journal, *Stocksbridge Gazette*, between 1981 and 1993. He is a regular contributor to the *Aspects* series.

10. THE SHEFFIELD WORKHOUSE NEAR KELHAM ISLAND

Tim Caulton was born and educated in Nottingham before studying economic history at Sheffield University, eventually gaining a PhD for research into working-class housing in Sheffield. After brief spells with South Yorkshire County Council and the British Antarctic Survey, Tim joined Kelham Island Museum shortly before it opened in 1982, staying with Sheffield City Museums until 1990. From 1990–3 he was a member of the team developing Eureka! The

Museum for Children in Halifax. In 1993, he left Eureka! to work freelance developing new museums, and in the following year began lecturing at the University of Sheffield, where he is course tutor on the MA in Arts and Heritage Management programme. Tim has written a number of articles and museum publications, and is currently finishing a book on the management of hands-on museums. Tim lives in Eckington with his wife, Angie, and two teenage children, Ben and Eleanor.

11. A CHANGING LANDSCAPE: DARNALL IN THE NINETEENTH CENTURY

Sue Turton submitted a dissertation entitled 'Change and Continuity in Darnall between 1841 and 1881', as part of the requirements of a University of Sheffield MA degree in Local History, awarded in 1993. Her article is based on the research she undertook for that dissertation. In her experience, most people perceive the history of Darnall as being largely that of Attercliffe. It is her contention that Darnall has its own unique history and a story worth telling.

12. PARADISE LOST? SHEFFIELD'S HISTORIC PARKS AND GARDENS

Joan Sewell was born and educated in Glasgow. After taking Geography at Glasgow University, she studied Landscape Architecture at Sheffield University. Joan worked as a landscape architect for Sheffield City Council for three years and thereafter as a freelance landscape architect and garden design consultant. In 1992, she took up a part-time lectureship in planting design at the Department of Landscape, Sheffield University and now works as a studio tutor in the Department. Her research focuses on the historic parks and gardens of Sheffield. Studies include a *Register Review of South Yorkshire* commissioned by English Heritage in 1994 and *A Strategy for the Heritage Parks and Green Spaces of Sheffield*, recently commissioned by Sheffield Leisure Services Department. Joan is studying the life and work of Robert Marnock for a PhD. She lives in Bakewell with husband, John, and children, Rowan and Freya.

13. ENDCLIFFE HALL: THE RESIDENCE OF A GENTLEMAN INDUSTRIALIST

Julie Goddard was born and educated in Sheffield. She attended Bradfield and Ecclesfield Schools before taking a BEd at Sheffield University in 1980. After teaching for two years she began her own business restoring and selling antique furniture in Oughtibridge. In 1996 she was invited to become manager of an antiques centre in Ecclesfield to which she transferred her own business. She is currently studying part-time at Sheffield Hallam University for an M.Phil on Sheffield's nineteenth century furniture industry.

14. THE GUITES OF SAMEHILL FARM, RIVELIN

Valerie Answer was born, and has lived all her life, in Sheffield. In the last few years she has become interested in tracing her family, and much to her surprise has found the family tree extended to the Shemeld and Pearson families. The Shemeld family played a prominent part in the affairs of the town from 1560. She has always been interested in local history and has written articles on the subject and one book: *Sheffield's Traditional Craftsmen*.

INDEX OF PEOPLE AND PLACES

PEOPLE